In the churches of Africa, as Baba Simon, the barefoot missioner from Cameroun, put it: The time has come to "reinvent Christianity, so as to live with our African soul."

Jean-Marc Éla, *African Cry*

Reinventing Christianity

AFRICAN THEOLOGY TODAY

John Parratt

WILLIAM B. EERDMANS PUBLISHING COMPANY
GRAND RAPIDS, MICHIGAN / CAMBRIDGE, U.K.

AFRICA WORLD PRESS, INC.
TRENTON, NEW JERSEY

© 1995 Wm. B. Eerdmans Publishing Co.

Published jointly 1995 by
Wm. B. Eerdmans Publishing Co.
255 Jefferson Ave. S.E., Grand Rapids, Michigan 49503 /
P.O. Box 163, Cambridge CB3 9PU U.K.
www.eerdmans.com
and by
Africa World Press, Inc.
P.O. Box 1892, Trenton, New Jersey 08607

Printed in the United States of America

00 99 98 97 96 95   7 6 5 4 3 2 1

Library of Congress Cataloging-in-Publication Data

Parratt, John.
Reinventing Christianity: African theology today / John Parratt.
        p.   cm.
Includes bibliographical references.
ISBN-10: 0-8028-4113-9 / ISBN-13: 978-0-8028-4113-1 (pbk.: alk. paper)
1. Theology, Doctrinal — Africa, Sub-Saharan — History — 20th century.
2. Christianity and other religions — African. 3. Africa — Religion — 20th century.
I. Title.
BT30.A438P37   1995
230′.096′09045 —dc20   95-36685
                                      CIP

Africa World Press ISBN 0-86543-523-5

Contents

Author's Note

The main text of this book first appeared in 1991 under the title of *Theologiegeschichte der dritten Welt: Afrika* in the series *Theologiegeschichte der dritten Welt*, edited by Theo Sundermeier and Norbert Klaes. I am most grateful to the editors, and to Kaiser Verlag, for their permission for the publication of an English edition.

A great deal has happened on the African continent since the original book appeared. South Africa has achieved majority rule, and several other states have moved away from one-party rule towards more open and democratic forms of government. Several parts of the continent, too, have witnessed a "third wave" of Christianity, as the Pentecostalist movements have begun to have a noticeable impact on the older mission churches and the independent churches. New issues, too, have come to the forefront in Christian theology in Africa, and some of the older issues have been rethought and redefined. I have tried to take account of what seemed to me the most important of these developments, and the majority of the chapters have been revised, some quite extensively. I am acutely conscious, however, that much has been left unsaid and that there is a very great deal of theologizing, especially at the "grassroots" vernacular level, with which I have been unable to deal. Nevertheless, it is my hope that the publication of an English edition of this book may help to make some of the riches of African Christian theology more widely known, and that it may contribute to the ongoing fraternal dialogue between African and Western theologians.

I must again thank Kwesi Dickson, Hans Gensichen, Theo Sundermeier, and Maurice Wiles, who were kind enough to comment on the earlier draft. More recently I have gained much from discussions with Kwame Bediako and Itumeleng Mosala on trends in cultural and political theology in Africa. I also owe a great debt to my former students in Malawi and Botswana and, more recently, in New College, Edinburgh, for their sharp and critical insights into doing theology from the African context. I am grateful to two former colleagues at Chancellor College, University of Malawi: David Bone read the original draft and pointed out numerous obscurities, and Dr. Francis Chilipaine untangled several particularly tricky bits of philosophical French. I am also grateful to Theo Sundermeier, Hans Gensichen, and Pierre Federlé, who kindly loaned me materials in German and French that would otherwise not have been available to me; to Evelyn Salu Maseko (Zomba), Diana Mogatle (Gaborone), and Ruth Scott (Edinburgh) for their typing and transcription skills; and to the Universities of Malawi and Edinburgh for research grants.

JOHN PARRATT
Carlisle, 1994

Abbreviations

Books

ATER   *African Theology en Route* (papers from the Pan-African conference of Third World theologians held at Accra, 1977), ed. K. Appiah-Kubi and S. Torres (Maryknoll, 1979).

BRAB   *Biblical Revelation and African Beliefs* (papers from the consultation of African theologians held at Ibadan, 1966), ed. K. A. Dickson and P. Ellingworth (London, 1969).

BTSAV   *Black Theology, the South African Voice* (papers from various conferences held in South Africa, 1971), ed. B. Moore (London, 1973).

CIA   *Christianity in Independent Africa* (papers from the conference held at Jos, 1975), ed. E. Fasholé-Luke, R. Gray, A. Hastings, and G. Tasie (London, 1978).

EG   *The Emergent Gospel, Theology from the Underside of History* (papers from the ecumenical dialogue of Third World theologians held at Dar-es-Salaam, 1976), ed. S. Torres and V. Fabella (Maryknoll, 1978).

Journals

AFER   *African Ecclesiastical Review* (Tabora & Eldoret).

ATJ   *Africa Theological Journal* (Makumira).

CONTENTS

BTA   *Bulletin de Théologie Africaine* (Kinshasa).
JRA   *Journal of Religion in Africa* (Leiden).
JRT   *Journal of Religious Thought* (Washington).
JTSA   *Journal of Theology for Southern Africa* (Braamfontein).
RAT   *Revue Africaine de Théologie* (Kinshasa).
RCA   *Revue du Clergé Africaine* (Mayidi).

I

The Emergence of Christian Theology in Africa

1. Historical Roots of African Theology

It is becoming increasingly clear — however unpalatable it may appear to Western theologians — that the focus of the Christian faith is moving steadily away from Europe and America to new centers in the Third World. Andrew Walls,[1] writing in 1976, pointed out that within the last three centuries the position of Christianity had changed from being a kind of "tribal religion of the Caucasian peoples" to becoming a truly world religion. Today the greatest areas of Christian strength are no longer in the West; and in Europe in particular Christianity is, in Walls's words, "in marked recession, losing in adhesion, respect and influence." Its main strength lies rather in Latin America, Western Africa, the Rift Valley, and the Pacific, where it has most adherents and where its impact upon society is most widespread. It seems imperative, then, that European Christian theologians should take the Third World's contribution to Christian thought seriously.

Though developments in Latin America have, since the emergence of the theology of liberation in the 1960s, caught the attention of Western theologians, and though there are increasing signs of an interest in

---

1. Andrew Walls, *Towards an Understanding of Africa's Place in Christian History in Religion in a Pluralistic Society,* ed. John Pobee (Leiden, 1976), 180.

Asian Christian theology, African theologians have been strangely and unjustly neglected in the West. Theological traffic between Europe and Africa has thus continued to proceed down a one-way street, with the theological riches of the West — as well as a certain amount of its theological poverty — being exported to the African continent, and very little African theologizing making the return trip to Europe. Part of the reason for this state of affairs, no doubt, has been that Western theology, because of its long and dignified heritage, has tended to lay claim to a universal validity and has consequently, until fairly recently, not readily acknowledged that it may learn from the newer Christian world. Such a claim to universal validity is now rightly being questioned.[2]

Christian theology in Africa is relevant for the ecumenical church for two reasons. First, in its struggle to relate the Christian message to the traditional background of primal religions, African Christianity is repeating in our own time the encounter that characterized the early centuries, between the infant faith and the pagan milieu in which it found itself. That many of the factors in this encounter, which helped to form and shape the Christianity of the patristic age, are relevant to Africa today has been demonstrated with great insight by Kwame Bediako.[3] The encounter that is going on in Africa today also mirrors to some extent the conflicts between paganism and Christianity in the early centuries in European lands. Second, and perhaps more important, Christian theology in Africa is deeply concerned to seek a Christian

2. So, e.g., Desmond Tutu: "[F]or too long western theology has wanted to lay claim to a universality that it cannot too easily call its own. Christians have found that the answers they possessed were answers to questions that nobody in different situations was asking. New theologians have arisen, addressing themselves to the issues in front of them" (address to the Presbyterian Church Assembly, 1978, reprinted in *A Voice of One Crying in the Wilderness* [London, 1982]). To similar effect see E. Mveng's complaint, at the VIth conference of the Ecumenical Association of Third World Theologians in Geneva in 1983, that theologians from the Third World had been all but ignored by their counterparts in the West, and that there had been no real dialogue but "only a monologue of the poor and those left out of account" ("A Cultural Response to Doing Theology in a Divided World," *Doing Theology in a Divided World,* ed. V. Fabella and S. Torres [Maryknoll, 1985], 72-75).

3. In his doctoral dissertation *Identity and Integration: an inquiry into the nature and problems of theological indigenisation in selected early hellenistic and modern African writers* (University of Aberdeen, 1983), published as *Theology and Identity: The Impact of Christian Thought on the Second Century and on Modern Africa* (Oxford, 1992).

response to the contemporary social and political issues that affect the African continent. This is most clearly seen in South African "black theology," but, as will become clear, a similar concern with present-day problems is a characteristic of Christian theology throughout the continent. As the theology of liberation has opened up Western theology to the cardinal importance of the "gospel of the poor," so, it is to be hoped, the emergent Christian theology of Africa may bring to light other new dimensions of the gospel.

The concern of this book is twofold. Primarily its purpose is to seek to expound what Christian leaders of thought in Africa are actually saying, and to analyze their ideas as systematically and sympathetically as possible. All true theology, however, must lay itself open to critique. My secondary aim therefore is to subject African theology to critical analysis in the hope that this may lead to a refinement that will be of benefit to the church worldwide.

While the origins of the church in Africa are lost in obscurity, biblical and historical traditions trace the introduction of Christianity into the continent back to the earliest times. The Acts of the Apostles indicates that the introduction of the Christian faith into "Ethiopia" dates from the early decades of the first century,[4] and a strong tradition credits St. Mark with the founding of the church in Alexandria.[5] In any case, it has been well said that in the early days of Christianity "Christian Africa looked across at pagan Europe," and for many centuries it was Africa that was the seed bed of Christian theology. Towards the end of the second century the North African church entered the light of Christian history with thinkers such as Tertullian, Cyprian, and Augustine, while to the east Egypt produced its Origen, Clement, and Athanasius. Most of our Christian doctrines were formulated by these early African theologians, and, one might argue, most of the early heresies had their origins here too. Africa has therefore left an indelible mark on the history of theology. What Robin Boyd has called the "Latin Captivity"[6] of the church is at root an African captivity, for Latin theology originated in North Africa before it took hold on Rome.

But these developments properly belonged to the Mediterranean world. "African" though they were in a geographical sense, the vast expanse

4. Acts 8:22ff.
5. Eusebius, *Church History,* II.xvi.
6. Robin Boyd, *India and the Latin Captivity of the Church* (Cambridge, 1974).

3

of "black Africa" had to wait many centuries for the Christian message. What were the origins of indigenous Christian theology in Africa south of the Sahara? Perhaps it was during the period of the Portuguese colonization. Somewhere around the year 1700 a young African girl of aristocratic birth, Kimpa Vita, was converted to Catholicism and baptized under the name of Béatrice. She began to receive visions and claimed to have experienced death and resurrection.[7] St. Anthony appeared to her, and, like the saint, she gave away all she had and began to preach. The Portuguese found her preaching alarming; she protested against church rules and ceremonies, and forbade fasting and the singing of the Ave Maria and Salve Regina. She taught that Jesus was an African and had appeared in San Salvador, and that the apostles were also black. Christ, she claimed, was the Savior who identified himself with the oppressed against their colonial masters: this black Christ would return to establish a paradise on earth and to restore the old Congolese kingdom to its former glory. Around the year 1706 Kimpa Vita was arrested and burnt at the stake. Tradition has it she died with the name of Christ on her lips.[8]

As Bosch[9] has suggested, Kimpa Vita has a good claim to be called the first black African theologian. The claim to spirit possession, the rejection of asceticism, the identification of Jesus and the apostles with the African race, the stress on the poor and the oppressed, the millenarian conception of a black paradise on earth — these ideas all have, in one way or another, characterized Christianity in Africa, not least among the African independent churches.

Kimpa Vita's call for the indigenization of the church in Africa found in the following century more orthodox echoes in Samuel Ajayi Crowther, the first African bishop south of the Sahara.[10] Although Crowther was firmly convinced of the uniqueness of the Christian faith, he was equally concerned that it should not destroy the African char-

7. There is a strong tradition in Central Africa that outstanding charismatics, especially witch-finders, undergo death and resurrection before beginning their work.

8. For a more detailed account of Kimpa Vita, see Marie-Louise Martin, *Kimbangu, an African Prophet and his Church* (Oxford, 1975).

9. Bosch, "Currents and Cross-Currents in South African Black Theology," *JRA* 3, no. 2 (1974): 1-22.

10. At least among non-Catholics; in Congo a prince of the royal house, given the baptismal name of Don Henriques, had been consecrated bishop as early as 1518, although this proved a very short-lived experiment in indigenization.

acter. While asserting that "Christianity has come into the world to abolish and supercede all religions," he nonetheless believed that "it should be borne in mind that Christianity does not undertake to destroy national assimilation."[11] "Holy" James Johnson, the Sierra Leonean who also ministered in Nigeria, went further: for him the church was "not an exotic but a plant become indigenous to the soil."[12] Johnson was open to the virtues of traditional religion, and sought information on Yoruba beliefs from a local Ifa priest.[13] He was equally convinced of the need to bring about a Christian faith with an African face:

> Christianity is a religion intended for and suitable for every race on the face of the globe. Acceptance of it was never intended by its founder to denationalise any people, and it is indeed the glory that every race and people may profess and practise it and imprint upon it its own natural characteristics, giving it a peculiar type among themselves without losing any of its virtue. And why should there not be an African Christianity as there has been a European and Asiatic Christianity?[14]

Johnson may well have been influenced by — and he was certainly familiar with — the writings of Edward Blyden. While Blyden did not reject Christianity (he was himself ordained, although he never seems to have ministered in the church) he is better known for his vigorous campaign for Africans' mental and political freedom from foreign domination.[15]

11. Quoted in J. A. Ajayi, *Christian Missions in Nigeria 1841-1891: The Making of a New Elite* (London, 1965), 224. But on Crowther's ambivalent attitude to other religions, see P. McKenzie, *Inter-Religious Encounters in West Africa: Samuel Ajayi Crowther's attitude to African Traditional Religion and Islam* (Leicester, 1976).

12. Ajayi, 235. The same imagery was used by the Nyasaland Tonga Y. Z. Mwasi in his seccession statement in 1933: "The time has now come for the native church to take up its responsibilities alone, as the churches planted by the Apostle Paul did, without fear that the absence of mission is death to the Christianity of the soil" ("My Essential and Paramount Reasons for Working Independently," reproduced as *Sources for the Study of Religion in Malawi* no. 2, Zomba, 1981).

13. Ajayi, 235.

14. Quoted by E. A. Ayandele in *CIA*, 613; see further his *Holy Johnson, Pioneer of African Nationalism, 1883-1917* (London, 1970).

15. Especially in his *Christianity, Islam and the Negro Race* (London, 1889).

Blyden's ideology of blackness perhaps bore its most spectacular fruit not among the mission-based churches but in the emergence of the so-called independent churches, and it is in these churches that some have discerned the origins of indigenous theology in Africa.[16] The commonly accepted nomenclature is indeed misleading, for they are "independent" only in that these bodies are not organically allied to the mainstream churches that were established by Western missionary effort. They have, however, been a potent factor on the African scene since the beginning of the century. The literature on these churches is vast and shows no sign of abating, and their classification is complicated.[17] Here I wish to note simply that the independent churches in many respects show a more "African" approach to the Christian faith than do their more orthodox counterparts in their adoption of new styles of worship, in their hierarchies of power, and in their frequent assimilation of elements from African culture and religions. They are also significant in that they highlight the place of the charismatic within the community and generally lay less emphasis upon doctrinal orthodoxy than do the established churches. But it would be wrong to regard them as "prophetic" in the classic sense of the word, or as valuing orthopraxis above orthodoxy. On the contrary their impact on social and political issues has been relatively insignificant, and in those cases where they have come into conflict with their governments (whether colonial or independent) it has usually been over matters purely of religious autonomy.[18] Even in South Africa, despite the involvement of some independent churches in the land alienation problem, they were not especially in the forefront in either the struggle against racial oppression or the quest for a more just society.[19]

Their contribution to African theology is difficult to assess, for as yet we still have comparatively few in-depth studies of the doctrines of

16. So Bosch.

17. Much of the credit for the documentation on the African independent churches must go to Harold Turner; see especially his pioneering *Bibliography of New Religious Movement in Primal Societies* (Boston, 1977) and *Religious Innovation in Africa* (Boston, 1979). It would be true to say, however, that we are now in the midst of a "third wave" of Christianity in Africa, that of the charismatic movements.

18. As, e.g., with the Lenshina (Lumpa) Church in Zambia or the Maria Legio in Kenya.

19. See, e.g., B. Sundkler, *Bantu Prophets in South Africa* (London, 1961).

these churches. Furthermore there has been, until relatively recently, an absence of trained theologians within these movements themselves. The spectrum of theological opinion within them is very wide, stretching from the solidly orthodox at the one extreme to the avowedly nativistic at the other. Some African theologians, it seems to me, have been somewhat too enthusiastic in their commendation of the theological stance of the independent churches. Others, while recognizing their genuine potential, have at the same time subjected them to a more critical appraisal in the light of the Bible and Christian tradition.[20] A comprehensive investigation of the theology of the African independent churches is one of the urgent tasks facing African theologians today, but it lies beyond the scope of this book. In a number of ways they have awakened the mainstream churches to important issues like the concept of "Africanity," lay participation, and, perhaps most important, the real value of African rites and beliefs. In their reaction against white missionary control of the church in Africa the independent churches began early in the century to pave the way for a truly indigenous church.

Among theologians of the mainstream churches themselves, attitudes to the European missionary expansion have been ambivalent. Probably few would wholeheartedly agree with Alioune Diop's assertion that Western religion "succeeded in converting African Christians into a people without soul or visage, a pale shadow of the dominating pride of the Christian West."[21] But at a time when the scholarly debunking of missionary hagiographies of an earlier age has gone hand in hand with political independence and African nationalisms, it has been scarcely surprising that many African theologians have come to have a negative view of the effect of Christian missions.[22] Those aspects of

---

20. H. G. Muzorewa, e.g. in his book *The Origins and Development of African Theology* (Maryknoll, 1985), 35ff., shows a too easy acceptance of the view that the theology of the independent churches is essentially biblical. Sawyerr ("What is African Theology," *ATJ* 4 [1971], reprinted in *The Practice of Presence, the Shorter Writings of Harry Sawyerr*, ed. John Parratt [Edinburgh, 1995]) and Kwesi Dickson (*Theology in Africa* [London, 1984], 10, 113) are more critical.

21. Diop continues: "At the very heart and centre of the Church in Africa we have in fact witnessed the mutilation of African personality and the trampling of human dignity in Africa" (*First International Conference of Africanists*, held in Accra, 1962 [London and Oxford, 1964], 50-51).

22. Though it would probably also be true to say that the last few years have

missionary expansion that have especially aroused the condemnation of African theologians have included missionaries' involvement in colonial rule, denigration of traditional rites and customs, attitudes of racial superiority and of paternalism, and an unhappy desire to keep the African church for as long as possible under European control. A statement along these lines came out of the conference in Dar-es-Salaam in 1976:

> In the early phases of western expansion the churches were allies of the colonial process. They spread under the aegis of the colonial powers: they benefitted from the expansion of empire. In return they rendered special service to western imperialism by legitimising it and accustoming their new adherents to accept compensatory expectations of an eternal reward for terrestrial misfortunes, including colonial exploitation.[23]

And regarding the general attitude of missionaries towards traditional customs, a West African theologian has observed:

> Western missionaries stressed aspects of discontinuity between Christianity and African cultures and traditional religion to such an extent that they excluded the aspects of continuity between Christianity and African cultures and traditional religion. They condemned without proper evaluation African religious beliefs and practices and substituted Western cultural and religious practices.[24]

---

witnessed the beginnings of a more positive attitude to "developmental" aspects of Christian missions.

23. The statement continues: "The Gospel was used as an agency for a softening of national resistance to the plunder by the foreigners and a domestication of the minds and cultures of the dominated converts. In fact, foreign powers often gave Christians a privileged position within their arrangements for the administration of the countries. In the process Christian teaching got badly tainted by the search for selfish gain of the peoples who called themselves Christians and exercised power in the name of emperors and spiritual rulers" (*EG*, 266); so also 222-23, which speak of the churches as accomplices in exploitation and cultural subjection, and of the theology of the colonizers as "attuned to the justification of this inhumanity."

24. E. Fasholé-Luke, *CIA*, 357.

There can be no doubt that in many respects such judgments are justified, for the earlier missionaries were in many ways children of their age and products of what were often arrogantly colonial cultures. While there were undoubtedly cases (Malawi and Kenya provide examples) of missionaries who were found on the side of their African converts against the colonial masters, these were perhaps too few and far between to affect greatly the popularly accepted impression. It is scarcely surprising, therefore, that at times theologians in Africa have adopted a highly critical stance toward Western-dominated Christianity, a stance illustrated by the call for a moratorium on foreign personnel by the All Africa Council of Churches in 1974, and by the exclusion of whites from the Dar-es-Salaam conference two years later.

The Dar-es-Salaam statement, quoted above, draws attention to one aspect of the missionary endeavor that has had a not altogether wholesome effect on theology in Africa: the fact that Protestant missions were often characterized by a kind of other-worldly piety that did not involve itself to any great extent in practical needs and issues. Manas Buthelezi, writing against the background of the racial oppression of blacks in the Republic of South Africa, sees this pietistic aspect of the missionary movement as an attempt to recreate in the African mission field the kind of theocratic paradise that the European missionaries could no longer find in the modern Western world from which they came.[25] The inadequacies of such a pietism in the face of blatant racial inequalities led Buthelezi and his compatriots to a radical political theology, which has not, however, abandoned a genuine conviction of the love of Christ for the oppressor as well as the oppressed. The problem here is the difficult one of standing apart from the present situation and trying to assess the history of the church in Africa dispassionately, a task the more difficult for the African theologian who has suffered the less positive effects of missionary zeal in the history and culture of his own people.

But, as a number of African theologians are now pointing out, simply to attack the sins of the European fathers of the African church is becoming a negative and sterile exercise, and may be simply used as an excuse for diverting attention away from the needs of the present and from the exploitation of Africans by Africans in the independent

25. Manas Buthelezi, "Towards an Indigenous Theology for South Africa," *EG*, 63-64.

African states. Fasholé-Luke, for example, while himself reacting against the involvement of missions in colonial exploitation and against the general political conservatism of the mission-founded church, goes on to note that it was easier to fulminate against the oppression of blacks by a white government of South Africa than to expose the exploitation of blacks by blacks elsewhere in the continent.[26]

The early calls of men like Crowther and Johnson for an indigenous expression of the Christian faith were but little heeded until fairly recent decades. In French-speaking Africa the debate may be said to have received a good deal of impetus from the publication in 1945 of Placide Tempels's *Bantu Philosophy*.[27] To castigate Tempels's book for its patronizing and colonial attitudes may indeed be justified,[28] but it is also to betray a misunderstanding of its real importance in the development of African thought. It was the first attempt to come to grips, other than in a purely descriptive way, with African thought forms, and to treat them both analytically and as a coherent system. It also set out to show the importance of the study of language and oral lore, as well as the accepted methods of ethnology, in bringing to light religious and philosophical ideas. In particular, Tempels's identification of "life-force" as the ground of Bantu ontology has contributed to our understanding of African thought in general and has provided a base from which several of his successors have worked.[29] Tempels's lead was followed by several Catholic African priests, most notably Kagame, Lulufuabo, and Mulago. The former's *La Philosophie Bantu Rwandaise de l'Être*[30] made wide-ranging use of linguistics and oral tradition, and marks a considerable achievement in the field of ethnophilosophy. It is perhaps most interesting — and controversial — for its employment of Aristotelian

---

26. E. Fasholé-Luke, *CIA*, 358-9. Tutu's paper in the same volume makes a similar point ("Whither African Theology?" 368-69).

27. The English translation, published by Présence Africaine, did not appear until 1952. For a sympathetic treatment of Tempels see Benézét Bujo, *African Theology in its Social Context* (Maryknoll, 1992), 56-58. He believes that the appearance of *Bantu Philosophy* was the real starting point of African theology.

28. See, e.g., Paulin Houtonji, "Comments on Contemporary African Philosophy," *Diogenes* 71 (1990): 109-17.

29. Though this is not to imply that his category of "vital force" is valid for all African societies.

30. Brussels, 1956.

categories as applied to Bantu thought forms. All three mentioned above have made substantial contributions to African Catholic theology.

Explorations such as these by French-speaking Catholics bore their theological fruit in the publication in 1956 of the symposium *Des Prêtres Noirs s'interrogent*. This volume came out of the association of young priests in Paris, and included among its contributors Kagame and Mulago. It was a very remarkable achievement indeed when one recalls it was produced nearly a decade before Vatican II. The book was a serious attempt to emphasize the need to take into account the African heritage in developing a valid theology for Africa. As such it built upon Tempels's thesis that Christianity could be developed only upon a substratum of African philosophy. The outward-looking decrees of Vatican II itself, of course, gave a new impetus to this movement by French-speaking priests, but less in the way of introducing a new direction than of validating what was already in progress.

The Faculty of Catholic Theology at Kinshasa early on came to the forefront in tackling indigenous theology in its annual colloquia. Of especial significance was the interchange between Tshibangu and Vanneste, sparked off by the former's *Vers une théologie de couleur africaine*,[31] in which he took as his point of departure the need to integrate the Christian faith and African culture, by which he meant "African life, mentality and the way of looking at things." Vanneste, by contrast, denied the validity of any attempt to integrate elements of African traditional religions and philosophy into Catholic theology.[32] The whole issue became the subject of the 1968 Kinshasa Colloquium, which took African theology as its theme. The commission that it set up identified various important areas for further research and chose to group them around the central idea of "life." Its conclusions were epitomized in Mulago's affirmation that there could be no universal theology, and that it was no longer possible to put the clock back and deny to African theologians the freedom to elaborate a Christian theology that would not be foreign to the African milieu, tradition of thought, mentality, and culture.[33]

---

31. *RCA*, 15, 333-46.

32. *RCA*, 346-52. For a brief summary of the debate, see Tshibangu, *Le Propos d'une Théologie Africaine* (Kinshasa, 1974), 12ff.

33. The French reads: "Personne ne peut nous deconseillir ou nous faire remettre a plus tard l'aboration d'une théologie qui ne soit pas étrangère à nôtre milieu, à nôtre tradition de pensée, à nôtre mentalité, à nôtre culture."

On the Protestant side a consultation on Christianity and African Culture had taken place in Ghana as early as 1955.[34] Despite the eminence of some of its contributors, however, it does not seem to have set in motion any real movement for the development of African theology. It was the Ibadan Conference, organized under the auspices of the All Africa Council of Churches, a decade later that marked a new beginning.[35] Scholars from widely different parts of the continent came together, including francophone and Catholic delegates. The conference was in many ways an exploratory one, and revealed the deficiencies as well as the potential strengths of African theology. The most evident weakness that emerged was the lack of sound biblical scholarship. It was, however, an important event, and one that gave impetus to future studies, especially with respect to the use and abuse of traditional religion in relation to Christian theology. Some of the contributors were to make more substantial contributions to African theological studies. In the same year, 1965, Bolaji Idowu published his lectures calling for the indigenization of the practice, ritual, and liturgy of the church in Nigeria.[36] Harry Sawyerr also sought to relate indigenous concepts and rituals to Christian thought in his *Creative Evangelism*,[37] while Mbiti attempted a similar task in the more limited field of eschatology among a particular ethnic group of Eastern Africa.[38] Some of these efforts had been foreshadowed in the pioneering work of the Scandinavian Bishop Bengt Sundkler in South Africa, who as far back as 1960 had argued that African theology should focus on "the African interpretation of existence and the universe."[39]

The 1970s produced an increasing number of conferences of all descriptions, sponsored by such bodies as the AACC,[40] the WCC, the

---

34. C. G. Baeta, ed., *Christianity and African Culture* (Accra, 1955).

35. The proceedings were published in both English and French as *Biblical Revelation and African Beliefs*.

36. Bolaji Idowu, *Towards an Indigenous Church* (Oxford, 1965); the broadcast talks were actually given in 1961.

37. Harry Sawyerr, *Creative Evangelism, towards a New Christian Encounter* (London, 1969).

38. John Mbiti, *New Testament Eschatology in an African Background* (Oxford, 1971).

39. Bengt Sundkler, *The Christian Ministry in Africa* (London, 1960), 183.

40. For a useful account of the role of the AACC, see Muzorewa, 57ff.

Lutheran World Federation, and subsequently the Ecumenical Association of African Theologians and the Ecumenical Association of Third World Theologians.[41]

2. Currents and Influences

Several factors — not all of them theological — contributed to the call for a Christian theology "with an African face." The emergence of independent nations from former colonial territories, and indeed the preindependence political movements themselves, certainly played a significant role. So also, especially in French-speaking Africa, did the philosophy of *négritude* developed by Senghor and others. In South Africa the black consciousness movement, which sought to assert the dignity of African personhood within a context of white exploitation and oppression, was a crucial factor in the rise of black theology. Even in the seventies however, as Fasholé-Luke pointed out,[42] the term "African Theology" was in no sense a definition; it was merely a label. But it was a label that arose out of a deep dissatisfaction with, and even protest against, the westernized theology as currently accepted by the African church. Bolaji Idowu expressed himself with characteristic warmth in this vein at the Ibadan conference when he complained that the church in Africa had for too long been preaching about "the strange God of the white man."[43] Africans began to talk in terms of the inward struggle between their Africanness and their adopted religion. President Kenneth Kaunda of Zambia, for example, confessed that he found

41. An increasing number of these conference proceedings are now available in published form, often sponsored by the Orbis Press. For a summary of conferences up until the end of the 1970s, see E. J. Schoonhoven, "The Bible in Africa," in *Exchange* (Leiden, 1980), 25.

42. E. Fasholé-Luke, "The Quest for African Christian Theology," *JRT* 32, no. 2 (1975): 74.

43. Bolaji Idowu, *BRAB*, 13. Nearly ten years later Idowu reiterated his complaint, but this time with the confidence that Africans were now doing something about it: "There are in Africa men of faith who are finding the prefabricated theology imported into Africa inadequate for her spiritual and academic needs. . . . [They are] advocators and promoters of theology which bears the stamp of original thinking and meditation of Africans" (*African Traditional Religions: A Definition* [London, 1973], xi).

within himself a "tension created by the collision of two world-views, which I have never completely reconciled."[44] Desmond Tutu also complained that the African "suffered from a form of religious schizophrenia" because of the struggle between his Christianity and his Africanness, which Tutu felt to be "violated" by the new religion.[45] There was a widespread feeling of alienation from Western theology, a conviction that the Christian faith, as it had been presented, lacked immediacy and relevance to the African situation and that it had failed to take African traditions seriously. Consequently, the need to integrate the traditional worldview into Christian theology became an emerging theme.[46] Several African theologians, especially in West Africa, began to enunciate guidelines as to the directions such a theology should take. Harry Sawyerr, with the awareness that theology should serve the pastoral and evangelistic needs of the church, noted:

> The church in Africa is faced with a clamant demand for an interpretation of the Christian faith in a sanguine hope that such an interpretation, when produced, would provide the means of bringing home to Africans the truths of the Christian gospel in an idiom related to the African situation.[47]

Sawyerr did not deny the essential unity of the Christian faith, but he pleaded for its "interpretation in terms of the African soil," which would provide a view of the Christianity that would enable the African

---

44. Kenneth Kaunda, *Letter to my Children* (London and Lusaka, 1973), 17, in the essay entitled "Faith and Values."

45. Desmond Tutu, "Whither African Theology?" *CIA*, 366.

46. Compare the similar comment by Busia: "For conversion to Christianity to be more than superficial, the Christian church must come to grips with traditional beliefs and practices, and with a world-view that these beliefs and practices imply" (*Christianity and African Culture*, 2). From the Catholic standpoint Léopold Senghor, the apostle of négritude, wrote: "Catholicism cannot ignore traditional African religion without very serious risk. In these countries with their sandy plains, nothing solid or lasting can be built except on the foundations of African traditional religion" (*Vues sur l'Afrique Noire, or assimiler non être assimilés*, translation in J. Reed and C. Wake, *Senghor: Prose and Poetry* [London, 1956], 41-42).

47. Sawyerr, 8. Sawyerr believed that such an interpretation of a *theologia africana* might provide one way for African and non-African to "think together, first in the African continent and then perhaps in other parts of the world."

"to feel at home in his new faith."[48] Sawyerr's younger compatriot, Edward Fasholé-Luke, saw the quest for an African theology in terms of the exposition of biblical truths for the present generation in the context of the social and political life of Christian communities and in categories and thought forms that modern people in Africa could understand. To accomplish this, he believed the biblical categories had to be translated into the social milieu and thought forms of the African continent.[49]

Kwesi Dickson[50] saw the problem in terms of the paradoxes and tensions within African Christianity, which arose from the very history of the faith in Africa. In his view, many Africans were unclear in their minds as to the nature of the church they had joined, which led in turn to some converts' attempt to adopt a wholly alien European manner of life. He noted also that in several important areas of life experience African Christians did not relate their needs to Christ as much as to the traditional practices of their non-Christian heritage. In consequence, Dickson felt, "the Christ preached was a particular Christ who did not speak with any clarity to the many Africans in the church,"[51] and the theology of the church was quite unsuited to the circumstances of the people. On the other side of the coin, there remained the persistence of traditional beliefs, despite the adoption of Christianity and of the Western way of life. Dickson therefore sought to point the way by which the gospel might be related to African life and thought.[52] Not that this would be an easy task: indeed, he warned that we might have to wait a very long time before a real *theologia africana* emerged. Nor could it be artificially created, for it would have to evolve spontaneously out of the life of the church.[53]

---

48. Sawyerr, 21, 23, referring to Welbourne and Ogot's study of an independent church.

49. Fasholé-Luke, *CIA,* 74ff.

50. Kwesi Dickson, "African Theology: Origin, Method and Content," *JRT* 30, no. 2 (1975): 34-45.

51. Dickson, "African Theology," 37.

52. Kwesi Dickson, "Towards a Theologia Africana," *New Testament Christianity for Africa and the World,* ed. E. Fasholé-Luke and M. Glasswell (London, 1974), 198ff.

53. As Christian Baeta had warned earlier: "We cannot artificially create an 'African Theology' or even plan it: it must evolve spontaneously as the Church teaches and lives her faith in the extremely complex situation in Africa" (*Christianity in Tropical Africa* [London, 1968], 332).

However, he believed the church in Africa was already involved in theologizing, in both its liturgy and its preaching and teaching.[54] The need now was for a more systematic approach.

What these theologians were pleading for was that Christianity should be incarnated within a particular culture. Such an assumption has indeed characterized the adaption of the Christian faith to the circumstances in which it found itself throughout church history. It takes its stand, albeit within a different context, on what Paul Tillich called a theology of culture, in that it seeks to analyze what lies behind all cultural expressions as a preparation to relating them to a systematic Christian theology.[55] The implication of this is a pluralistic approach to the Christian faith and the acknowledgment that there can be no final theology.[56] On the Catholic side such an approach is found, in a modified form, in the decrees of Vatican II, and more clearly in Pope Paul's address to the Ugandan bishops in 1969, when he declared:

> The expression, that is the language and mode of manifesting the one faith, may be manifold, suited to the style, the character, the genius and the culture of the one who professes the one Faith: you may, and you must, have an African theology.

This theme was subsequently taken up by Ngindu Mushete, who argued that unity and plurality in the church are not in opposition, but rather complement and complete each other.[57]

---

54. See also Mbiti's comments on oral theology in Africa in his paper "Cattle Are Born with Ears, Their Horns Grow Later," *ATJ* 8, no. 1 (1979): 15-25.

55. Tillich understood theology "as the statement of the truths of the Christian message and the interpretation of those truths for every generation." He also pointed out that "the pole called situation cannot be neglected in theology without dangerous consequences," this being defined as "all the various cultural forms which express modern man's interpretation of existence" (*Systematic Theology*, vol. 1 [London, 1978], 5).

56. This is succinctly put by MacQuarrie: "Recognition of the cultural factor is equivalent to acknowledging there is no final theology" (*Principles of Christian Theology*, rev. ed. [London, 1977], 14); so also Maurice Wiles, "Theology and Unity," in *Theology* (1974), 77.

57. Ngindu Mushete, "Unity of Faith and Pluralism in Theology," *EG*, 50-55. John Pobee has introduced a further dimension into the discussion by pointing out that in Africa there is a religious, not merely a Christian, pluralism: "The church, as she faces Africa and propounds her theology, must recognise the pluralism of African societies

Such a theological pluralism is evident even within the African continent itself in the controversy over whether one may speak of "African theology" (in the singular) or "African theologies" (in the plural). Clearly there are within Africa wide varieties of social, cultural, and religious systems;[58] and even within a linguistically homogenous group, differences are often more in evidence than similarities. These cultural differences will inevitably be reflected in constructions of Christian theology. Fasholé-Luke pointed out that "what is significant for one area, may not be meaningful in another."[59] This kind of plurality raises, among others, the question of the language of theology in Africa. It has been usual for Africans to work in English or French (or Portuguese) in line with the colonial heritage of their states. This helps to ensure a more widespread exchange of views both within a continent that has over eight hundred languages and in ecumenical Christendom as a whole. There may, however, be cogent reasons for doing theology, at least at the more "popular" level, more in the vernacular than has hitherto been customary, and such a trend is becoming to some degree evident in the field of African literature. Certainly there may well be cases where a direct translation from the Biblical languages into the vernacular, without going through the medium of a European language, may be more meaningful, and some African tongues may be able to capture the nuances of biblical terms rather better than English or French.[60] As yet, written — as opposed to "oral" — theology in African languages is but little advanced, but the question "whom are African theologians seeking to address?" is one that is now demanding an answer.

---

and recognise her contribution is only one alongside others such as Islam, traditional African religions, secularism, and even atheism" ("The Church and Community," *African and Asian Contributions to Theology,* ed. J. Mbiti [Geneva, 1977], 81).

58. For a useful overview of African cultures, see Basil Davidson, *The Africans* (Harmondsworth, 1973), and for general surveys of African religions, see E. G. Parrinder, *African Traditional Religion* (London, 1962), B. C. Ray, *African Religions* (New Jersey, 1961), J. Mbiti, *African Religions and Philosophy* (London, 1969), E. Dammann, *Die Religionen Afrikas* (Stuttgart, 1963).

59. Fasholé-Luke, *CIA*, 74.

60. See, e.g., the comments of D. Wambtda, "Hermeneutics and the Search for a Theologia Africana," *ATJ* 9, no. 1 (1980): 27-39; on the use of the vernacular in theology, see also Dickson, *Theology in Africa*, 4-5.

17

Pluralism in African theology is evident not only because of linguistic and cultural differences; perhaps more important are the regional differences of theological emphasis that have come about as a result of the history of missionary penetration. The emphasis of West African Protestants on the place of the Bible stems from their exposure to the kind of Bible-centered missionary societies that, in the eighteenth and nineteenth centuries, established Christianity in those regions. By contrast the dominant influence in French-speaking Central Africa has, until fairly recently, been one of Catholic sacramentalism, into which, from time to time, a degree of traditional Thomism has been injected. Similarly the rise of black theology in South Africa can be understood only against the history of the exploitation of blacks in that country, justified by an ideology of the racial superiority of whites that was derived, however perversely, ultimately from a scriptural base. Theology in Africa thus is a multiheaded animal, which draws its special emphases from the cultural and historical contexts from which it emerges, and this diversity should warn us against simplistic generalizations. Nevertheless there does not seem to be any compelling reason for a pedantic insistence upon the plural designation of "African theologies." The bases of all the theological variants we find in Africa today are the same — the Bible and Christian tradition, African religious traditions, and the contemporary situation. We shall therefore speak of Christian "theology" in Africa, but with the full recognition that it contains several very divergent trends.

A further question that has raised some debate among African theologians has been that of the role of non-Africans in the development of African theology. John Mbiti has more than once protested against this involvement, and has accused some of "wanting to meticulously sabotage" the onward march of indigenous theology in Africa.[61] He felt, probably rightly, that non-Africans have been far too free with advice on how to do African theology. However, before proclaiming a moratorium on future non-African involvement in African theology, two points at least need to be kept in mind. First, it can hardly be denied that several non-Africans have made a very useful and seminal contribution in opening up and stimulating Christian theology in Africa

61. John Mbiti, "The Biblical Basis for Present Trends in African Theology," *ATER*, 90.

— Tempels, Sundkler, Taylor, and Barrett to name but a few. However much in need of correction their views may be, they had considerable importance in raising issues and setting the debate on African theology moving. Second, there is the question first raised by Sawyerr, of what, in any case, "African" means in this context. For Sawyerr the word is primarily what he calls a "mythological" term, expressive of love for the continent and commitment to an ideal.[62] Fasholé-Luke seems to agree with this; for him the gospel is all-inclusive, and he has argued that, even in South Africa, white and black should be working together on the theological task.[63] And strangely enough, nowhere has white involvement in theology in Africa been so evident as in the emergence of black theology in South Africa.[64] At any rate, the issue at the present time is of a rather different order, namely that of how seriously Western theologians are prepared to take African theology and make use of its insights in their own work.

Perhaps a more relevant aspect of the question of European and American influence is the extent to which African theologians themselves have been shaped in their own theological education. A majority of leading African theologians even today — both Catholic and Protestant — have been nurtured in the context of a Western-style system of theological education, and many have at the higher levels pursued studies in Europe and America. There are indications that this commonly accepted pattern is showing signs of strain: teaching at the postgraduate Catholic Seminary in Nairobi and attempts to found Protestant colleges of similar status elsewhere in the continent are now well under way. The WCC has also attempted, though with a variable degree of success, to direct potential postgraduate and undergraduate candidates to theological centers within Africa and elsewhere in the Third World. This does, however, pose problems. One serious problem is that in those countries that do possess considerable theological excellence — especially in West Africa — universities are often closed down for political reasons for

---

62. Sawyerr, 23: on Sawyerr's definition, a non-African who has lived and worked in Africa may, if he or she is committed to this ideal, be as "African" as an African who has been domiciled outside Africa for a long period.

63. Fasholé-Luke, *CIA*, 75.

64. In the early period of South African black theology, Basil Moore and Theo Sundermeier, among others, edited important symposia.

considerable periods, which makes them unattractive to intending scholars from elsewhere in the continent. Another is that there is still a lack of suitably trained African staff in many of these theological institutions, and thus to direct an African student to an institution within Africa is not necessarily to ensure that he or she will be taught by fellow Africans or in such a way that the studies will be relevant to African issues. There is also the danger that even Africans teaching in such institutions may be tempted simply to pass on to their students the same kind of theological education that they themselves have received from their European mentors. In such cases, to study at an institution within Africa may be little more stimulating to specifically African theological innovation than to study at Oxford, Rome, or Tübingen. These are real problems with which the church in Africa will need to continue to grapple if theology in Africa is to break free from the restrictions of the Western theological tradition.

There are two sides to this issue. The first is how far, in fact, African theologians do make use of Western theological writings. Catholics tend, as one would expect, to be more aware of the European heritage of their church than do Protestants. Among the latter the Lutherans (especially in South Africa) do seem to have their roots firmly in Reformation ground. But on the whole — and certainly as contrasted to some Asian theologies — African theologians have paid comparatively little attention to the Western theological tradition, and the dominant figures of twentieth-century European theology have been widely ignored.[65] Whether this is entirely a matter of loss is not under discussion here: my point is simply that, on this level, it is not really the case that Africa is dominated by Western theology.

The other side to this question is probably more fundamental, and has been exposed by Kwesi Dickson.[66] As Dickson sees it, the real problem has been that of the theological method adopted in theological training in Africa. On this view the categories that have been employed reflect a Western approach to theology, so that Africans have been constrained "to do theology in terms of areas of thought defined in the west." This methodological straitjacket, while not freely imparting all

65. There has been rather more interest in Moltmann and Metz, whose theologies seem to have more immediate relevance to Third World problems.
66. Kwesi Dickson, *The African Theological Task*, 46-49; *Theology in Africa*, 119.

the findings of Western scholarship, compels Africans to think along Western lines and thus hampers originality of thought.[67] Dickson in consequence pleads, "as a matter of urgency (that) training for the ministry should be re-examined in order to give greater impetus to the development of ideas and rooting of commitment such as the quest for an African theology would thrive on."[68] He is seeking here a new approach, a genuinely African methodology. We shall return to this issue below.

On this same level of methodology, there is perhaps more to be said in support of the view that African theologians have been more influenced by the theology of liberation of Latin American and by North American black theology. From the late 1970s it became evident that the lasting message of liberation theology was being applied to Africa with considerable insight, and that its dominant ideas — concern for the poor and oppressed and for social justice, the supremacy of orthopraxis over orthodoxy — were becoming more and more important in Africa. However, there is little evidence outside of the rather special case of the second stage of South African black theology[69] that the classical Marxist social analysis on which Latin American liberation theology partially relies is playing any significant role in Africa. In most African countries the lines of social conflict are drawn in a rather different way than in Marxist theory, which thus has a limited relevance only.[70] Afri-

---

67. Okot p'Bitek made a similar criticism of the approaches of Christian theologians like Idowu and Mbiti to African traditional religions (*African Religions and Western Scholarship* [Nairobi, 1971]).

68. Dickson, *Theology in Africa*, 47.

69. See below, chapter 7.

70. See, e.g., Peter Worseley's comments (*The Third World* [London, 1967], 122-23). It is surprising therefore that explicit reference to Marxism found its way, presumably under the influence of Latin Americans, into the official statements of conferences at which Africans were present. Sergio Torres, in his introductory remarks to the proceedings of the Dar-es-Salaam EATWOT conference, implied that all Third World theologians subscribed to findings of Marxist social analysis ("The theologians of the Third World have their own interpretation. . . . There is a crisis in theology because there is a crisis in the culture of western scientific rationalism. And there is a crisis in the culture because there is a change in the mode of production, which has not been able to resolve the injustices of the world and overcome different forms of oppression." *EG*, 14; so also *ATER*, 191). Kwesi Dickson was later to comment that there was a "detectable difference" between the attitude of the Latin Americans and that of the

can theologians also have pointed out that issues vitally important to Africa, such as race, gender, and religious pluralism, were hardly addressed by liberation theology in its initial stages.

North American black theology has been a factor, especially in its influence on theology in South Africa.[71] Black American churchmen participated in several conferences with their African counterparts, for example, at Dar-es-Salaam (1971), New York (1973), and Accra (1977). The papers of the last-mentioned, however, betray a certain wariness on the part of West Africans over the influence of American blacks. James Cone's contribution[72] was to some extent a reaction to John Mbiti's article, published in 1974,[73] in which he drew a sharp division between American black theology and African theology. According to Mbiti, the former grew out of pain and oppression, and seeks to propagate a distinctive ideology. African theology, on the other hand, "grows out of our joy in the experience of the Christian faith," and has no such ideology. Accordingly, black theology could have little understanding of or relevance to African theology. Mbiti comments:

> Black theology hardly knows the situation of Christian living in Africa, and therefore its direct relevance for Africa is either non-existent or only accidental.[74]

Cone agrees that black Americans cannot play a major role in formulating African theology and that they live in a quite different

---

Africans at this conference, and that the latter were unhappy about the Latin American "doctrinnaire analysis of society and making theology sound almost exclusively like political action" (*Theology in Africa,* 126). It would be probably true to say that in the intervening years Latin American theologians have become more open to culture as an "other side" of human liberation.

71. For a useful summary of the debate between African and American black theologians (from an American viewpoint) see G. S. Wilmore, "Afro-American and Third World Theology," *ATER,* 196-208. Emmanuel Martey's *African Theology, Inculturation or Liberation* (Maryknoll, 1993) seems to me greatly to overstate the role of American black theology in the formative years of the development of African theology.

72. James Cone, "A Black American Perspective on the Future of African Theology," *ATER,* 176-86.

73. John Mbiti, "An African Views American Black Theology," *Worldview* 17 (1974): 41-44.

74. Mbiti, "An African Views," 43.

situation. He believed, however, that a useful dialogue could ensue for two reasons. First, both Africans and black Americans share what he calls "a common historical option" in the liberation of the black world from European and American dominance, and both therefore seek to reinterpret history and theology from the viewpoint of the oppressed. Second, Cone points out that they share a common faith. In Cone's view American black theology shares — or should share — with African theology a theological "dimension." This dimension is based on the political and economic realities that separate the rich from the poor nations, that is, on a shared social context. For Cone the future of theology in Africa lies in its political ingredient as a theology of liberation for black people.[75] With this approach it is understandable that Cone's main affinity should be with South African black theology. However, as Allan Boesak pointed out,[76] the latter operates in quite a different sociopolitical context and was called upon to deal with a quite different set of problems. This makes it somewhat unconvincing to draw too close an equation between the two different manifestations of black theology, even though liberation, in its broad sense, is a common denominator. Outside of South Africa, American black theologians seem to have had little real influence on African theology, for they have little to contribute to the relationship between Christianity and African cultural reality that is its main thrust. Pobee has indeed argued that American blacks (despite attempts in modern times to discover their historical roots in Africa) have not retained the traditional structural and social institutions of Africa: they have therefore tended to romanticize Africa. The preoccupation of American black theology with liberation from racial oppression, he believed, limited severely its relevance outside the Republic of South Africa.[77]

A Catholic evaluation of American black theology, as found especially in the writings of Cone and J. Deotis Roberts, has come from Nyamiti.[78] While he finds a number of useful and positive elements in

75. "The future of African Theology, and all Third World theologies, is found in the attempt to interpret the Christian Gospel in the historical context of the people's struggle to liberate themselves from all forms of oppression." Cone, 184.

76. Allan Boesak, *Black Theology, Black Power* (London, 1978), 142ff.

77. John Pobee, *Towards an African Theology* (Nashville, 1979), 38-39.

78. Charles Nyamiti, *African Tradition and the Christian God* (Eldoret, n.d.), 32-37.

these theologians, Nyamiti (like Pobee) is not happy with Cone's exclusive emphasis upon liberation from social and racial oppression as the main theme of theology. He points out that for the Christian theologian there are other and equally important aspects of liberation, the foremost of which is liberation from the slavery of sin. "By limiting the redeeming activity of Christ," writes Nyamiti, "to social liberation in this world, Cone runs the risk of reducing Christianity to a mere instrument for social and political advancement."[79] He is equally unhappy with the assumption that "blacks are the standard and criterion for theological realities," and he believes that the forces of black liberation themselves need to be judged by the standards of Christ. Nyamiti also draws attention to the superficiality of Cone's views of suffering, which is inadequate in the light of the biblical teaching that suffering may be a means to a higher good.

These warnings are salutary and are an indication that the African theologians are pursuing their own areas of primary theological concern. While they may draw upon the insights of liberation and American black theology, they are in general maintaining an independent and critical stance. African theologians seem rightly to be doing their own theological thinking according to the demands of the contexts in which they work. Theology in Africa today may draw inspiration and encouragement from Christian theologies elsewhere in the Western and non-Western world, but it has its own peculiar sets of circumstances in which it operates, and as such it seeks to work out its own solutions to deal with those peculiar contexts.

79. Nyamiti, 34.

II

The Theological Method

1. African Theology and Black Theology

It has become customary to divide Christian theology in Africa into two main areas, "African" and "black" theology. The former is usually taken to mean Christian thought that concerns itself fundamentally with the relationship of Christian theology to African culture, and that evinces a particular concern to relate this to the Bible and Christian tradition. It finds its foremost exponents in West African Protestants and among Catholic theologians of French-speaking Africa. "Black" theology, by contrast, usually refers to the response of South African blacks to the need to reinterpret the gospel in the light of their political and social deprivation under the apartheid governments of the Republic of South Africa. It therefore represents a "political" theology as opposed to the "cultural-biblical" theology found elsewhere in sub-Saharan Africa.[1]

This broad classification may be accepted as useful and convenient to give an overview of theological development within the continent of Africa, and it will be in general adopted in this book. It stands in need of some refinement, however, if it is not to give a misleading picture of the rich variety of theologizing within Africa, and this for two reasons.[2]

1. E.g., H. J. Becken: "On our sub-continent we today observe two major trends in theology which deserve our attention. They are known by the terms 'African Theology' and 'Black Theology'" (*Relevant Theology for Africa* [Durban: Lutheran Publishing House, 1973], 6-7).

2. See further my "Theological Methodologies in Africa," *Verbum SVD*, fasc. 1 (1983):

First, while the emphasis of South African black theology has, as one may expect, been deeply concerned with the role of the Christian faith in confronting the social and racial problems in that country, it would not be true to regard it as wholly disinterested in traditional cultural religious values. Indeed, there is a sense in which its roots are firmly within that tradition, in that it was a powerful affirmation of the dignity of black culture as opposed to the white ideologies of the South African government. Furthermore, there is no absolute rejection of traditional African values on the part of leading black South African theologians. Allan Boesak, for example, has clearly affirmed that black theology "believes it is possible to recapture what was sacred in the African community long before the white people came: solidarity, respect for life and humanity, and community."[3] Boesak does not reject the value of past traditions or their usefulness for the Christian life; rather, for him the mere re-creation of the past is inadequate if it has no immediate relevance to present issues. Manas Buthelezi makes a similar point. In his view one cannot eulogize the past if at the same time human dignity is being trampled underfoot in the present generation. "Who can blame the man," he asks, "who can see no sense in writing theological poetics about the golden age, while at the very same time his present human dignity is daily being systematically destroyed?"[4] There is here no absolute denial of the value of the past cultural traditions; rather, they are inadequate in and of themselves to deal with present issues.

But it is equally untrue to characterize theology north of the Limpopo as disinterested in the political dimension of the Christian faith. This indeed was only partially the case in 1972, when Mbiti drew attention to the neglect of the political element in African theology.[5] In

---

47-62. The supposed dichotomy between what he calls "inculturation theology" and "liberation theology" seems to me exaggerated in Martey's recent book *African Theology*.

3. Allan Boesak, *Black Power, Black Theology* (London, 1978), 152.

4. Manas Buthelezi, "Ansätze Afrikanischer Theologie," in I. Tödt, ed., *Theologie in Konfliktfeld Südafrika: Dialog mit Manas Buthelezi* (Stuttgart and Munich, 1976), 117. Pobee, from the standpoint of "African Theology," makes a similar point when he rejects an outmoded traditionalism as "fossil religion" (*Towards an African Theology* [Nashville, 1979], 18).

5. John Mbiti, "Church and State: a Neglected Element in Christianity in Contemporary Africa, *ATJ* 1 (1972).

West Africa Senghor's Catholicism had already opened up possibilities for theological reflection, and the Ujamaa doctrine of Julius Nyerere and Kaunda's African Humanism had also begun to attract the attention of African churchmen.[6] In West Africa, too, theologians began to examine more closely the implications of political developments for a relevant theology.[7] More recently the churches have been active initiators and participants in the "second independence struggle," the movements towards democracy and away from one-party states in Kenya, Zambia, and Malawi, and in peace initiatives in Mozambique. Though these developments have produced little formal written theology, they are indication enough that political theological praxis is by no means absent from Africa north of the Limpopo. Clearly political theology in independent Africa is very different from that in apartheid South Africa; the issues, the pressures, and, thus, the responses are quite other. However, it is clearly not accurate to characterize Christian theology outside South Africa as concerned only with the relationship of the Bible and Christian dogma to African traditions, any more than it is correct to describe theology within the Republic as concerned only with politics. Theology throughout Africa finds its common ground in three basic elements — in the Bible and Christian tradition, in African culture and religion, and in the contemporary sociopolitical situation. The divergences are ones of emphasis, and the emphasis placed on each of these three elements will vary in intensity according to the situation in which the African theologian finds himself or herself. But there is nevertheless an underlying unity in Christian theology throughout Africa that derives from common basic sources. Theo Sundermeier noted even in the 1970s that the two approaches of African and black theology were showing signs of coming closer together.[8] This he attributed to the realization by leading representatives of African theology that a one-sided emphasis on the past was leading them into a blind alley, and that they needed to address themselves also to contemporary issues if they were to remain relevant to today's Christians.

6. See further chapter 6 below.

7. E.g., Edward Fasholé-Luke's contribution to *CIA*, 358-63; also Pobee, "Church and State in Ghana 1949-66," *Religion in a Pluralistic Society*, 121-44, and "Political Theology in the African Context," *ATJ* 2, no. 2 (1982): 168-75.

8. T. Sundermeier, *"Theologie zwischen Kultur und Politik," Zwischen Kultur and Politik*, ed. Theo Sundermeier (Hamburg, 1978), 24.

Within this general framework of similarity of concerns and of theological sources, the main emphases of African and black theology can now be isolated. The latter is unique in that it arose within a colonial situation of white rule, thus within a context quite different from elsewhere in the continent. To understand black theology therefore demands an appreciation of the political situation of blacks under apartheid. It will receive separate treatment in chapters six and seven. Elsewhere in Africa there has been a broad division between Catholic and Protestant scholars in their approach to Christian theology. The former have from the beginning paid more attention to formal theological methodology, and some, for example Nyamiti, have gone to some lengths to explicate their theoretical approach to doing theology. The contribution of Protestant scholars has been less systematic, but has constantly reiterated the need to keep the Bible as the fundamental basis of theology, alongside traditional culture and religions. In the remainder of this chapter we shall examine some of the most significant contributions to the method of doing theology in Africa from both these points of view.

2. The Catholic Contribution to the Theological Method

The Catholic interest in the formulation of an African theology emerged, as we noted earlier, in the publication in 1957 of *Des Prêtres Noirs s'interrogent*. Kalilombe has suggested that the concept of "adaptionism"[9] in contemporary African theology may be traced to this book. For the contributors to *Des Prêtres Noirs*, adaptionism "meant that evangelization should take people's way of life seriously (and that) Christianity was to espouse the forms of local culture,"[10] by which was meant its context and thought-forms. It was thus a method that concerned itself not only with reflective theology but also with Christian practice — the preaching of the gospel and the reformation of the liturgy and of Christian rites. Fundamentally, of course, such an approach

9. Or "adaptationism": I have throughout used the shorter (and older) form.
10. P. Kalilombe, "Self-Reliance of the African Church, a Catholic Perspective," *ATER*, 38.

was not new. Indeed a good case could be made out for its place within the New Testament documents themselves, an irrefutable case for its implementation, for good or ill, in the writings of the North African and Egyptian church fathers. Within the Roman Catholic Church it has an impressive pedigree. Ezeanya, after alluding to the role of the adaptionist method in the early fathers, goes on to quote the remarkable statement of the Sacred Congregation for the Propagation of the Faith in 1659, which urged missionaries:

> [D]o not show any zeal and do not for any motive try to persuade peoples to change their rites, customs and habits unless they are most openly opposed to religion and good morals. For what could be more absurd than to transplant France, Spain or Italy, or any other part of Europe to China?[11]

Or indeed to Africa. As students of missions point out, this kind of approach has characterized, among others, men such as Francis Xavier, Matthew Ricci, and Robert de Nobili. In our present period, and within Africa, it was stated, as we have noted above,[12] by Pope Paul, and also finds its support in the outward-looking decrees of Vatican II's approach to other religious traditions.[13]

Ngindu Mushete has attempted to trace the development of this approach within Africa in his *History of Theology in Africa*.[14] According to Mushete theology in Africa has developed in two stages, which he terms "the theology of adaptation" and "critical African theology." The former, he believes, seeks to "adapt the practices of the western church as much as possible to the socio-cultural life of African peoples."[15] Such a method has been proposed, among others, by Tempels, Mulago, Lulufuabo, and Kagame. Mushete regards the major defect of these attempts

11. Quoted by Ezeanya, "Gods, Spirits and the Spirit World," *BRAB*, 31.

12. See above, p. 16.

13. See, e.g., the *Decree on the Church's Missionary Activity*, which speaking of the younger churches declares: "From the customs and traditions of their peoples, from their arts and sciences, these churches borrow all those things which can contribute to the glory of the Creator, the revelation of the Saviour's grace, or the proper arrangement of the Christian life."

14. Ngindu Mushete, *ATER*, 23-35.

15. Mushete, 27.

to be their tendency to equate the Christian revelation with the systems of thought in which it has found its historical expression, and in consequence he believes its results have been somewhat meager. "Critical African theology," on the other hand, seeks to purify the African milieu, which paves the way for an "incarnation" of the gospel by "seeking to establish closer contact with the Bible" and "opening up wholly to the African milieu and its problems."[16] It is difficult to see how this neat developmental distinction can be successfully maintained. The differences between the representatives of Mushete's two schools, where they exist, are really differences of emphasis rather than of method. It is probably more accurate to regard the representatives of adaptionism as following a similar basic approach to the construction of Christian theology in Africa but with both regional and individual variations in the emphasis.

What then should be understood by adaptionism? It is evident in the first place that it represents not so much a methodological dogma as a certain drift or tendency in the approach to Christian theology in Africa, a tendency first explored in *Des Prêtres Noirs*. Ezeanya gave the following statement of this approach at Ibadan:

> It is necessary, therefore, that all scholars, teachers and heralds of the gospel should co-operate actively in the task of seeking to understand the essence of African religion. We are convinced that there are in African life and thought hidden treasures, precious gems, provided by God for the embellishment of the Gospel. The present generation has inherited a precious tradition from its forebears — a tradition that puts God first in everything, a tradition in which the spiritual takes precedence over the material.[17]

One of the outstanding earlier examples of the adaptionist approach, and one that well exemplifies the philosophical approach of francophone African Catholics, was Abbé Mulago gwa Cikala's *Une Visage africaine de Christianisme: l'unité vitale bantu face a l'unité vitale écclesiale*, which appeared in 1962.[18] Mulago's main thesis was that the

---

16. Mushete, 29.
17. Quoted by Ezeanya, 46.
18. Mulago, *Une Visage africaine de Christianisme: l'unité vitale bantu face a l'unité*

church must seek in its evangelism to give meaning to the aspirations of the people it seeks to convert. To do this there is need to

> undertake a laborious journey to the sources of the practices and customs of the people, in order to discover the mainspring and centre of their organisations and their traditions. Once he has discovered the centre of gravity he must transplant there the message of the Christian mystery.[19]

It needs to be emphasized that Mulago was not advocating a superficial drawing of parallels by which aspects of traditional religion are (sometimes all too naively) related to aspects of Christian doctrine. He was seeking rather to uncover the fundamental focus of each traditional thought-system. Among the Bantu of Rwanda-Burundi Mulago sees that center of gravity in the concept of vital union, which is epitomized within family relationship. In its strict sense this embraces the immediate family only, but in its wider application it includes all blood relations. Tribal unity can be regarded as an extension of the family, which may be widened still further by treaties and alliances between different clans. The essence of vital union for Bantu life then is communion, one with the other. Such communion survives even death, for a fundamental idea of Bantu religion, as Mulago interprets it, is the link between the living and their dead ancestors, who are the intermediaries between the living and God, the ultimate source of all life. The cult of the ancestors thus unites the two worlds, the visible and the invisible. Humans can exist only in the community and for the community. Vital union thus has a twofold function, corresponding to the "vertical" and "horizontal" dimensions of religion. It is the link with God, the ultimate source of life, and at the same time the link between man and his fellow and the world of things. Vital union is therefore neither exclusively

---

vitale écclesiale (Paris, 1965); see also his contribution, along similar lines, "Vital Participation," *BRAB*. For a detailed discussion of Mulago, see Bediako, *Theology and Identity* (Oxford, 1992), 347-85, and Benézét Bujo, *African Theology in its Social Context* (Maryknoll, 1992), 58-60. The latter describes Mulago as "the first African who can be called an African theologian."

19. Mulago, *Une Visage africaine*, 233ff.: for convenience, quotations are taken from the English summary.

corporeal life nor exclusively spiritual life; rather, it is life in the totality of its being, in its full integrity. As such it is "superempirical," for life here and now and life beyond the grave are inseparable and interdependent.

Mulago broadly accepts the concept of a hierarchy of beings as expounded in Tempels' Bantu *Philosophy*[20] and developed in modified terms by Alexis Kagame.[21] Beings are ranked in order of potency and are broadly divided into the invisible and visible worlds. Within the former, *Imana* (God) is supreme; then in descending order come the founders and the spirits of culture heroes, then deceased parents and relations. The hierarchy of the visible world is headed by the King and Queen Mother, broadening out into a kind of pyramid with the ranks of the chiefs, patriarchs, and family heads, and finally, as the base, the ordinary family members. Animal, vegetable, and inanimate created things are regarded as part of the total existence of those to whom they belong. Beings can influence each other for good or ill, to the increase or decrease of their vital power. *Ntu* (man) is thus a dynamic entity, rather than a static one, capable of both growth and decline as he is influenced by other beings. Those beings closest to *Imana*, the source of all life, are capable of exerting the most potent influence. A basic concept here is that of symbol. Through symbol contact is made with invisible power; it thus has a kind of "priestly" function. But it is also through symbol that the duality between man and the world is overcome and that unification of the "All" is achieved. Being is fundamentally one, for all beings are interconnected. Humans are not separate from other beings, and only the supreme being can exist independently of other beings. The unifying factor, the cement that holds all things together, is vital union, which transcends the merely visible and biological and reaches out to the invisible world.

Mulago has now identified his "mainspring," the center of gravity of the Bantu-Rwandan tradition, as vital union. His second task is to translate this into a base for Christian theology. The mirror, the Christian response to vital union in traditional thought, he finds in the doctrine of the church and the Trinity.

20. Although Mulago later pronounced Tempels's thesis "philosophically unsound" but probably "justified from a phenomenological standpoint" ("Vital Participation," 137 n. 2).

21. Alexis Kagame, *La Philosophie Bantu-rwandaise de l'Être* (Brussels, 1956).

The life connection which is the basis of communities and individuals among the Bantu, this vital communication, participation and vital means, this effort of growth, of going beyond, of ontological enrichment, finds an answer and a sublime and transcendental realisation in the Church of Christ, which is a community of life, and of which the vital principle is a participation in the life of the Trinity, made more human in the Word of God made man. This participation is never completed in this world, and tends constantly to intensify itself more and more in likeness to the Son of God, founder of this "clan" descended from heaven, the church.[22]

The sharing community of traditional culture is here transcended in Christian teaching into the sharing community of the church, "the community of those associated in the supernatural life." And the Godhead itself, the Trinity, provides the supreme example of mutual participation. The Christian community, furthermore, is characterized by growth. It cannot find completeness in this world, but is in the process of being transformed into "the likeness of the Man from Heaven." The thirst of the Bantu to participate in and to communicate with greater forces finds its fulfillment in the church of God. The desire for symbolism, through which in traditional thought contact with the deity was effected, can be fulfilled in the seven sacraments of the Catholic Church. Each of these, according to Mulago, has its counterpart in traditional life. Baptism can be regarded as corresponding to traditional initiation into the Nyangombe hero cult, and confirmation to "second degree" initiation; anointing of the sick finds its counterpart in the traditional rubbing of butter on the corpse, the eucharist in the blood pact,[23] and so on. In this way the church has its archetype in the clan, the tribe, and the kingdom. The Christian community becomes

the true answer to the aspirations of the Bantu, a transcendental and supernatural answer, an answer not in the sense that nature is, as it were, prepared for the supernatural gift, but in the sense that in God's

22. Mulago, *Une Visage africaine*, 240.
23. This parallel had previously been developed in "Le pacte de sang et la communion allimentaire, pierres d'attente de la communion eucharistique," in *Des Prêtres Noirs s'interrogent*, 171-87.

plan man has since his creation been raised freely and without any merit on his part to the supernatural order.[24]

How far is Mulago's approach valid? Its essence is that there is a single "center of gravity" in Bantu-Rwanda religious thought, namely, the concept of vital union, that gives it a fundamental rationale. It will be recalled that the earliest attempt to discover the centripetal focus of Bantu religion (although with a different group, the Luba) came to the conclusion that it was to be found in the idea of "vital force" — and indeed, with some reservations, Mulago broadly accepts many of Tempels's propositions in his own work. The problem here is not so much whether these writers have correctly isolated basically important concepts in Bantu thought-systems — that can scarcely be denied; it is rather whether one special aspect can be viewed as so dominant that it forms the basis of the system as a whole. It is partly this attempt to reduce African religion to one major concept, in the manner of Tempels, which may then be readily related to an analogous aspect of Christian theology, that has led to the characterization of the adaptionist method as one "bequeathed by the missionaries."[25]

A related problem with Mulago's work is his readiness to relate too easily specific aspects of traditional culture to Christian rituals, especially the sacraments of the Catholic Church. That there are indeed points of similarity between some forms of traditional initiation rites and some Christian rites is undeniable. But such similarities are not peculiar to Africa, still less to one particular African culture, for rites of passage, the sacred meal, and so on form part of the common religious heritage of humankind.[26] The Christian theologian may indeed use them as indications of a spiritual desire that finds its outlet in such rites, and they may therefore be, in a sense, a *preparatio evangelica*, or a point of contact between the traditional and the Christian. But this is a different thing from postulating some kind of special relationship between Christianity and African religions, which Mulago's adaptionist approach seems to do.

24. Mulago, *Une visage africaine*, 242.

25. So S. Sempore, "Conditions of Theological Service in Africa: Preliminary Reflections," *CIA*, 517.

26. The comparative literature is vast; here we may allude only to Van Gennep's pioneering *The Rites of Passage*.

Though he lays great stress on the value of Bantu tradition, Mulago at the same time acknowledges the ultimacy of the Christian revelation. The task of theologians, as he sees it, is to purify the various aspects of the Bantu concept of vital union, so that it can be fittingly introduced into Catholic theology:

> The introduction must be an assimilation, an incarnation, but above all a liberation, an elevation, a transfiguration, a supernaturalisation, a new way of being, a seizure in and by Christ, in and by the Church.[27]

Such a theology will have a pastoral concern, for "in order that the Bantu may feel at home the church must show universality and love." The way to this is adaption in all fields — theological, catechetical, pastoral, and disciplinary, and "the unashamed affirmation of the church's négritude."[28] A subsequent important contribution from the adaptionist francophone school was Tshibangu's brief *Le propos d'une théologie africaine*.[29] Tshibangu begins by affirming the need for plurality in Christian thought, corresponding to the multiplicity of languages and philosophical systems throughout the Christian world. While all Christian theology must be based on biblical exegesis and the history of dogma, these — if they are to be relevant — must lead on to subsequent "interpretation," and it is at this point that Christian Africa can make its special contribution to theology. For Tshibangu there are steps in the theological method. The first is what is "given" in revelation; this must then, secondly, lead on to the elaboration of the given in terms that make it intelligible to each and every people. Finally — and this is the task of African theology proper — are the attempts at a more elaborate interpretation and systematization. In an earlier paper,[30] Tshibangu had pleaded for the place of culture to be taken seriously in the development of theology. His point of departure is Christianity's enlivening *(animation)* of African life, mentality, and outlook, and the whole of African culture.[31] According to Tshibangu, African

---

27. Mulago, *Une visage africaine*, 242.

28. Mulago, *Une visage africaine*, 242.

29. Tshibangu, *Le Propos d'une Théologie Africaine* (Kinshasa, 1974).

30. Tshibangu, "Vers une théologie de couleur africaine," *RCA* 15 (1960): 333-46.

31. Tshibangu, *d'Une Théologie Africaine*, 12: "il s'agit de plus que simplement

thinking is characterized by a spontaneous trust in the faculties of intuitive and intellectual knowledge[32] and by a vision of the world that is global, dynamic, and vitalistic, a kind of ontological-existentialist view of humankind.[33] Furthermore, African religion has both concepts and institutions that may be used to throw light on certain aspects of theological issues. These points of contact provide the avenues for developing "a theology of African color."

Tshibangu's indebtedness to earlier writers is clear. From Tempels he has taken the concept of vital force as the basic feature of the African worldview.[34] Being is identified with vital force. The emphasis on the symbolical nature of African thought is supported by Griaule's research, and justification for the characterization of negro reasoning as discursive but not synthetic draws heavily on Senghor. It was perhaps this overreliance on such Western or Western-inspired writings that aroused the criticism of Sempore,[35] and indeed, serious question marks have been raised against all those authors to whom Tshibangu is heavily indebted. But to question the appropriateness of his sources is not necessarily to destroy Tshibangu's theological method. While it may indicate his references are out of date (or out of favor), it does not invalidate his plea that the Christian faith should enliven and animate African life in its wholeness.

Mulago and Tshibangu belong to what Charles Nyamiti has called the speculative school of Catholic theology in Africa.[36] Nyamiti himself has set out his theological methodology in several papers, but most fully in his *The Way to Christian Theology in Africa*.[37] Nyamiti recognizes that

---

l'inimation et l'information par l'ésprit chrétien de la vie africaine de sa mentalité, de sa manière de voir les choses, et un mot de sa culture."

32. The French reads: "une conflance spontanée dans les facultés de connaissance sensible et intellectuelle, orientant vers une philosophie du sens commune, par un recours spontané et foi à la connaissance par intuition" (Tshibangu, *d'Une Théologie Africaine*, 5).

33. "Une ontologie existentielle des personnes."

34. Tshibangu does not refer to Tempels, although he does mention Bergson, whose "élan vital" is very similar to Tempels's "force vitale."

35. Sempore, 517 n. 3.

36. So C. Nyamiti, "Approaches to African Theology," *EG*, 31. This paper provides a useful summary of Nyamiti's own position.

37. Charles Nyamiti, *The Way to Christian Theology in Africa* (Eldoret, n.d.). This constitutes a revision of his earlier *African Theology, Its Nature, Problems and Methods* (1971) and *The Scope of African Theology* (1973).

there are several approaches to theology within Africa, for cultural divergences make for a plurality of theologies. His own approach is concerned with "the building up of African systematic or scientific theology,"[38] which takes as its primary data the Bible, tradition, and history, and in which philosophy plays an important role. For Nyamiti Catholic theology is essentially bound up with tradition and the official teaching of the church: he therefore regards those approaches to theology that focus on particular issues — such as liberation, political systems, and so on — as one-sided and "unable to deal with the entire problems of theology and the African situation."[39] He claims his own approach, while it has historically been developed especially in the West, has a "universal bearing." African theology therefore should be the "very self-same Catholic doctrine expressed and presented in accordance with African mentality and needs," and at the same time should be based both on Christian revelation and on African culture and situations.[40] Christian teaching has an essentially "unchangeable kernel of revelation," which has to be applied to the African milieu. The fundamental dogmatic content is primary, while the African aspects are secondary, in the sense that these African elements have to be subordinated to the kernel of revelation and be modified to fit it.[41]

Nyamiti's method seeks to unite three distinct approaches to theology, which he calls the pastoral, the apologetical, and the pedagogical. Fundamentally "the pastoral motivation should permeate and determine all theological efforts."[42] Consequently theology is an activity of faith as well of intellect. The apologetic method has two aspects: negatively it consists in exposing the insufficiency and deficiency of non-Christian religions, and in showing that Christianity "answers to, and surpasses, human needs and aspirations."[43] This approach will therefore necessitate a deep study of both the sources and philosophies of African religions and those of the Christian faith. Nyamiti writes:

38. Nyamiti, *Way to Christian Theology,* Preface (not paginated), 2.
39. Nyamiti, *Way to Christian Theology,* Preface, 3.
40. Nyamiti, *Way to Christian Theology,* i.
41. Nyamiti, *Way to Christian Theology,* ii.
42. Nyamiti, *Way to Christian Theology,* 3.
43. Nyamiti, *Way to Christian Theology,* 4.

A theology resulting from such a method would necessarily have an African colour. Not only would the accent in theology be determined by the African mentality through the choice of theological themes more directly corresponding to the apologetical needs of the African, but also the arguments employed would partly be determined by the African way of thinking. All this would lead to the employment of new categories in theology and to a new way of theological presentation.[44]

The pedagogical approach involves the systematic exposition of Christian doctrine with the aid of philosophy, including a "critical African philosophy," and other sciences. Some of the fundamental ideas that might provide an entrance into African philosophy would be the African concepts of humankind, the world, destiny, suffering, and death, and African beliefs about God. These, together with other important cultural ideas — such as dynamism, solidarity and participation, the sacred, anthropocentrism — could be used to inform and contribute to a Christian theology. Nyamiti is, however, quite aware that theology may become a sterile exercise if it fails to deal with contemporary factors, and he therefore also emphasizes that issues such as the meaning of liberation, the tackling of social and political problems, and the engagement of the Christian faith with other religions and ideologies should play an important role in theologizing.[45]

The typically African elements may be used in constructing an African Christian theology in various ways. At one level they may be a *praeambula fidei*. More in line with the approach of Mulago and Tshibangu, they may also become points of departure for the exposition of Christian doctrines. For Nyamiti, prominent African concepts can provide the way into Christian dogma, which will then be able to build upon ideas and experiences that are truly African. This is, as we have seen, the essence of the adaptionist approach. However, Nyamiti emphasizes that the "kernel" of Christianity is to be found only in the Bible and in the tradition of the church and that it should be this kernel that penetrates and transforms African religions and that supplies what they lack.

44. Nyamiti, *Way to Christian Theology*, 5-6.
45. Nyamiti, *Way to Christian Theology*, 19.

It is this kernel which, while remaining absolutely unchanged, has to penetrate and transform the teaching of the African religions. The christianisation of the African elements will depend on their nature: those which are equally found in Christianity will have to be adopted as such; the elements analogous to the Christian mysteries will receive a Christian dimension corresponding to the mysteries to which they are analogous: the superstitions or erroneous elements will have to be eliminated. As Christianity surpasses the African religions, one will have to search in the Christian doctrine for the missing elements from the christianised African religious and moral doctrines. The missing elements should then be organically integrated in the African theology.[46]

Nyamiti's approach has its roots firmly in the traditional bases of Catholicism. While it seeks, along the lines of the adaptionist method, to utilize and incorporate into Christian theology all that is good in African religious culture, it retains a critical stance towards the traditional heritage and recognizes that there are elements that may be incompatible with the Christian faith.

Few Catholics have devoted the same energies to the method of theology as Mulago, Tshibangu, and Nyamiti. Others have used the term "adaptionism," however, in a much looser way. This has led, in some circles, to something of a reaction, as a result of which the very term itself has come to have a pejorative connotation. Much of this criticism, it seems to me, has failed to give due credit to the adaptionist approach and to appreciate its real importance in the advance of Christian theology in Africa.[47] Whatever the shortcomings of the adaptionist ap-

---

46. Nyamiti, *Way to Christian Theology*, 55, is raising, but not addressing, the very large issue of how such a kernel can be identified when it can only be conveyed and apprehended through a particular culture.

47. Shorter (*African Christian Theology* [London, 1975], 150) tends to dismiss adaptionism (though without any discussion of its leading exponents) because in his view "the idea this term suggests is one of the western missionary announcing the gospel in the terms of his own culture, and of the young, mission church adapting this message to suit local idiosyncrasies. The word 'adaptation' cannot help but convey an activity that is peripheral, non-essential — even superficial." This is a gross caricature of the adaptionist approach. Its most able exponents, far from succumbing to Western impositions, were in fact protesting vigorously against it! Shorter himself favors the term "incarnationism": this term was actually used by Mulago as far back as 1965. Shorter's

proach, it represents a genuine attempt to come to grips with the problem of the relationship between Christian theology and African culture and thought. It does not, in the hands of its most able exponents, focus attention only on the past to the neglect of contemporary issues, nor does it concentrate only on peripheral similarities between Christianity and traditional culture to the exclusion of the broader worldview. On the contrary, it has opened up new paths for Christian theology in Africa that are still being profitably explored, and that we shall examine in more detail in chapter four.

3. The Protestant Contribution to the Theological Method

The most significant of the earlier Protestant contributions to theological methodology came predominantly from West Africa, and may be traced back to the Ibadan conference of 1965. Indeed, we may regard this colloquium as practically an extended exercise in the adaptionist approach, although its final results, as Kwesi Dickson was later to remark,[48] were not entirely successful. The underlying assumption at Ibadan was that African culture had a genuine value and therefore should play a vital role in rendering the Christian faith relevant to Africans. The introductory statement deserves to be quoted in full for the light it throws on the way the participants went about their task:

> We believe that God, the Father of our Lord Jesus Christ, Creator of Heaven and earth, Lord of History, has been dealing with mankind at all times and in all parts of the world. It is with this conviction that we study the rich heritage of our African peoples, and we have evidence that they know Him and worship Him.

---

methodology, based as it is on the wholesale, and somewhat uncritical, use of Western anthropological writing, is open to just the criticisms he himself levels against adaptionism. One of the problems here seems to me to be that critics of adaptionism seldom make allowances for the fact that it represents not so much a solidly identifiable school as a drift that is used by writers from varying points of view.

48. Kwesi Dickson, "Towards a Theologia Africana," in *New Testament Christianity for Africa and the World*, ed. E. Fasholé-Luke and M. Glasswell (London, 1974), 204.

We recognise the radical quality of God's self-revelation in Jesus Christ; and yet it is because of this revelation we can discern what is truly of God in our pre-Christian heritage; this knowledge of God is not totally discontinuous with our previous knowledge of Him.[49]

This statement is important for its theological assumptions. It affirms that God has been active in all cultures at all times, that traditional African religion is indeed in a sense the worship of the true God, and that there is a continuity between African religions and Christian revelation. At the same time, the revelation in Christ represents a radically new element, which sheds light on the traditional past, revealing all that is truly of God in it. The two foci of this approach are therefore African traditional religions on the one hand, and Christian revelation on the other. This affirmation was to be reiterated in somewhat stronger terms a few years later by one of the leaders of the Ibadan conference, Bolaji Idowu. Writing of the need to construct a truly African theology he declared:

[T]he only way by which this worthy end can be obtained is for African theologians to apprehend African spiritual values with the African mind, while at the same time they possess the requisite knowledge of the fundamental facts of the faith which they are seeking to express and disseminate in an indigenous idiom.[50]

The earliest consistent, albeit brief, exposition of this kind of theological methodology was Harry Sawyerr's paper that attempted to answer the question, "What is African Theology?"[51] in which he introduced a number of important issues that have proved increasingly relevant. Sawyerr noted that the impact of such concepts as "African personality" and "négritude," while considerable, had been imprecise. These ideas had, however, performed a useful function in forcing African theologians to begin to reinterpret their faith in terms which Africans could understand and to which they could relate. For Sawyerr himself, theology should be

49. *BRAB*, 16.
50. Bolaji Idowu, *African Traditional Religions: A Definition* (London, 1973), x.
51. Harry Sawyerr, "What is African Theology," *ATJ* 4 (1971), reprinted in *The Practice of Presence, the Shorter Writings of Harry Sawyerr*, ed. John Parratt (Edinburgh, 1995), 8ff.

essentially practical, and should not be separated from worship. He fully acknowledged the importance of traditional religion, but firmly rejected the view that would seek to replace the Old Testament with the traditions of African religion. For him the heritage of Israel is integral to the Christian faith and essential for an understanding of the New Testament. Nor again should traditional African culture be taken in isolation from its modern counterpart of present-day secularism. Sawyerr was not enthusiastic about the contribution of the independent churches, whose theology — especially christology and soteriology — he regarded as seriously defective at several points. The African theologian therefore cannot use the independent churches as a yardstick. Sawyerr is in basic agreement with Mulago that there exists much common ground between African traditional religions and Christianity, and he sees the key to this in a proper acknowledgment of the place of the spirits, both ancestral and otherwise, within the African worldview.[52] Equally important is the need to establish a firm philosophical basis for theology. This means carrying out a "searching investigation into the content of traditional religious thought-forms with a view to erecting bridgeheads by which the Christian Gospel could be effectively transmitted to African peoples."[53] An important starting point here might be the concept of the cultic community, of which the African feels himself or herself a part, and which extends also into the supernatural sphere. If this is taken as central, other cardinal concepts, vital to both traditional religion and the Christian faith, such as birth and death, sin and sickness, health and forgiveness, could be introduced. In this way Christian theology in Africa would be more concerned with function, rather than with any radically new content. At the same time Sawyerr urges African theologians to stand fully within the mainstream of Christian theological traditions by a vigorous pursuit of systematic theology.[54]

Sawyerr's practical and pastoral concern — the "function" of the-

52. The "Christian theologian who seeks to use the ingredients of 'the African soil' to build a theology designed to meet the African situation must recognise the place of the spirits ancestral and otherwise — in the African world-view." Sawyerr, "What is African Theology," 17.

53. Sawyerr, "What is African Theology," 20.

54. "To the present writer, the answer lies in the vigorous pursuit of systematic theology, based on philosophical thought-forms of African peoples." Sawyerr, "What is African Theology," 24.

ology in his terms — had been developed a few years earlier in his *Creative Evangelism.*[55] This book was an attempt to integrate traditional religious ideas and rituals into the Christian faith. Sawyerr discusses the main aspects of the African interpretation of existence — the concept of God, the ancestors, evil, and so on — and then seeks to relate them to the needs of evangelism. While some aspects of traditional religions may be assimilated into the Christian faith, they are not, according to Sawyerr, entirely adequate. He therefore regards it as imperative to recognize the basic role of Hebrew and Jewish concepts as found in the Old Testament,[56] which have their culmination in the incarnation.[57] The liturgical approach to the indigenization of theology finds its focus, in Sawyerr's view, in the eucharist, into which salient features of African worship may be incorporated, thereby being transformed and trans-figured.[58] Central to this transformation of traditional ritual through Christian liturgy is the role of the priest. The Christian ministry in Africa should be a genuinely sacerdotal one, making full use of African ideas of priestcraft, since "priestcraft and with it confession, absolution and sacrifice are deeply ingrained in the life-setting and thought of the peoples."[59] Sawyerr's aim is to renew the Christian liturgy by the assimi-lation of certain refined aspects of traditional worship. He notes:

> If we are patient enough to distil from the corpus of African tradi-tional beliefs and practices such factors as are consonant with Chris-tianity, we shall ultimately redeem them into the obedience of Christ.[60]

Besides his emphasis on the pastoral and liturgical needs of the church, another feature of Sawyerr's book is his concern for what he calls "sound doctrine." He thus devotes a considerable amount of space to the examination of the biblical evidence for the central Christian dogmas — God, creation, christology, covenant — and is also at pains

---

55. Harry Sawyerr, *Creative Evangelism* (London, 1968).
56. Sawyerr, *Creative Evangelism,* 33ff.
57. Sawyerr, *Creative Evangelism,* 56.
58. Sawyerr, *Creative Evangelism,* 134-53.
59. Sawyerr, *Creative Evangelism,* 157.
60. Sawyerr, *Creative Evangelism,* 158.

to point out the absolute need for a clear appreciation of the Scriptures and the history of dogma, which will avoid the pitfalls of a superficial fundamentalism.[61] This in turn leads him to subject African beliefs to a penetrating scrutiny in the light of Christian doctrine and to reject those aspects that he finds inadequate as vehicles for the Christian faith.

Sawyerr's plea was echoed by Edward Fasholé-Luke.[62] For Fasholé-Luke the essence of African theology is "to translate the one Faith of Jesus Christ to suit the tongue, style, genius, character, and culture of the African peoples."[63] It must therefore be incarnational in the sense that it must be implanted in every society, and the form it assumes should be determined by the needs and character of that society. Such an incarnation of the gospel into African culture ought to be coextensive with evangelism. As such a theology is still in its embryonic stage, Fasholé-Luke addresses himself to the task of expounding the foundations on which African theology should be built.

Its primary source must be the Bible. Fasholé-Luke therefore firmly rejects a neo-Marcionite approach, which seeks to replace the Old Testament with traditional religions, as destructive of the wholeness of Christian revelation. While admitting that much Christianity in Africa is unduly fundamentalist in character, he recognizes the importance of the emphasis found therein on the uniqueness and finality of revelation in Christ as an essential one. He pleads, however, for an interpretation of the Bible that sees it both as the Word of God and the word of man, an approach that he feels will correct some of the present fundamentalist aberrations in Africa, and lead to a more fruitful use of the Bible in the construction of a relevant theology. Here he rightly laments the failure of the African church to produce genuine biblical scholars, and insists that until this happens African theology will be "sterile, bankrupt and unworthy of the African tradition which nourished Tertullian, Cyprian and Augustine."[64]

If the Bible is to be the primary source, then African religions and philosophy are next in importance, and Fasholé-Luke recommends a

61. Sawyerr, *Creative Evangelism*, 67ff.

62. E. Fasholé-Luke, "The Quest for African Christian Theology," *JRT* 32, no. 2 (1975).

63. Fasholé-Luke, "Quest," 77.

64. Fasholé-Luke, "Quest," 80.

wider use of anthropological findings and a thorough study of oral traditions in the analysis of African religions, with a view to their use in Christian theology. Alongside the two foundations of biblical and anthropological studies, Fasholé-Luke, like Sawyerr, stresses the need for a closer examination of the heritage of the church. Rejecting the extreme position that dismisses Western theology as irrelevant, he notes that the pluralism in Western theology itself makes it possible for the African theologian to select those insights that are meaningful while rejecting those that are culturally conditioned.[65] While he recognizes the place of independent churches and advocates a close examination of the theology of these bodies, Fasholé-Luke stresses that their teaching may be unsystematic and needs to be critically assessed.[66] In sum, the quest for Christian theology in Africa should be the search for a "medium by which Africans and non-Africans can think together about the fundamental articles of Christian faith in Africa."[67]

Like Fasholé-Luke, the two leading Ghanaian theologians, Kwesi Dickson and John Pobee, see the foundations of theology in Africa as the Bible and the African religious heritage. Kwesi Dickson's views were first put forward in a number of disciplined papers and later developed in his *Theology in Africa,* which is perhaps still the most sustained defense of cultural theology to come out of Africa. Dickson drew attention to certain paradoxes in African Christianity, which gave rise to the tensions that brought forth African theological reflection.[68] This reflection, emerging first of all in informal oral theologizing in hymn, prayer, and preaching, he believes now stands in need of deeper systematization. Dickson therefore addresses himself to the question of how the Christian faith may be adjusted to be meaningful to the African context.[69]

According to Dickson, the African theologian may proceed along several avenues. One, following the line of liturgical renewal, is the rewriting of services to suit African realities. Another is a return to a thorough study of the Bible, which he believes has been woefully ne-

---

65. Fasholé-Luke, "Quest," 82.
66. Fasholé-Luke, "Quest," 83-84, 89.
67. Fasholé-Luke, "Quest," 89.
68. Kwesi Dickson, *Theology in Africa* (London, 1984), 16ff.; Kwesi Dickson, "African Theology: Origin, Method and Content," *JRT* 30, no. 2 (1975): 42.
69. Dickson, *Theology in Africa,* 109ff.; "African Theology," 34ff.

glected by the Church in Africa,[70] with unhappy results. Dickson sees the Old Testament especially as one area in which Biblical concepts can be easily related to African ones.[71] This is not to be accomplished by a naive parallelism, but through a deep penetration of the fundamental concepts of both religious traditions. It is to be hoped that the result would be a "theology of self-hood," relevant to both the plurality of the African religious scene and to those situations in which oppression and injustice are to be found. Some of these ideas were developed in Dickson's contribution to the Sawyerr *Festschrift*. Here he again emphasized the need to make the Christian church a fundamentally African institution — "one which belongs to the African world" — rather than something that is predominantly Western. He comments:

> It would be strange indeed, at a time when the Christian world in general is questioning its role in an increasingly secularised world, for the Church in Africa to wear the garments fashioned a good many generations ago.[72]

Dickson visualizes this process of rethinking the African nature of the church as an ongoing one, which is as yet only in its early stages. An important facet of the African religious situation, in Dickson's view, has been the emergence and proliferation of the independent churches. While not all that these churches do is meaningful, and while they sometimes have a tendency to misinterpret the Bible, they have at least sought to bring about a spontaneous synthesis between Christianity and the African cultural and religious heritage, and they are a factor that a study of theology in Africa cannot ignore.[73]

Dickson's own approach to theology develops around two poles, the biblical and the cultural. On the one hand, he emphasizes the need to base African theology on a sound biblical foundation. He freely

70. Dickson, "African Theology," 42. On the problems of biblical hermeneutics in African theology, see chapter 3.

71. Dickson, *Theology in Africa*, 141ff.; "African Theology," 43ff. See also his "The Old Testament and African Theology," *Ghana Bulletin of Theology* 4, no. 4 (1973): 31-41, and "Continuity and Discontinuity between the Old Testament and African Life and Thought," *ATER*, 95-108.

72. Dickson, "Towards a Theologia Africana," 198-208.

73. Dickson, *Theology in Africa*, 10, 113.

admitted that the Ibadan consultation contributed little in this respect. *Biblical Revelation and African Belief,* he felt in retrospect, sprang out of an approach that was built upon a faulty methodology: it was inadequate, in his view, to proceed "by first making a value judgement of certain facets of African life and thought, then seeking sanction from biblical revelation for their incorporation into the expression of Christian faith."[74] For Dickson this is a reversal of what should be done. He thus regards the only valid approach to be to move from the biblical revelation to the traditional religion, and not vice versa.[75] The study of the Scriptures then should be primary, for they are the indispensable source of theology.[76] But the study of the Bible must always, in his view, be done in relation to the African situation.[77] The Scriptures themselves are a witness to the revelation of God mediated through particular events in a particular historical and cultural context. The church therefore, wherever it may be situated, should relive the Scriptures in its own experience, so that it becomes the living word of God and speaks to each people's real-life situation. In this respect, Dickson believes that African theologians should feel free to develop theological categories of their own that would suit the task in hand, rather than being dominated by the categories of Western theology:

> African Christians wanting to restate Christian teaching for themselves and their people should not work from the assumption that traditional categories of doctrinal statement are immutable.[78]

The fundamental tools of the Bible and Christian doctrine should therefore provide the basis of African theology, but should not be a straitjacket by which Africans are constrained, and should not stifle innovation.

Dickson's second emphasis is upon culture. He takes culture very seriously indeed as a source for theology, arguing that Christian theology

---

74. Dickson, "Towards a Theologia Africana," 204.

75. Dickson's criticism could be applied with some force to the Catholic representatives of adaptionism discussed above.

76. Kwesi Dickson, *The African Theological Task,* 47; *Theology in Africa,* 16ff.

77. Dickson, *Theology in Africa,* 19ff., 182.

78. Dickson, *African Theological Task,* 49; *Theology in Africa,* 119-20.

can only be done in a particular cultural context and that from its inception the gospel has been culturally colored.[79] Culture is therefore an important formative factor because the saving activity of God in Christ "embraces different people who speak different tongues and live their own differing but authentic life-styles, whom God in his wisdom has created." This "obliges the Church to expect that there will be different understandings and expressions of the same fact."[80] In Africa culture and religion are bound inextricably together. Dickson isolates several elements in African culture that may have an impact on doing theology. These African cultural values include the concern for a just society and a communalism that eschewed extremes of wealth and poverty. In this sense, therefore, an awareness of African cultural realties can lead to sociopolitical questions being on the agenda. At the same time, the Christian theologian will need to take African religion seriously, seeking a fuller understanding of its internal rationale as well as of its rituals, and examining how it continues to affect human life and behavior today, despite all the modern influences that have been brought to bear on it.[81]

John Pobee shares Dickson's biblical and cultural emphases. For him the task of theology in Africa is "to translate Christianity into genuine African categories."[82] *Homo africanus* to him is a "multi-headed hydra," and there is a multiplicity of cultures within the continent. Pobee therefore believes that we ought to speak of "theologies" in the plural. His book seeks to deal only with his own culture, and is an attempt to show how the Christian message may be communicated to the Akan — although he suggests that his own particular study may well be meaningful elsewhere in Africa. To speak of "African culture" is not to confine oneself to past traditions. Humans in Africa are not museum pieces, nor may one reconstruct a "fossilized" traditional religion. Rather, African people have grown in mentality, outlook, and culture as they have partaken of the pluralistic modern world of change and development. Pobee's focus is very much on the relevance of African culture as present existential reality. He believes that

79. Dickson, *Theology in Africa*, 17.
80. Dickson, *Theology in Africa*, 28-29.
81. Dickson, *Theology in Africa*, 37, 85, 137ff.
82. John Pobee, *Towards an African Theology* (Nashville, 1979), 17.

African theology is concerned to interpret essential Christian faith in authentic African language in the flux and turmoil of our time, so that there may be genuine dialogue between the Christian faith and African cultures.[83]

In Pobee's view certain aspects of the Christian faith are non-negotiable. Consequently African theology needs to be rooted in the traditionally accepted bases of Christian theology — that is, in the Bible (taking into full account all that modern biblical criticism can contribute to its interpretation), and in the historical dogmas of the church. This will ensure that theology in Africa is not insular but ecumenical. However, to be relevant to Africa, theology should at the same time concern itself with "revelation in African religion."[84] In uncovering the values of African religions, Pobee favors an impartial phenomenological approach, which will involve the collection, analysis, and elucidation of oral literature — myths, prayers, proverbs, and so on. The raw materials of African theology thus are biblical-theological materials on the one hand, and the oral traditions of African religion on the other. How are these to be used?

The center of the Christian faith, according to Pobee, is the Christ event. Christian theology, therefore, within any given context "should reflect on the implications of that Christ event for those who see the world in a particular way"[85] — that is, it should seek to discover what the Christ event looks like when seen from within a particular worldview. Such an interpretation of the faith is specific to each and every historic community, for "theology implies participation." Consequently the function of theology within an African context should be to ask what statements can be made about Christ when his person and work are seen and are reflected upon from within African culture. Such statements will use African concepts and the African ethos as vehicles for the communication of the gospel. For the Akan the question of existence ultimately depends upon a sense of belonging; it is *cognatus ergo sum*, I am related by blood, therefore I exist.[86] This is indeed, in Pobee's view, a concept that the Akan share with other African peoples and that is also closely related to the biblical view of

---

83. Pobee, *Towards an African Theology*, 22.
84. Pobee, *Towards an African Theology*, 21.
85. Pobee, *Towards an African Theology*, 28.
86. Pobee, *Towards an African Theology*, 49.

solidarity. Here, therefore, is one point of contact between Christianity and Akan society, and similarities of this kind can become a starting point for a dialogue between the two traditions. Such similarities provide the basis for the theological method of "adaption, localization, or indigenization," which finds its ultimate doctrinal justification in the fact that Christ himself was incarnated in a specific culture. In Pobee's hands the adaptionist method proceeds by discussing the essence of Akan religion to see "how far it is consonant with Christian worship." Pobee therefore asks such questions as, Can the Akan idea of God, especially as contained in the praise names, help in capturing what the Christian faith has to say about God? How far does the cohesion of the family help our understanding of the Church? How can Akan ethics and cosmology assist us in understanding good and evil?

Clearly, in Pobee's view, not everything in African cultures may be useful for the purposes of adaption — some elements have to be purified and others may have to be rejected outright. What is needed is for African theology to be couched as far as possible in African terms and categories, without thereby losing anything of its authentic and essential Christian character.[87]

Perhaps Pobee's most illuminating elaboration of this approach is in his examination of christology, to which we shall return below. Here it may be noted that his method seeks to bring out the real value of African culture, while at the same time subjecting it to penetrating criticism in the light of the Bible as the fundamental source of Christian revelation. One outstanding feature of his book is his adroit use of Akan proverbs and sayings, by which he attempts to bring out the folk wisdom of Akan religion. While other writers have paid lip service to the importance of oral literature, few have so painstakingly delved into religious and moral oral tradition as Pobee does here. In this he has opened up new possibilities for exploring common ground between African religions and the Christian faith.

4. Feminist Perspectives

In common with American black theology (and indeed Latin American liberation theology), women's issues were not in the forefront in the

87. Pobee, *Towards an African Theology*, 79.

early debates about African theology. One reason for this, no doubt, was the paucity of theologically trained women, a situation that is now rapidly being rectified. Feminist theology in Africa has not been as strident as in some parts of the Western world, and it would probably be right to characterize it (like its sister movement in Asia) as concerned with women's role in the wholeness of a single humanity rather than in feminism as a revolutionary countermovement. The earliest sustained exposition to come from an African woman, Mercy Amba Oduyoye's *Hearing and Knowing*, indeed argues that feminism implies "a particular way of addressing itself to what it means to be human"[88] and that "women's experience should be an integral part of what goes into the definition of being human."[89] Feminist theology, then, is a way of bringing the neglect of women by the church and by theology out into the open and of redressing the present imbalance between sexes. It is thus a "second-generation" liberation theology. Part of the problem here is that women have been traditionally valued only in relation to men, as daughters, wives, mothers, rather than as individuals in their own right. Thus even in matriarchal societies a woman has no real power or status, and is defined only in relation to others.[90] The other side of the problem is that this traditional way of regarding women has been carried over into the church — "the women are very much concerned about the church, but the church is not so much concerned with women," Oduyoye remarks. She argues that the feminine perspective and women's experience must be taken seriously as part of the data for theological reflection.[91] Ideas and language that legitimize the domestication and sidelining of women need to be seriously challenged. Both the mythology and oral tradition of African religion and the sources of the Christian theological tradition need to be confronted so that the integrity and contribution of women can become integrated into the theological task.

While Oduyoye is deeply concerned to redress the marginalizing

88. Mercy Amba Oduyoye, *Hearing and Knowing; Theological Reflections on Christianity in Africa* (Maryknoll, 1986), 120.

89. Oduyoye, *Hearing and Knowing*, 121.

90. The Indonesian theologian Marianne Katoppo's *Compassionate and Free* (Geneva 1979) argued that woman is conceived as "the other" or "the threatening other" rather than as a person in her own right.

91. Oduyoye, *Hearing and Knowing*, 135.

of the feminist perspective in much African theology, her use of the Bible stands firmly within the Protestant tradition, both cultural and liberational.[92] The Nigerian Catholic Teresa Okure, in a short study of the narrative of the appearance of the risen Jesus to Mary Magdalene in John 20:11-18,[93] has presented a more distinctive African feminist hermeneutic. Okure rightly rejects the interpretation that the phrase in v. 17a "do not touch me" implies that pollution would result from Jesus being touched by a woman. On the contrary, the phrase implies no rebuke but rather is part of her commissioning. The substance of the commission is that now, for the first time in the Gospel, God is "your Father," that is, that "they and Jesus share the same parent or ground of being in God."[94] Further, the plural "your" implies a new relationship between the followers of Jesus themselves: "[T]hey relate to Jesus as blood brothers and sisters relate to one another. Hence Jesus' relationship with his Father and with them now becomes the norm of their relationship with one another."[95] Thus, according to Okure, the cardinal New Testament conviction, that believers are in the fullest sense children of God, derives from the Easter message entrusted to a woman. Okure's application of this insight in the modern world is to see the church as a family united by blood, the blood of Christ shed on the cross, which nourishes the church in the symbolism of the eucharist. Her paper is an indication that feminist exegetical insights are now enriching the agenda of African theology.[96]

The possibility of feminine language and symbolism in theology has also been the concern of both male and female African theologians. Nyamiti, for example, argued strongly that African tradition has a rich variety of female symbols for God, including God as Mother, and the

---

92. Oduyoye, *Hearing and Knowing*, 56-119.

93. Teresa Okure, "The Significance Today of Jesus' Commission to Mary Magdalene," *IRM* 81, no. 322 (1992): 177-88. This whole issue is devoted to women in mission. See also Teresa Okure, "Women in the Bible," in *With Passion and Compassion*, ed. V. Fabella and M. Oduyoye (Maryknoll, 1988), 47-59.

94. Okure, "Jesus' Commission," 182.

95. Okure, "Jesus' Commission," 183.

96. See further the volumes *With Passion and Compassion* and, more recently, M. Oduyoye and M. Kanyoro, eds., *Tabitha Qumi!* (proceedings of the convocation of African women theologians) (Ibadan, 1990). See below, chapter 6, for the writing of African women on christology.

assumption of such characteristics as life, fruitfulness, and generation power.[97] Boulaga, on the other hand, used the figure of the archetypal Mother to explicate the central mystery of rebirth.[98] The Kenyan feminist theologian Nyambura Njoroge has focused on the inadequacy of scientific language to convey the mysteries of Christian faith. For her the canticles contained in the Lucan narratives, and uttered in that context by women, provide new possibilities of holistic expression. Thus the language of stories, myths, symbols, dance and song, ritual and drama, but more especially the language of grassroots communities, can point forward to new ways of communicating the meaning of faith.[99] The role of language in African theology is now one that is firmly on the agenda.

The main contribution to theological methodology of the scholars discussed above has broadly been twofold. First, they have emphasized the need to take seriously the Bible as the foundation document of the Christian faith and the primary basis for a lasting theology in Africa. Second, they have stressed the need for a sympathetic, but at the same time critical, treatment of African cultures, in order to make the Christian faith relevant and comprehensible within the African context. These two basic sources were clearly affirmed at the Pan-African Conference of the Third World Theologians in Accra in 1977:

> The Bible is the basic source of African Theology, because it is the primary witness of God's revelation in Jesus Christ. No theology can retain its Christian identity apart from Scripture. The Bible is not simply an historical book about the people of Israel; through a re-reading of this scripture in the social context of our struggling for humanity, God speaks to us in the midst of our troublesome situation. This divine word is not an abstract proposition but an event in our lives, empowering us to continue to fight for our full humanity.
>
> The God of history speaks to all peoples in particular ways. In

---

97. Charles Nyamiti, *African Tradition and the Christian God* (Eldoret, n.d.), 13-15.

98. For a discussion of F. Eboussi Boulaga, see below, chapter 5.

99. Nyambura Njoroge, "Confessing Christ in Africa Today," in *Exploring Afro-Christology*, ed. J. Pobee (Frankfurt am Main, 1992), 131ff.

Africa the traditional religions are a major source for the study of the African experience of God. The beliefs and practices of the Traditional Religions in Africa can enrich Christian theology and spirituality.[100]

In the following two chapters we shall first seek to assess how far and in what way the Bible is in fact being used by Christian theologians in Africa. We shall then examine the assumption that African traditional religions constitute a genuine divine revelation and look at examples of how aspects of traditional religions are being used to elucidate certain Christian doctrinal beliefs.

---

100. *ATER,* 193. The statement includes also among the sources of African theology, African cosmology, African independent churches, and "other African realities" such as cultural expressions, commonality, and the struggle against social, economic, and racial oppression.

III

Scripture and Revelation

1. The Biblical Hermeneutic[1]

In our discussion of theological methodologies we noted that African theologians in general are agreed that the Bible is the foundation document of the Christian faith, as important and basic for theology in Africa as elsewhere. It will be helpful, therefore, to consider the question of the place that the Bible is actually playing in theology in Africa and the way in which it has been used.

John Mbiti, in a paper first published in 1978,[2] attempted to give evidence for the view that "the potential and actual influence (of the Bible) in shaping African theology and Christianity is tremendous."[3] Mbiti noted the great influence that translations of the Bible have had upon the continent — despite the wide variation of literacy rates — especially, as he puts it, in integrating the biblical world with the traditional African world at all levels.[4] Mbiti divides theology in Africa into three categories, which he terms the written, the oral, and the symbolic.

1. See also my "African Theology and Biblical Hermenutics," *ATJ* 12, no. 2 (1983): 88-94. The special case of the use of materialist exegesis in South African black theology will be considered in chapter 7.

2. John Mbiti, "The Biblical Basis for Present Trends in African Theology," *ATJ* 7, no. 7 (1978): 72-85, reprinted in *ATER*, 83-94, from which the page references are taken.

3. Mbiti, "Biblical Basis," 84.

4. Mbiti, "Biblical Basis," 83.

By symbolic theology Mbiti means the expression of Christian belief through ritual,[5] a theme to which we shall return below in connection with the Christian sacraments. Oral theology is for Mbiti an important concept, and one that he has expounded in more detail elsewhere.[6] It is largely a prerequisite to written theology and consists in popular, usually vernacular, reflection on the faith produced by Christians in their preaching, teaching, evangelizing, and worship. It is usually local and limited in character, and seldom recorded.[7] Mbiti's main concern, therefore, was to document written theology. On the basis of some three hundred articles and books available to him at that time, Mbiti believed that "African Christianity has the Bible as its forefront, and the Bible is shaping much of its development both explicitly and implicitly."[8]

On closer examination one is forced to the conclusion that this view was only partially correct and that Mbiti was perhaps oversanguine. At a popular level it was true that a good deal was being produced within Africa on "Bible study." At the level of serious academic work, however, the position was — and to a degree still is — much less encouraging. Mbiti's own *New Testament Eschatology* and several papers by writers such as Sawyerr, Dickson, and Pobee stand out in the formative period of African theology in that they were the work of scholars trained to high standards in biblical studies. But in general the contributions of African scholars in the field of biblical exegesis have fallen short of their corresponding contribution to the study of African religions.

There were several reasons for this state of affairs. Fourah Bay, of course, had taught theology since 1874, and was thus well to the forefront in biblical studies. For most African countries, however, biblical scholarship is a very recent phenomenon. Further, within those several African universities that have departments of religion, biblical and theological studies are only one area of study out of several in multireligious communities (African religions and Islam often being

---

5. Mbiti thus gives quite a different meaning to symbolic theology than does MacQuarrie.

6. John Mbiti, "Cattle Are Born with Ears, Their Horns Grow Later," *ATJ* 8, no. 1 (1979): 15-25.

7. Although some attempts have been made to record sermons, pioneered in H. W. Turner's analysis of texts in his *Profile through Preaching* (Edinburgh, 1965).

8. Mbiti, "Biblical Basis," 91.

9. Compare Dickson's comments in *The African Theological Task*, 47.

as important).[9] The biblical disciplines consequently have much less time devoted to them than is customary in Europe. Some departments of religion, for reasons that may be quite valid locally, teach little or no Hebrew or Greek, and among those that do, books and materials are still often in short supply. Theological colleges have tried to correct this in providing instruction in biblical languages, but these institutions often tend to operate at a less academic level. Those colleges that offer degrees (e.g., the Lutheran College at Makumira) often do so outside the aegis of their universities, although at a lower level some countries (Malawi, Uganda, Zimbabwe) have a theological diploma that is accredited by their respective national universities. It is also perhaps unfortunate that so many talented African scholars have in the past opted to specialize in traditional religion to the loss of biblical scholarship. These are serious problems, which are likely to affect the development of African theology for some time to come. Fasholé-Luke indeed drew attention to this dilemma as long ago as 1974. After stressing the need for African theologians to be first-rate biblical scholars, highly competent in biblical languages, he went on:

> Unfortunately, there are few African theologians with the necessary source-material, of sufficiently high quality, so that African Christian theologies will rise above the level of the banal and peripheral. This calls for the training of well equipped biblical scholars in Africa and a radical reappraisal of the policies in our University Departments of Religious Studies, Theological Colleges, Seminaries and even Bible Schools.

He then commented caustically:

> I suspect that the major reason why consultations, conferences and seminars on African Theology simply affirm the uniqueness of Christianity and the primary status of Scripture and then quickly pass on to African Traditional Religions and the impact of Westernized Christianity upon them, is that many of those present at these Conferences are not well grounded in the Bible.[10]

10. E. Fasholé-Luke, "The Quest for African Christian Theology," *JRT* 32, no. 2 (1975): 80.

In Fasholé-Luke's view, however fascinating comparative religion may be, it is no substitute for a rigorous study of the Bible. Since those words were spoken there has been a welcome and perceptible shift to a greater emphasis on biblical and theological factors in formulating Christian theology in Africa, but there is equally some way to go before the affirmation of the basic role of the Bible in African theology becomes a practical reality. Equally, African theologians outside of South Africa have given little direct attention to the theoretical and philosophical issues in determining a biblical hermeneutic, and it may be claimed that their hermeneutic is more often implicit than explicit.

It is perhaps understandable that one approach to the Bible has been to attempt to relate it to the African cultural heritage. Certain areas of biblical studies ought indeed to relate fairly closely to African traditions. Sundkler, for example, drew attention to what he termed "remembrance" in both traditions.[11] In his understanding, African religious rites are a source of remembrance, by means of which the existential involvement of the present generation in a past or mythical event is secured, through the reenactment of festivals and the recital of certain events. The closeness of this method of preserving traditions to certain interpretations of the Bible is evident.[12] Another area of similarity is that of oral tradition. This has played an increasingly important role in biblical criticism, and we are now beginning to understand the Bible less as a collection of documents than as the end product of a process of development in which traditions were born, developed, and transformed, and in which a period of oral transmission preceded the actual writing of the books themselves. The study of traditional religions has also been giving more and more attention to the place of oral tradition.[13] We are fortunately beginning to have at our disposal impressive collections of African oral religious literature, and Christian theologians are now using these.[14] The dichotomy between a written religious tradition (the Bible) and an oral one (African religions) is therefore no longer wholly valid. Both share a similar development from the oral to the written.

11. Bengt Sundkler, *The Christian Ministry in Africa* (London, 1960), 285-86.
12. E.g., in Mowinckel's *Psalmenstudien* (1923).
13. J. Vansina, *Oral Tradition* (Harmondsworth, 1973).
14. E.g., J. Mbiti, *The Prayers of African Religion* (London, 1975); A. Shorter, *Prayer in the Religious Traditions of Africa* (Nairobi, 1975); C. Gaba, *Scriptures of an African People* (New York, 1977).

A more frequent method of relating African traditions to the Bible has been to draw attention to the close parallels between the biblical world and that of traditional Africa. It needs scarcely to be emphasized that the traditional world was, like that of the Gospels, one in which supernatural powers impinged on the world of humans at all points, and in which all life was subject to the influence of spiritual powers. This is nowhere more seen perhaps than in those areas that cause some embarrassment to European exegetes, such as demon possession and the personalization of evil. Mbiti, for example, has drawn out the parallel between the African spirit world and the evil spirits in the Gospels.[15] The Kings put it more picturesquely: "The New Testament world of spirits buzzing round, super-imposing themselves on human spirits, being beaten off by stronger than they, comes alive in Africa."[16]

This is but one aspect of the view, common to the biblical writers and African traditional thought, that causality is not simply a matter of natural consequence but of the interplay of spiritual powers. Cultural similarities between the biblical and African worldviews have also been noted. Mbiti refers to such socioreligious factors as respect for parents and authority, family coherence and marriage customs, ties to the land, the place of festivals, and the all-pervading concept of God.[17] While such cultural parallels are useful, they also have their limitations, especially from a methodological point of view. Many of these aspects, as Dickson has pointed out, although helpful for a basic understanding of what he calls "the total consciousness of Israel," are not really essential to the main thrust of the biblical message.[18]

---

15. John Mbiti, *New Testament Eschatology in an African Background,* 185.

16. N. Q. and D. J. F. King, "Towards an African Strack-Billerbeck," *Religion in a Pluralistic Society,* 83. This is a characteristic of the African worldview that has come to the forefront through the work of Archbishop Emmanuel Milingo; see *The World in Between: Healing and the Struggle for Spiritual Survival,* ed. with an introduction by Mona MacMillan (London, 1984).

17. John Mbiti, "Christianity and African Culture," *JTSA* 20 (1977): 35. Mbiti notes, "[T]he Bible is close to African peoples because of the many items in common between their cultural life and the cultural life of the Jews as contained in the Bible." See also E. Isaacs, "Relations between the Hebrew Bible and Africa," *Jewish Social Studies* 26, no. 2 (1964): 87-94.

18. Kwesi Dickson, "African Traditional Religions and the Bible," in *Jerusalem Congress on Black Africa and the Bible,* ed. E. Mveng and R. J. Werblowsky (Jerusalem, 1972), 158.

Kwesi Dickson himself has been especially concerned with the importance of the Old Testament,[19] and has argued strongly against the approach that would relegate it to a place of secondary importance in the Christian revelation. He points out that a good deal of Christianity in Africa (especially within the independent churches) has shown a considerable predilection for the Old Testament. One reason for this he sees in the legalistic attitude fostered by some of the earlier missions, which stressed law rather than grace. Such an approach, according to Dickson, coincided well with the observance of ritual and other regulations that were important in the traditional life.[20] Furthermore, the Old Testament gives us a picture of a people struggling against political and social oppression, which was of especial relevance in colonial Africa.[21] Finally, Dickson points out that religion in the Old Testament, as in traditional Africa, covered all aspects of life, family, social, agricultural, and so on. Dickson is not advocating here drawing of superficial parallels, but rather arguing that interpreting the Old Testament primarily within its own context will illuminate its significance within the African world. The characteristic uniqueness of the Old Testament will thus be preserved.[22]

Dickson's discussions of the role of the Old Testament in African theology have stressed the dual aspects of its continuity and discontinuity with African life and thought. He finds a basic theological continuity between the two traditions in that the Old Testament, although a particular story of specific people, nonetheless contains within itself the seeds of universality, for in it we find "an invitation to those outside the Israelite tradition to see themselves as sharing that tradition."[23] Dickson

19. Kwesi Dickson, *Theology in Africa* (London, 1984), 141ff.; "The Old Testament and African Theology," *Ghana Bulletin of Theology* 4, no. 4 (1973): 31-44: "Continuity and Discontinuity between the Old Testament and African Life and Thought," *ATER*, 99-108.

20. "When one realises that the observance of ritual and other regulations occupies an important place in African traditional life and thought, the attachment to the Old Testament becomes understandable." Dickson, *Continuity and Discontinuity*, 98; compare *Theology in Africa*, 151ff.

21. Dickson, "Continuity and Discontinuity," 98. This concept appears in the use of "exodus theology."

22. "The study of the Old Testament begins with the recognition that it was the people of Israel who interacted with God in peculiar circumstances." Dickson, "Continuity and Discontinuity," 98; also *Theology in Africa*, 154ff.

23. Dickson, "Continuity and Discontinuity," 99; *Theology in Africa*, 17ff.

is here emphasizing the universalist trend in ancient Judaism, contained especially in the early chapters of Genesis and the prophetical writings. One aspect of this is that God is the Lord of the whole earth, concerned with the Gentiles as well as with Israel, and at work among them as well as among his covenant people. Dickson has also seen a religiocultural continuity between the two traditions, in that various elements in the African religiocultural ethos recall ancient Israelite beliefs and practices. He isolates three such elements: the theology of nature, spirit possession, and the sense of the community.[24] In all of these areas there are marked similarities between the ancient Israelite worldview and that of African tradition. In all areas there are equally elements of contrast. In the understanding of the community, for example, the Old Testament uniformly condemns the veneration of the ancestors that is so important in Africa. The Old Testament also, as we have seen, at times rises above a narrow sense of the community to a more universalistic outlook.

Dickson also draws attention to what he terms a hermeneutic or interpretative continuity. Hermeneutics, according to Dickson, should initially interpret the Old Testament in the light of its original setting. However, this is only a first step, for "[s]ide by side with this approach, another task of the interpreters has come to be recognised: in approaching the text they must keep in mind the questions of their own period." In other words, there are "two unavoidable guidelines for the study of the Bible; it is important to know the biblical story *as it is,* and, the exegete should come to the Bible armed with questions relevant to his circumstance."[25]

This aspect of biblical interpretation, of "not leaving behind the questions and problems that matter to us," has in Dickson's view been neglected by African theologians until recently. The discontinuity here means seeing the Old Testament in the light of the New, and exposing both the Old Testament Scriptures and the religious life and thought of African traditions to the new revelation in Christ, especially to the event of the cross. Thus

the radical nature of the cross-event spells discontinuity. Yet in this cross-event Christ's involvement with society is clearly seen: for the

---

24. Dickson, *Theology in Africa,* 168ff.
25. Dickson, "Continuity and Discontinuity," 106; *Theology in Africa,* 142.

radical nature of the cross serves to underline the extent to which God would go to identify himself with humankind in the totality of human circumstances.[26]

Kwesi Dickson's discussions of the place of the Old Testament are important because he attempts to produce a genuine biblical hermeneutic. The simple comparison of the Old Testament with African religions is for him superficial: he asks that its meaning in its original context be used to illuminate its meaning in Africa today, and that all interpretation of the Old Testament be subjected to the critical judgment of the Christian revelation.

Historically the missionary penetration of Africa was done, in the main, by Europeans with a fundamentalist view of the Bible, and such an approach is still characteristic of a large proportion of African Christians. As several African theologians have pointed out, this fact has tended to circumscribe biblical studies on the continent.[27] Fasholé-Luke, while himself eschewing such an approach, rightly points out that it is not entirely negative in that it emphasizes the uniqueness and finality of revelation in Christ. A fundamentalist approach to the Bible has often been an underlying assumption, rather than a well thought out position, as in the West and America. It has, however, found an apologist in the Nigerian B. H. Kato.[28] According to Kato, all "liberal" (i.e., nonfundamentalist) theology fails because it is at root "syncretistic universalism," which represents a denial of the uniqueness and finality of Christ, and is therefore a perversion of the Bible. Kato sees these trends at work in the World Council of Churches and the AACC. The current interest of African theologians in African religions, Kato sees as "syncretism." For him African religion can only locate the problem, but points away from the solution in Christ.

Despite the fact that Kato seems to have uncritically swallowed the

26. Dickson, "Continuity and Discontinuity," 107.

27. Fasholé-Luke, "Quest," 78; Bolaji Idowu, "The Teaching of the Bible in Africa," in Mveng and Werblowsky, 200; Dickson, *Theology in Africa*, 16-17.

28. Kato's views were set out in his *Theological Pitfalls in Africa* (Kisumu, 1975), which originated as a thesis at Dallas Theological Seminary, and in various articles in *Bibliotheca Sacra*. According to Mbiti, Kato modified his views before his early death (*The Biblical Basis for Current Trends in African Theology*, 85). A critical treatment of Kato may be found in Bediako, *Theology and Identity* (Oxford, 1992), 325-86, and in Mercy Amba Oduyoye, *Hearing and Knowing; Theological Reflections on Christianity in Africa* (Maryknoll, 1986), 61ff.

opinions of his North American mentors, and despite its sometimes uncharitable tone, his book does make some salient points. It is indeed true that a large number of African Christians share his very conservative standpoint, and any African theology that is to be viable will need to take this into account. The reminder of the centrality of Christ is also very salutary at a time when the focus of theological studies in Africa is still very much upon building bridges between the Bible and African religions. Basically, however, Kato's approach is faulty on the grounds both of biblical interpretation and of the history of theology. Like fundamentalism in general, it imposes upon the Bible an artificial viewpoint instead of allowing it to speak for itself.[29] It also fails to make allowance for the fact that throughout its history Christianity has had to come to terms with the cultures in which it has been implanted and to reformulate itself in the appropriate thought-forms. Christian theology in Africa cannot avoid the same obligation. Kato does not make any specifically African contribution to theology, but is content to reiterate the position of a particular brand of western Christendom.

That a literalist interpretation of Scripture is so widespread is perhaps surprising in the light of the similarities between the mythological language used in parts of both Old and New Testaments and in African oral literature. Sundkler, as we have seen, believed that much traditional African thinking was mythological in character. He indeed advocated an interpretation of theology starting from "the fundamental facts of the African interpretation of existence,"[30] and saw the clue to this in the myths "which constitute an original revelation, which is reenacted in the annually recurrent festivals, in a rhythm which forms the cosmic framework of space and time."[31] Sundkler then draws out similarities between myths among the Hebrews and in Africa, which he feels may provide a point of contact for the African.

Sundkler's suggestion has been sharply criticized by Sawyerr.[32]

---

29. It would probably be true to say that although the dominant tradition in African Protestant Christianity remains broadly conservative, the lines are much less sharply drawn than in the West. In this respect Kato introduced into the debate in Africa a largely foreign controversy.

30. Sundkler, 285.

31. Sundkler, 281-82.

32. Harry Sawyerr, *Creative Evangelism, towards a New Christian Encounter* (London, 1969), 43ff.

Sawyerr is especially unhappy at what he feels is Sundkler's overvaluation of African myths and at his claim that they constitute an "original revelation." For Sawyerr, divine revelation, apart from that in Christ, is found only in the Old Testament. The issue raised by Sawyerr here is a more fundamental one than simply that of the similarity between certain literary forms found in the Old Testament and in African oral literature. It is basically the question of how far the concepts of God in African thought and in the Old Testament — or indeed in the New Testament — are identical. Put another way, the problem is one of the continuity or discontinuity of the apprehension of God in the African and the Judeo-Christian traditions. To this problem we now turn.

2. God and Revelation

One of the underlying assumptions of the adaptionist approach, in its broadest sense, is that it postulates, explicitly or implicitly, some kind of relationship between the Christian revelation and the pre-Christian traditions of African religions. It builds, in other words, on what traditional Christian theology has called "general revelation,"[33] and it believes (in Pobee's words) that "the biblical faith allows the possibility that natural man, otherwise described as 'heathen,' like our traditional African, has some intimation of God through creation."[34] The term "general revelation" may indeed be misleading, but if it is taken as implying "the universal possibility of revelation,"[35] few except the committed Barthian would deny its usefulness.

John MacQuarrie (whose concerns are in general quite other than those of African theologians) has an interesting paragraph that, taking its cue from Zaehner, lucidly illustrates the close association between the adaptionist standpoint and general revelation:

> "In the early centuries", writes R C Zaehner, "the Catholic Church rejoiced to build into herself whatever in paganism she found com-

---

33. For a classic exposition from the Reformed standpoint see G. C. Berkouwer, *General Revelation* (Grand Rapids, 1955); also MacQuarrie's discussion of "natural theology" in *Principles of Christian Theology*, rev. ed. (London, 1977), 43ff.

34. John Pobee, *Towards an African Theology* (Nashville, 1979), 73.

35. MacQuarrie, 43.

patible with and adaptable to the revelation of which she deemed herself the repository". Perhaps it is even more necessary that we should be prepared to do this in the contemporary world. Without in any way taking away from the historical and eschatological work of Christ, we can recognise its continuity with that universal reconciling work of God in all creation, a work that has as its goal the gathering of all creaturely beings into the commonwealth of love.[36]

The biblical writers themselves, of course, recognize that God may be apprehended not only in the works of creation (e.g., Ps. 19:1-4) and in the common ethical responsibility of person to person (e.g., Amos 1–2), but also in humans' innate sense of the divine (e.g., the Pauline speeches of Acts 14:15-17 and 17:24-29; cf. Rom 1:19-21). As William Temple pointed out, there is a sense in which revelation in Christ is continuous as much with "general revelation" as it is with the "special revelation" contained in the Old Testament.[37] Within the context of African theology, what is being argued is that African religious traditions constitute a genuine revelation of God. This revelation may be seen as a kind of *praeparatio evangelica* or, more radically, as having a real salvific value in itself.

Some African theologians have sought to obliterate the distinction between general and special revelation at a very basic level by affirming the intrinsic identity of God in the African and Christian traditions. According to this view there can be but one God, who has revealed himself to humankind both in the Bible and also in African religions. Few have set out this position more vehemently and more often than Bolaji Idowu,[38] for whom the Ibadan Consultation was basically an attempt to find an answer

> to the delicate question of whether there is any correlation between the Biblical concept of God and the African concept of God; between

36. MacQuarrie, 327.

37. "Only if God is revealed in the rising of the sun can he be revealed in the rising of the Son of Man from the dead. . . . Only if nothing is secular can anything be sacred." William Temple, *The Nature of God* (London, 1934), 306-7.

38. Bolaji Idowu, *BRAB*, 13, 17ff.; *Towards an Indigenous Church* (Oxford, 1965), 25ff.; *African Traditional Religions: a Definition* (London, 1973), 62ff. For a detailed critique of Idowu's position see Bediako, 267-302.

what God has done and is doing according to the Biblical record and teaching, and what God has done and is doing in Africa according to African traditional beliefs.[39]

Idowu takes his stand on the findings of older investigators, such as Schmidt and Lang, that even the most primitive peoples believe in one supreme God, and are to that extent "monotheists."[40] He has an intense dislike of the commonly accepted term "High God" to describe the supreme deity in Africa.[41] This term, in his view, not only permits each (European) scholar to give to the High God the attributes the scholar wishes, but also — more seriously — introduces a "pluralism," so that each people has its own High God, "with the result that the whole place is overrun with high Gods of various brands."[42] For Idowu, God, through creation, has made humankind able to respond to his revelation and has "revealed himself primarily to them all, each race apprehending the revelation according to its capability."[43] Further, argues Idowu, the understanding of God in modern Western theology itself is far from clear, and both the history of dogma and the Bible indicate a degree of unknowability in the nature of God. He therefore favors a more experiential approach — the knowledge of God consists in the experience of humans as his creatures.[44] He goes on to outline the main characteristics of the deity in Africa — his reality, uniqueness, control of the world, universality. Africans, he concludes, "have their own distinctive concepts of God. . . . God according to African traditional belief is not a 'loan-word' from the missionaries."[45] Consequently, revelation means that God "has left his mark upon the

39. Idowu, *BRAB*, 13.
40. Compare his earlier book *Olodumare: God in Yoruba Belief* (London, 1962), in which, by a remarkable theological tour de force, he attempted to demonstrate that the Yoruba pantheon should be understood as aspects or attributes of the supreme God; see further my "Olorun and the High God Pattern," *Ghana Bulletin of Theology* 3, no. 1 (1970): 1-10.
41. The High God concept is for Idowu a "heresy" (*African Traditional Religion*, 61), "an academic invention, an intellectual marionette, whose behaviour depends upon the partiality of its creators," and which stems from "emotional resentment and deliberate refusal to accept the facts on the part of some European scholars." *BRAB*, 18-19, 29.
42. Idowu, *BRAB*, 19.
43. Idowu, *BRAB*, 20.
44. Idowu, *BRAB*, 23.
45. Idowu, *BRAB*, 29.

created order and his witness within men — every man" and this is "meant for all mankind, all rational beings, irrespective of race and colour."[46]

Idowu clothes his arguments in passionate, even emotive, language, but I believe his very eloquence covers up a logical fallacy in his position. I am not here concerned with the rightness or otherwise of the use of the term "High God" by writers (both European and African) to describe the supreme God in Africa.[47] What is, I believe, basically problematic about Idowu's approach is the blurring of the edges between the real existence of God and man's conceptions of him. John Baillie once pointed out that theology "may mean either the reasoned and reasonable statement of the nature of God, or the reasoned and reasonable statement of what men and women thought and think about him."[48] This distinction is obscured in Idowu's writings. To say that there is one God is not the same thing as to say that he reveals himself equally to all people and in the same way, still less as to say that all people in all cultures (or even that gifted people in all cultures) apprehend and understand him to the same degree. That the real point at issue is one of the human apprehension, rather than real existence, of God is indeed assumed by Idowu himself when he states (quite rightly) that "we should realise Africans have their own distinctive concepts of God,"[49] which are different from those of Christianity.

Idowu has exposed the thorny theological problem of what exactly the difference is between "general" and "special" revelation — or, put in another way, between revelation in all religions (here especially in African religions) and revelation in the Judeo-Christian tradition. It is not very clear from Idowu's writings (as it is from those of Sawyerr and Dickson) that the Bible presents us with a different kind of revelation at all, or in what (in the words of the Ibadan declaration) the "radical quality of self-revelation in Christ" consists. Kwame Bediako has sug-

---

46. Idowu, *African Traditional Religions*, 12, 56.

47. This seems to me a terminological red herring: it is undeniable that the attributes of the High God as set out by, e.g., E. Dammann (*Die Religionen Afrikas* [Stuttgart, 1963], 26ff) are extremely relevant.

48. Quoted by John McIntyre in "Theology and Method," in *Creation, Christ, and Culture*, ed. R. McKinney (Edinburgh, 1976), 205.

49. Idowu, *BRAB*, 29.

gested that perhaps Idowu is less interested in the theology of the Christian faith for its own sake than "insofar as it provides a means of establishing African identity."[50] This is a perceptive comment, for it seems that often in Idowu's writings Christian theological categories are used as a vehicle for his portrayal of African religions.[51] The preoccupation with the idea that there is, after all, little real difference between the concept of God in the Bible and in African religions is perhaps possible for Idowu because he pays very little attention to the place of Jesus Christ in revelation. The result of this is not only to obscure the uniqueness of the Christian faith, but also to cast doubt on the unique nature of the African concept of God, for which Idowu himself vigorously pleads.[52]

John Kibicho and Gabriel Setiloane have advocated a more radical approach. Kibicho's views were set out in his paper "The Continuity of the African Concept of God into and through Christianity: a Kikuyu Case-Study."[53] His basic question is:

> Was the God of ATR (known by different names as Mulungu, Mungu, Asis, En-Kai, Akuj, Tororut, Ngai etc.) the One True God whom we Christians worship in Christianity, the Father of our Lord Jesus Christ? If so, as most Africans believe, did our forefathers really know him adequately for their religious needs (salvation) or was their knowledge of him only partial and preparatory to the coming of the full revelation of Christianity?[54]

---

50. Bediako, 352. S. I. Tyrell's often quoted comment about liberal theologians might perhaps be reshaped: Idowu looks into the well of the Bible and sees there reflected the image of African traditional religion.

51. See further chapter 8.

52. Idowu, *BRAB*, 29, quoted above. Nor indeed can we speak very meaningfully of "the African concept of God": while there may be a certain pattern in the delineation of the Supreme God in Africa, regional variations are considerable. Idowu's understanding of God in Africa is perhaps too much dominated by his own interpretation of Yoruba religion.

53. John Kibicho, "Tha Continuity of the African Concept of God into and through Christianity: A Kikuyu Case-Study," *CIA*, 370-88. Similar views were advocated earlier in his "African Traditional Religion and Christianity," *A New Look at Christianity in Africa* (Geneva, 1970).

54. Kibicho, "Continuity of African Concept," 370-71.

For Kibicho (as for Idowu) any discussion of the relationship between Christianity and African religions begins with "the relation of the Mungu of African Traditional Religion and the God of Christianity."[55] He argues for a radical continuity of African traditional religion, particularly of the African concept of God, even into and through Christianity.[56] Kibicho's argument is involved and in places difficult to follow, but I shall attempt to summarize it below.

The Kikuyu concept of God (Ngai or Mugai) is basically monotheistic. The names of God in Kikuyu express the belief that he is owner of all things (Nyene), source of all mysteries (Mwene-Nyaga) and omnipotent (Murungu); he is also the Great Elder (Githuri) and Father (Baba). It is believed that God is invisible, spiritual and omnipresent, transcendent and immanent, sustainer and controller of all things, benevolent towards humans. He was addressed not only in times of need but also in thanksgiving and for guidance. This traditional idea of God, Kibicho affirms, continued after the christianization of the Kikuyu and still remains the basic concept of Kikuyu Christians. Western missionaries however, in Kibicho's view, in general failed to recognize the true character of Ngai, and concluded that the Kikuyu were in total ignorance of the true God and retained only a vague yearning for something higher. Hence the missionaries demanded a radical abandonment of the traditional religion, believing that "God was only to be found and seen truly in Christianity, not in traditional Kikuyu religion and culture."[57] They thus advocated "fulfilment through radical discontinuity." While the name Ngai was adopted in the Kikuyu Bible, this was in name only, for "the content had to be different." African traditional religion was therefore regarded as incomplete; its adherents had no real knowledge of the One God, and it could at best be only a preparation for the gospel.

Against this "radical discontinuity" between the African conception of God and the Christian one Kibicho vehemently protests. In his opinion this represents "a relic of the old prejudicial evolutionary view of African religion."[58] By contrast, he seeks to demonstrate a radical

---

55. Kibicho, "Continuity of African Concept," 371.
56. Kibicho, "Continuity of African Concept," 371.
57. Kibicho, "Continuity of African Concept," 379.
58. Kibicho, "Continuity of African Concept," 380.

continuity between the concepts of God in the two traditions. He takes, first, the example of the resistance movements to colonial powers.[59] The leaders of these movements, Kibicho argues, "from Waiyaki to Mau Mau . . . were among some of the most religious and God-fearing men and women in Kenya, in continuance of African traditional religions," and these movements included also many Christians. The freedom fighters "held on to the traditional African conception of God, which they also believed to be the true Biblical conception."[60] Both they and the colonial missionaries believed they were guided by the One True God. However, inasmuch as the missionaries, with few exceptions, sided with the oppressors, they "had lost the reality and vision of the One True God." This vision of the One True God was to be found among the believers in the Ngai of African traditional religion in their fight for justice and freedom.

Kibicho's second line of approach is to point to evidence of the continuity of the conception of Ngai into Christianity, as illustrated by the Kikuyu response to Christian evangelism. This response was, in Kibicho's opinion, not originally because people saw in Christianity a new God, but rather because of the material benefits that the missionaries brought with them to a people dispossessed of their land by the colonists.[61] The main point, asserts Kibicho,

> is that as far as the converts or non-converts to Christianity were concerned, God *(Ngai)* was never an issue. Despite the strange doctrine about the Son of God who became man, died and rose again (an element however that the Kikuyu could accept as part of the mysteries of the new religion), the *Ngai* the missionaries preached was the same *Ngai* whom the Kikuyu had always known and worshipped. . . . *Ngai* was not among the elements of their traditional

59. "In their response of resistance and struggle against their powerful and ruthless invaders and oppressors the Africans manifested and asserted a radical continuity of their conception of God." Kibicho, "Continuity of African Concept," 380.

60. Kibicho, "Continuity of African Concept," 382. This statement is somewhat difficult to follow: it seems to imply that non-Christian as well as Christian freedom fighters also accepted and believed in the true biblical concept of God.

61. Kibicho, "Continuity of African Concept," 383; hence conversion was described as *guthoma*, meaning literally "to read, become literate," and Christians were called *athomi*, "literates."

religion to be left behind. They moved with him into the new religion, or rather he was the same one worshipped in Christianity.[62]

For the converts the new feature of Christianity lay not in its doctrine of God, but rather in its scriptures, creeds, symbols of redemption, and so on. It is this radical continuity in the conception of God that Kibicho believes should form the basis for African theology. It implies that

> the God preached and worshipped in Christianity is the same God (*Ngai, Nyasaye, Asis, Mungu* etc.) who was fully-known, to the extent that any humans can know God, worshipped and trusted by their fore-fathers in the traditional religions of ancient times.[63]

Acceptance of this standpoint would lead to radical reinterpretation of other major Christian doctrines, including the Christian's attitude to other religions. It would, Kibicho believes, in fact enrich Christianity by making it more universal and more open to the "visions of God" in other religions.

Kibicho's approach has been endorsed by Gabriel Setiloane, who has gone further to argue that the concept of God among the Sotho-Tswana is in some respects higher than that of Christianity, or at least than that of what he calls "western theological tradition." According to Setiloane, *Modimo* is a "wider, deeper and all-embracing concept," which Christian theology itself needs to accept as the concept for its God, and he thus prefers to translate Modimo as "deity" or "divinity" rather than "God."[64] He finds himself in agreement with John Kibicho and Christian Gaba that the Christian use of African names for the supreme being is in some sense a "diminution":

> Put tauntingly it says that the western Christian theologians' "God" could easily die because he is so small and human. The Sotho-Tswana God, according to me, the Ngo people's God according to Kibicho,

62. Kibicho, "Continuity of African Concept," 385.
63. Kibicho, "Continuity of African Concept," 388.
64. Gabriel Setiloane, "How the Traditional World-View Persists in the Christianity of the Sotho-Tswana," *CIA*, 402-11; the quotation is from 411 n. 2.

could never die because it had no human limitations, and it is so immense, incomprehensible, wide, tremendous and unique.[65]

He accordingly finds that African Christians "Africanise the western Christian concept of God and thus raise it to the level of Modimo, which is much higher."[66]

These views clearly take us one step further than those of Idowu, for here the argument is not simply that God in African traditional religion is essentially identical with God in Christian revelation, but is in some sense a higher concept. This obviously calls for closer examination.

It is not always clear on reading Kibicho and Setiloane whether the thrust of their criticism is against the biblical concept of God or against certain brands of missionary and Western theology. Kibicho's "western missionaries" and Setiloane's "western theologians" may indeed have been guilty of a "diminution" in their idea of God; the former (or some of them) may have put colonial ideas before righteousness and justice, and the latter (or some of them) may have lost sight of certain fundamental aspects of the idea of God in the Bible. In this respect, in spite of their sweeping generalizations and lack of specific examples, Kibicho and Setiloane present a valid criticism of the approaches of some Western Christians. This is by no means the same thing, however, as dismissing the Christian concept of God as found in the Bible and Christian tradition as less adequate than that in certain parts of Africa. The inadequacy of the church's apprehension of the nature of God, and the inadequacy of its ability to put into practice what it does apprehend, in no way diminishes God himself or the biblical picture of him. Of course, it is possible to argue that certain African concepts of God are higher than those in Christianity; but one would imagine that it is difficult to sustain this position from the standpoint of a Christian theologian, which both Kibicho and Setiloane are.

I have one other problem with Kibicho's paper, namely his claim that the God preached in Christianity is the same God who was fully known in

65. Gabriel Setiloane, "Where Are We in African Theology?" *ATER*, 60; see further his *The Image of God among the Sotho-Tswana* (Rotterdam, 1976).

66. Setiloane, "Where Are We," 63; compare *A Statement of African Challenge, Uniting in Hope* (WCC Faith and Order Commission, Accra, 1974), 34.

traditional religion.[67] If God was "fully-known" before the advent of Christianity, then we must ask in what the uniqueness of Christianity consists and wherein lies the finality of revelation in Christ. Kibicho does not really address himself to this question any more than Idowu does. But this is precisely the kind of question with which African theologians should be struggling as they seek to relate the Christian faith to African religions. With Setiloane there is a further difficulty, his claim that the Christian God is inadequate (as compared with Modimo) because he is "small and human" and "could easily die." Such a statement betrays a fundamental misunderstanding of the biblical doctrine of God. One of the wonders of the Old Testament tradition was the conviction that God shared in the afflictions and sufferings of his people, a concept probably unique among the religions of the ancient world, and that has been rediscovered dramatically by Jewish scholars in this century.[68] The concept of God who suffers with and for his people is a central one for the Christian faith, where in the person of the Son God demonstrates his identity with the sufferings of humanity.[69] This is not a "diminution" of the Godhead, but, in the Judeo-Christian tradition, one of its crowning achievements and one that cannot be neglected without jeopardizing the whole basis of Christian faith itself. Another African scholar has expressed this view forcibly as follows:

> What is new to the African is the fact that God's power is manifest in weakness: in Christ's humility, meekness, forgiveness of sins, and — most astoundingly — in his suffering, his death on the Cross, and its glorious saving consequences in Christ himself and in the whole of creation.[70]

67. Setiloane, "Traditional World-View," 388.

68. See, e.g., Abraham Heschel's emphasis on the "pathos" of God as "emotional engagement" in his *The Prophets* (New York, 1962).

69. It was not a Western theologian but a Japanese who, in a book produced in 1946 after the horrors of World War II and Hiroshima, contended that the essence of the gospel is the "pain of God" (Kazoh Kitamori, *The Theology of the Pain of God* [ET Richmond, 1965]). Another leading Asian theologian, C. S. Song, while criticizing Kitamori for internalizing the pain of God as conflict between his wrath and love, agrees that "God's heartache is the beginning of theology" (*Third Eye Theology* [London, 1980], especially chapter 2); see also J. Moltmann, *The Crucified God* (London, 1974).

70. Charles Nyamiti, *African Tradition and the Christian God* (Eldoret, n.d.), 57. Theo Sundermeier, in a personal communication, has pointed out that Setiloane's thesis

However inadequate the views of Idowu, Kibicho, and Setiloane may be, they raise questions that are fundamental to African theology. They have also shown us — in contrast to some of the earlier missionary views — that the idea of God in traditional Africa should be taken very seriously indeed. At a time when a good deal of Western theology seems to be in danger of losing its sense of direction in its concept and experience of God, this may be salutory. As another African writer, from a very different context, has put it:

> [L]et African theologians enthuse about the awesomeness of the transcendent, when others are embarrassed to speak about the King, high and lifted up, whose train fills the Temple.[71]

If an examination of the traditional view of God in Africa can help the church towards such a rediscovery of such a conception of God, it will have performed a very useful function.

Not all African theologians, of course, take the extreme positions of those reviewed above. Harry Sawyerr also has a high view of the idea of God among African peoples: he is regarded generally as the creator and sustainer of all life, the apex of all existence; he may be invoked in times of need; and he protects humankind.[72] However, after subjecting the biblical view of God to scrutiny, Sawyerr is inclined to believe that Christian evangelism cannot proceed straight from the African concept of God to the gospel; it needs to go through the Jewish understanding of God for the preaching of the Christian gospel to be successful for "Africans who do not possess the basic attitudes to God which we know the Jews possessed." The Jewish idea of God is therefore the "bridge between the religious ideas of the pagan world and Christianity."[73]

---

was written during the brief popularity of "death of God" theology: this illuminates his stance vis-à-vis European theology.

71. Desmond Tutu, "Whither African Theology?" *CIA*, 369.

72. Sawyerr, *Creative Evangelism*, 13ff.; see also his *God, Creator or Ancestor?* (London, 1970).

73. Sawyerr, *Creative Evangelism*, 64: "The Jewish understanding of God as a God of History, who intervenes in the life and experiences of human beings, and as God who inspires His prophets to teach their people that true content of His will, is the prime basis of a full understanding of that manifestation in Jesus Christ which took

From the Catholic point of view the relationship between African and Christian concepts of God has been explored by Nyamiti in his monograph *African Tradition and the Christian God.* Nyamiti approaches his subject along the lines set out in his earlier methodological study,[74] which stressed the need for African theology to take seriously such traditional elements such as dynamism, solidarity, participation, anthropocentrism, and the place of the supernatural. He then deals with his subject from the three standpoints of the comparative-dialogal, the apologetic, and the pedagogical approaches. For our purposes here it is the first that is important.

Nyamiti seeks to open up dialogue between the Christian and traditional African concepts of God by drawing out comparisons between the common elements in both religions. There are several points at which we may discover "parallelisms." This is not surprising, in Nyamiti's view, since "God reveals himself to all people through their consciences and religious experiences, through creation, and even through supernatural revelation in faith."[75]

In Nyamiti's view "the God of traditional Africa is the God who reveals himself in the Bible" and thus "African teachings on God are very close to those of the Old Testament."[76] These similarities, however, should not obscure the equally important fact that there are significant differences between the two conceptions and that "judged from theological standards one of the main differences is that Christian theology is far purer and nobler than the African doctrines."[77] This is because, in Nyamiti's opinion, the traditional concept is "often mixed up with error and superstition." Furthermore, traditional religion sometimes stressed the immanence of God to such an extent that his personality

---

place at the Incarnation, as well as of a grasp of the love which prompted God to reconcile man to himself."

74. Charles Nyamiti, *The Way to Christian Theology in Africa* (Eldoret, n.d.).

75. Nyamiti, *African Tradition,* 4.

76. Nyamiti, *African Tradition,* 5; compare 19: "the African God is the God of the Bible, having the same nature and attributes."

77. Nyamiti, *African Tradition,* 5. See also his comments, which from his "apologetic" approach, seek to show that this ideal is fulfilled in Christianity: "The Christian conception of God is purer and more perfect, so that, by professing the Christian faith, the African will have the occasion to purify his theistic doctrine from superstition and error," at 19.

was compromised, and in other contexts stressed his transcendence to the detriment of his concern for humankind. Since God is not usually directly invoked for blessings in African religions, he in some sense is conceived of as sharing his power with other spiritual beings. The fundamental biblical concepts of covenant and of salvation history are also lacking. African religion tends to be materialistic, for "the African approaches God not chiefly in order to gain eternal life but rather to gain natural benefits demanded by human condition here and now."[78]

Positively there are aspects in the traditional idea of God that could help to enrich Christian understanding. These aspects are especially set out in the praise-names of God in Africa.[79] African religion also has its own characteristic symbolism for God — for example, God as mother — that could be fruitfully introduced into Christian theology.[80] There is, however, one very fundamental difference between the Christian and the African traditions, namely that the Christian understanding of God is essentially Christocentric in that the person and work of Christ "reveals a totally new relationship between man and God."[81] Nyamiti has here, it seems to me, identified the basic distinction between the African and Christian conceptions not only of God but also of revelation, and one that ought to be central to any African Christian theology. In the following chapter we shall examine the adaptionist approach in more detail, taking this central doctrine of the person of Christ as our point of departure.

78. Nyamiti, *African Tradition,* 6.

79. For a broad survey of praise names, see John Mbiti, *Concepts of God in Africa* (London, 1970), 327-36.

80. The motherhood of God, stripped of its physical connotations, represents God's generative powers, fruitfulness, and tenderness (Nyamiti, *African Tradition,* 15). Nyamiti is raising here the issue of whether terms other than "Father" might be more meaningful in African societies. Among some matrilineal peoples, e.g., might it not be appropriate to call God "maternal uncle," the member of the family group traditionally responsible for the care and welfare of the child?

81. Nyamiti, *African Tradition,* 7-8.

IV

African Religions and Christian Dogma

The main characteristic of the adaptionist approach, as has been noted, lies in its attempt to draw out the relationship between certain aspects of Christian doctrine and supposedly related aspects of African religions. In some areas — such as, for example, the concept of the religious community — there would seem to be fairly firm ground for comparison and a fair amount of overlapping of interests. In others the areas of agreement would at first glance appear to be slight. In this chapter I shall attempt to examine some of the more important areas of similarity and dissimilarity, taking as points of departure the problem of an African christology, the role of the community, and eschatology.

1. The Problem of Christology

As far back as 1925, Sydney Cave, himself well familiar with the issues of relating Christianity to non-Christian religions, described the problem of christology in the following way:

> We have to explore for ourselves the significance of Christ and His place in the experience of the Church, and then seek to express what

we discover in terms which shall be intelligible to our age and congruous with Christian values.[1]

On the African continent this intelligibility needs to be intelligibility within a specifically African context: in other words, what African theologians are seeking to do is to reinterpret biblical and historical christological dogma in categories that are both traditionally African and at the same time relevant to the Africa of today.[2] This should be, as Mbiti points out, at the center of African theology. He notes:

> Since his Incarnation, Christian Theology ought properly to be Christology, for Theology falls or stands on how it understands, translates and interprets Jesus Christ at a given time, place and human situation.[3]

However, it is only quite recently that christology has been put in its central place by African theologians.[4] One reason for its initial neglect perhaps lies in the discontinuity between the two religious systems in their view of history. African religions are not "historical" in the sense that they find their *raison d'être* in a historical founder, nor do they have a tradition of "sacred history." Their foundations are to be sought elsewhere, in the authority of the ancestors in the case of most Bantu systems, or in the combined authority of ancestors and deities in many parts of West Africa. However minimal some Christian theologians may consider our knowledge of the historical Jesus to be, the Christian faith claims to have its roots in events that involved a specific person at a

---

1. Sydney Cave, *The Doctrine of the Person of Christ*, 2nd ed. (London, 1930), 2.

2. As MacQuarrie points out, this is presumably what theology and christology are all about in any context, "trying to interpret today in categories of our time the Christ who meets us only in tradition." *Principles of Christian Theology*, rev. ed. (London, 1977), 307.

3. John Mbiti, *New Testament Eschatology in an African Background* (Oxford, 1971), 190; so also H. G. Muzorewa, *The Origins and Development of African Theology* (Maryknoll, 1985), 34: "African Theology can be Christian only if it is centred on Christ and his redemptive work" — though he unfortunately hardly begins to tackle this central area himself.

4. For a recent excellent symposium from a Catholic viewpoint, see R. J. Schreiter, ed., *Faces of Jesus in Africa* (London, 1992).

specific time in human history. It is just this kind of historical dimension that is lacking in African traditional religions.[5]

The lack of historical roots may also help to explain why some African theologians, perhaps taking their cue from Sundkler,[6] suggest that a "mythical" approach to christology may be more appropriate in Africa. Such an approach agrees well with the phenomenon, common in the history of religions, that those religions that lack a historical basis give more place to myth. Mbiti has indeed argued that in African religions the "mythical and mystical is often more valid, more solid, and more tenable than that which is otherwise too explicit and exposed," and he goes on to suggest that

> African Christians perhaps experience "our Saviour" more readily in the capacity of his myth and mystique than they would if they had a more historical grasp of Jesus and a spiritualised conception of salvation.[7]

What Mbiti seems to have in mind here is the understanding of the work of Christ in terms of deliverance from evil powers, both physical and spiritual, a theme to which we shall return later. Kofi Appiah-Kubi has made the similar claim that "the image of Christ comes to the soul of the African Christian through mythology."[8]

The lack of a genuine historical foundation in African religions

---

5. This is not to say that there are no important figures in African religions, but these are reformers and prophets rather than founders. Ranger and Kimambo (*The Historical Study of African Religion* [London, 1972]) argued convincingly for a genuine historical development in African religions, but they have not demonstrated the presence of founders in the sense indicated above. For a trenchant critique of their position, however, see J. Vansina's review in *International Journal of Historical Studies* 6, no. 1 (1973): 178-80. Kwesi Dickson agrees that African religions have no founders (*Theology in Africa* [London, 1984], 34).

6. In Bengt Sundkler, *The Christian Ministry in Africa* (London, 1960).

7. John Mbiti, "ὁ σωτὴρ ἡμῶν (Our Saviour) as an African Experience," in *Christ and the Spirit,* ed. B. Lindars and S. Smalley (London, 1973), 397-414.

8. Appiah-Kubi, a Ghanaian sociologist of religion, made the broad claim that "much African Christianity is mythical and mystical," which he then develops in terms of liberation from evil powers. Kofi Appiah-Kubi, "Some Christological Aspects from African Perspectives," in *African and Asian Contributions to Theology,* ed. J. Mbiti (Geneva, 1977), 55ff.

also perhaps explains why the attempts that have been made from time to time to compare the incarnation of Jesus with some specific belief of a particular African people do not afford a very solid basis for drawing together the two traditions. Mbiti finds partial parallels to the sonship of Jesus in the Ndebele "trinitarian" Father-Son-Mother concept of the deity and in the Shilluk belief that the king is the "first-born" son of God.[9] Appiah-Kubi refers to the traditions of a virgin birth among the Ashanti and Bare,[10] to which we may also add the "messianic" idea of the Akan.[11] But aside from the problem of whether these aspects of traditional religion have been correctly assessed, and their very tenuous links with Christian dogma, they would at best represent points of contact within a very limited area only, and could thus not provide a very firm basis for an African — as opposed to a purely local — christology. It seems clear that the lack of a historical founder in African religions represents a serious element of discontinuity between African religion and Christianity. This is not, of course, a new situation in the Judeo-Christian tradition. The same collision between the "historical" and the "mythical" traditions, reflecting perhaps different linear and cyclical concepts of time, marked the relationships between Mosaic religion and the pagan religions of the ancient Near East, and between early Christianity and the Greco-Roman world. This element of discontinuity needs to be carefully taken into account; put in another way, the nonincarnational character of African religions needs to be acknowledged so that the business of working out a valid christology (or christologies) for Africa can go ahead unmuddled.

The christological titles as used in the New Testament have not provided a promising basis for an African christology. Mbiti has commented that most of these titles — Messiah-Christ, Son of Man, Son of

---

9. John Mbiti, "Some African Concepts of Christology," in *Christ and the Younger Churches,* ed. Vicedom (London, 1972), 51ff. Muzorewa, apparently on the basis of this statement by Mbiti, goes so far as to ask what can be the significance of the historical Jesus for African theology "if we conclude that Africans already know him in pre-Christian ages." This kind of argumentation betrays a highly confused approach to biblical history (Muzorewa, 85).

10. Appiah-Kubi, 55-56.

11. For a criticism of the use of the Akan concept of "messiah" in christology, however, see Harry Sawyerr, *Creative Evangelism, towards a New Christian Encounter* (London, 1969), 103ff.

David — have no major significance in Africa since "they do not fit into the thought forms of African peoples."[12] Perhaps we should not expect them to do so; after all, a good deal of Western theology also inclines to the view that the importance of the christological titles has been exaggerated in recent discussion,[13] and that (in Tillich's words) they should be regarded as "symbols" rather than definitions.[14] New Testament scholarship itself has also been looking more to the general, if not so easily quantifiable, aspects of the Gospel accounts of Jesus, such as his authority[15] or his deeds,[16] as the material for an evaluation of the person of Jesus. The one term common to some African traditions and the New Testament, "the Word," does not seem to have attracted a great deal of attention.[17]

One of the most promising approaches to christology that has been advocated by African theologians has been a "functional," or existential, approach, which focuses on the deeds of Jesus in relation to the individual believer. This has been advanced by John Pobee, who seeks to answer the question, "Why should an Akan relate to Jesus of Nazareth, who does not belong to his clan, family, tribe or nation?"[18]

12. Mbiti, "Some African Concepts," 52. It is significant that Mveng, when discussing the title "Son of Man," understands it not in its usual (albeit probably wrong) theological interpretation of the divinity of Jesus, but rather of his humanity: "[The African] sees [Jesus] as also the Christ, the Son of Man, who became one with us. The mystery of the incarnation must be taken seriously. In time and space Christ takes our flesh, speaks our language, shares our fate with his concrete daily experiences" (E. Mveng, "Christus der Initiationsmeister," in *Zwischen Kultur and Politik,* ed. T. Sundermeier [Hamburg, 1978], 79. Compare also John Waliggo, "African Christology in a Situation of Suffering," in *Faces of Jesus in Africa,* 164-80.

13. MacQuarrie, 291.

14. Paul Tillich, *Systematic Theology,* vol. 2 (London, 1978), 84.

15. E.g., Bornkamm, *Jesus of Nazareth* (London, 1973).

16. E.g., Kümmel, *Theology of the New Testament* (London, 1974), 58ff.

17. On the concept of the Word in African religions see U. Beier, *The Origins of Life and Death* (London, 1974), 58ff., and, more speculatively, M. Griaule, *Conversations with Ogotemelli* (London, 1865).

18. John Pobee, *Towards an African Theology* (Nashville, 1979), 81. The same question could, of course, equally be put to European Christians. Kwame Bediako has addressed this issue with reference to the Epistle to the Hebrews in his monograph *Jesus in African Culture, a Ghanaian Perspective* (Accra, 1990), and in "Biblical Christologies in the Context of African Traditional Religions," in *Sharing Jesus in the Two Thirds World,* ed. V. Samuel and C. Sugden (Grand Rapids, 1993), 81-121.

According to Pobee the New Testament itself, unlike the creeds, expresses its christology in terms of Jesus' activity. This approach, Pobee believes, agrees with the Akan outlook, which prefers concreteness to abstraction. There are, he argues, several different christologies within the New Testament, but despite this diversity all agree on one essential: that Jesus is truly man and truly divine. "The humanity and divinity of Jesus," he writes, "are the two non-negotiables of any authentic Christology."[19] Jesus' divinity, however, is described in essentially functional terms and, in a certain sense, is displayed through the humanity: "The divinity of Jesus is to some extent mirrored through his humanity. In Jesus the disciples saw what man is meant to be; i.e. Jesus is the *imago dei*."[20]

The humanity has received a good deal of attention from African theologians, often with the stress on Jesus as the one who participates fully in the human community. Harry Sawyerr, for example, believed that the best approach to the incarnation in Africa was to emphasize the unity of experience between Jesus and his people: he was born as man, grew into manhood, suffered, and died as all humans do. Unity with Christ brings humans into a new community, which is his body. The church is the community that transcends the old clan, and so the "tribal affiliation of Christians gives way to the totality of the community of the church, with Jesus Christ as its founder member."[21] Jesus is thus the "first-born" among many brethren, who, with him, form the church "in true keeping with African notions." This kind of relationship between Jesus and his people finds some biblical support in the Pauline concept of mystical union. It can be meaningful for the African Christian, according to Sawyerr, and can illuminate the meaning of sonship with God, of Christ as the agent of creation, and of the re-creation of man's moral nature, and especially can bring home the sense of belonging to a great family whose head is Jesus himself.[22]

African theologians' emphasis on the humanity of Jesus is also shown in the interest in the way in which the Gospels portray Jesus as

19. Pobee, *Towards an African Theology*, 82.
20. Pobee, *Towards an African Theology*, 85.
21. Sawyerr, *Creative Evangelism*, 72.
22. Sawyerr, *Creative Evangelism*, 73-79. Throughout his discussion Sawyerr is at pains to bring out the biblical evidence for these concepts.

undergoing "rites of passage." These experiences are then compared to similar rites in African societies, and are taken as evidence that, as man, Christ "actually fulfils the conditions of a perfect member of the community."[23] Mbiti has pointed out that the birth of Jesus, his baptism (that is, his "initiation"), and his death correspond to the three main rites of passage in traditional religion. He sees in these events confirmation of the humanity of Jesus in that he "fulfils everything which constitutes a complete, corporate member of society."[24]

While this may provide the starting point for a discussion of the real humanity of Christ within the African context, there are nevertheless considerable dissimilarities between the crises in the life of Jesus and the traditional rites of passage. Mbiti himself points out that, on this view, one could regard the death of Jesus as a "symbol of completeness" rather than recognizing that the victory of the cross involved shame and humiliation. The birth of Jesus, too, according to the first and third Gospels and the historic creeds, was altogether unusual in that it did not follow the normal rules of procreation. And the baptism, furthermore, represented a unique affirmation of sonship that is far removed from simple initiation. In Mbiti's view there remains the danger that these events may be reduced to the level of Jesus' sharing in the common lot of humanity, and that the unique christological significance that they have in the New Testament will be minimized. Furthermore, there is one rite of passage, of very basic importance in the African life cycle, for which there is no evidence at all in the life of Jesus, namely marriage. This raises serious problems for those who would stress that Jesus underwent all the various stages that mark man in Africa. Again, the central feature of the apostolic preaching, the resurrection, has only very tenuous parallels in African religions. There is, it is true, a fairly widespread belief, especially associated with witch-finders, of a death and resurrection motif. But this is scarcely an adequate parallel, for the witch-finder's "descent" into death represents rather the end of his "normal" existence, and his resurrection indicates his endowing by the spirits for his work. The approach to an understanding of the humanity of Jesus through a comparison of the crises of his life with traditional rites of passage, then, is helpful in some

23. Appiah-Kubi, 56.
24. Mbiti, "Some African Concepts," 54.

respects only. It needs to be radically adjusted in order to bring out the unique significance in Jesus' life of those events — birth, baptism, and death — that do have partial parallels in African religion, and to be complemented by a clear emphasis on the equally unique event of the resurrection.

An alternative attempt to bring out the significance of Jesus in the African context has been to see his person in terms of African charismatic leaders.[25] The most obvious category here is that of the healer. Traditional religion knows many kinds of healer — the herbalist, the exorcist, the witch-finder, and so on — and these are often not mutually exclusive. Each is regarded as drawing, in one degree or another, on the power of the spirits or of the supreme God to effect his work. If this approach is followed in formulating an African christology, then the difference between Jesus and traditional healers needs to be clearly spelled out. As Pobee says:

> [T]he difference between Jesus and the healers would be the unprecedented scale on which he was ensouled with God: Jesus was in a perpetual state of holiness . . . unlike the traditional healer who had occasional experiences of it.[26]

Gabriel Setiloane has made the intriguing suggestion that the messianic idea in African thinking should be sought "somewhere in the area of the African *bongaka*," that is, the traditional African doctor.[27] As far as I am aware, neither he nor any other African theologian has followed this up in any detail, but it was developed with a rather different emphasis by Kibongi.[28] In the Zairean context in which Kibongi writes, *nganga* (a word commonly found in Bantu languages) means not only "medicine man" but also, according to Kibongi, "priest." The *nganga*'s

25. Jesus' ministry in the context of charismatics in first-century Palestine is discussed in Geza Vermes, *Jesus the Jew* (London, 1976).

26. Pobee, *Towards an African Theology*, 92.

27. Gabriel Setiloane, "Where Are We in African Theology?" *ATER*, 59-65. For a spirit-christology from a very different point of view see G. Lampe, "The Holy Spirit and the Person of Christ," in *Christ, Faith, and History*, ed. S. Sykes and J. P. Clayton (Cambridge, 1973), 111-30.

28. R. B. Kibongi, "Priesthood," *BRAB*, 47-56; for a different perspective see also Cece Kolié, "Jesus as Healer," in *Faces of Jesus in Africa*, 128-50.

function is to "interpose himself between man and all other agents of evil," such as sorcerers, bad medicines, ghosts, and even death. Furthermore, the *nganga* may act as a prophet, foretelling the future and also playing an important role in the political, economic, and social spheres. In the first of these roles he may divine and may destroy evil influences by various means, including animal sacrifice. Of course, the *nganga's* influence was not always wholly good, and he was responsible for conflicts arising from witchcraft accusations. Nevertheless the terminology itself and the ideas that surrounded the traditional *nganga* persisted into the Christian church, and Kibongi points out that "for good or ill Christianity has not always escaped the heritage of the *nganga*."[29] This heritage is seen not only in the term for missionary (*nganga Nzambi*) but also in a good deal of other terminology used within the church. Kibongi, standing as he does within the adaptionist approach, has emphasized, in a way that Setiloane does not, the discontinuous elements as well as the continuous. Though the *nganga* "throws into relief the idea of salvation or deliverance," it is only through Christ that this desire is fully satisfied. Thus the aspirations expressed in the traditional religion find their fulfillment in the Christian faith. While his approach is not as radical as Setiloane's, it can claim, as Kibongi himself points out, methodological justification in the theology of the Epistle to the Hebrews.

A related symbol for Christ is that of the "master of initiation," who plays an important role in many traditional initiation rites. His task is to school the novice and support him during the painful process of initiation. He is therefore the "master" who, because he has himself undergone pain in the same way, can become the guardian, guide, and elder brother.[30]

A third approach to African christology has been through the use of the offices or titles used in traditional African societies. We noted above that the biblical christological titles are not necessarily very helpful for a present-day understanding of the significance of Jesus within Africa. Some writers, however, have found partial points of contact in

29. Kibongi, 52.
30. So especially Mveng; A. Sanon, "Jesus, Master of Initiation," in *Faces of Jesus in Africa*, 85ff., and *Entrancer l'Évangile: initiations africaine et pedagogue de la foi* (Paris, 1988); M. Ntetem, *Die negro-afrikanische Stammesinitiation* (Munsterschwarzach 1983).

the titles of political leaders in Africa. The most obvious category here is that of the chief or king, which may be taken as corresponding to some extent to the New Testament "Lord." Aside from the fact that Jesus, in all probability, avoided titles with any marked political overtones, there are other objections to the chiefly symbolism, which have been cogently urged by Sawyerr.[31] He points out that colonial rule and subsequent independence have eroded much of the traditional authority of the chief, who now often occupies a somewhat precarious position. Furthermore, the chief in traditional Africa was never an absolute ruler, but was always subject to the restraints and councils of his elders. More important, the chief was often a figure remote from his subjects, not easily accessible to the ordinary man, and sometimes deliberately secluded. For these reasons Sawyerr regards the imagery of chieftainship as quite inadequate for constructing a christology for modern Africa.

A more attractive proposal, but along similar lines, has been advanced by Pobee. He sees a close parallel between the role of Jesus and the *okyeame*, the "linguist" who acts as official spokesman to the Akan chief. He is subordinate to the paramount but in public pronouncements represents the chief and exercises his chiefly authority. This symbolism Pobee regards as useful since it represents a "royal, priestly Christology" that would be relevant to Akan Christians.[32] He has, however, two reservations: first, it is limited in that it describes only the triumphant aspect of Christ's work — the chiefly analogy is, as he puts it, a *theologia gloriae*, not a *theologia crucis* — and second, it is only one of several possible christologies. Pobee indeed believes that there is a plurality of christologies in the New Testament itself, and thus we should look for several different christologies in present-day African theology.

Pobee's reference to the *theologia gloriae* reminds us that the most universal symbol for Christ in the New Testament is that of "Lord," a term that expresses both rank and commitment.[33] The lordship of Christ has attracted particular attention among African theologians, especially within the context of his lordship over evil and oppressive

31. Sawyerr, *Creative Evangelism*, 72-73; but for a recent more positive use of this title see Francois Kabasele in *Faces of Jesus in Africa*.

32. Pobee, *Towards an African Theology*, 94-95: "In Akan society, as in most other societies in West Africa, the royal priestly christology hopefully would speak to most African hearts."

33. MacQuarrie, 293.

powers that enslave the Christian. In traditional African religion humans are susceptible to attacks from powers outside themselves: disease, witchcraft, evil spirits, death. It is just these areas in which several theologians have seen the real significance of Jesus for the African church. Mbiti, for example, has pointed out that to the average African "savior" most meaningfully refers to deliverance from calamities that are primarily physical: "There is ample evidence to indicate the chief preoccupation of African Christians is 'redemption' from physical dilemmas,"[34] and again, "[D]aily and physical concerns of survival seem to have driven African Christians to see and experience 'our Saviour' in the role of physical rescuer and redeemer."[35]

With such a view Appiah-Kubi concurs.[36] Liberation, he believes, deals with the comprehensive needs of man's "total idea of liberation from fear, uncertainty, sickness, evil powers, foreign domination and oppression, distortion of his humanity, poverty and want."[37] These needs include protection against "spiritual powers" such as witchcraft and possession, but these things also are manifested in physical terms like misfortune, sickness, and death.

This view of the work of Christ as liberator has, of course, an impressive historical pedigree in the "classic"[38] view of the atonement, which has found its most persuasive modern defense in Aulen's *Christus Victor*. It sees the work of Christ as consisting in his triumph over demonic powers that enslave mankind. It has its origins firmly in the New Testament,[39] and seems to speak with much more immediacy to the African context than to the Western world, where it calls for some drastic demythologizing if it is to be relevant. However, within Africa it

---

34. Mbiti, "ὁ σωτὴρ ἡμῶν," 408; compare 405: "That which attacks, destroys and protects against these enemies of life is clearly salvatory. The enemies in traditional life are innumerable and include: sickness, witchcraft, sorcery, magic, barrenness, failure, troublesome spirits, danger, misfortune, calamity, and death as far as the individual is concerned; and drought, war, oppression, foreign domination, slavery, locust invasion, epidemics, floods, and so on as far as the wider community is concerned."

35. Mbiti, "ὁ σωτὴρ ἡμῶν," 411.

36. Appiah-Kubi, 57: "[T]he main preoccupation of many African Christians is redemption from physical dilemmas and evil forces."

37. Appiah-Kubi, 60.

38. So MacQuarrie, 317ff.

39. E.g., Mark 3:22-26; Col. 1:13 and 2:14-15.

has a serious limitation, namely its apparent failure to come to grips adequately with the problem of human sin and guilt. If the work of Christ lies in the destruction of evil powers outside of humankind, in what way does it deal with sin, and in what does redemption actually consist?

Part of the problem here perhaps may be that African traditional religions have a quite different concept of sin from that found in the Judeo-Christian tradition. In African thought sin tends to be regarded as that which disturbs the social order and the peace of the community. It is thus an offense less against the supreme God than against one's fellow humans or against the ancestral spirits.[40] For this reason the Christian doctrine of sin has seemed alien to some African writers. As Appiah-Kubi has it:

> The Euro-American Christian teaching on sin is such that it tends to be completely meaningless to the African; peaceful living with one's neighbors is far more important than any Western Christian teaching about sin.[41]

The vertical, God-ward aspect of sin, if not completely lacking, is nevertheless somewhat defective from a biblical point of view.[42]

---

40. See J. Mbiti, *African Religions and Philosophy* (London, 1969), 205ff., for an overview of sin and evil in African religions. Dickson's balanced discussion concludes that there is a tradition of sin against God in Africa, but that not all offenses are so regarded (Dickson, *Theology in Africa*, 67). It is true that many African peoples have myths of a "fall" of humankind. But the point behind these is probably not to give an "explanation" of the origin and nature of moral evil but rather to emphasize the distance between God and humankind, which then provides the rationale for ritual communication through intermediaries (so D. Zahan, *The Religion, Spirituality and Thought of Traditional Africa* [Chicago, 1979], 16).

41. Appiah-Kubi, 57. Appiah-Kubi does not make any attempt, however, to examine how far these "Western teachings" are related to the biblical understanding of sin.

42. Compare Pobee, *Towards an African Theology*, 118. Sawyerr's comment that the independent churches in Africa have generally failed to come to grips with the vicarious nature of the atonement may perhaps be relevant to some extent to the mainstream churches also. Harry Sawyerr, "What is African Theology," *ATJ* 16 [1971], reprinted in *The Practice of Presence, the Shorter Writings of Harry Sawyerr*, ed. John Parratt (Edinburgh, 1995).

These aspects of Christian doctrine are basically interlinked. The ultimate criterion for christology, as Tillich has pointed out, is soteriological, and is determined by the question of what salvation really means.[43] The Christian doctrine of the atonement, whatever its variations, claims to deal with the problem of humankind's alienation from God through sin and guilt. To view salvation as primarily deliverance from physical evil is to lead, in Mbiti's words, to "the eclipse of the atoning passion and the minimizing of sin."[44] This in turn will lead to an inadequate christology.

Little real attempt has been made as yet to interpret the atonement in African terms. Harry Sawyerr drew attention to the concept of "blood covenant," by which the living were bound both to each other and to the dead, and also to the agreement between African thought and the Book of Leviticus that "blood is life."[45] The most compelling interpretation of the cross in terms of African thought has, however, come from Kwesi Dickson.[46] Dickson has argued that just as Paul had no alternative but to express his understanding of the cross in terms of his own Jewish tradition, so the church has throughout its history derived its understanding of the death of Christ from the different cultural perspectives of its time. In the Western world death is usually regarded as a disaster, and such a view has tended to color traditional interpretations of the atonement. The death of Jesus consequently is often regarded as simply a stage in the process of redemption, the negative aspect of which finds its resolution in the raising of Jesus from the dead. The African view of death by contrast is rather one of fulfillment. While it does not deny the evil associated with death, it sees death as the gateway to greater life, both for the deceased, who becomes an ancestor able to grant benefits to the living, and also for the community, which receives such benefits. Furthermore, the deceased remains an integral member of the community of which during life he or she was a member. An African understanding of the atonement therefore "would not speak in muted tones but in glorious affirmation of the cross as that which is the basis of

---

43. Tillich, vol. 2, 146.

44. Mbiti, "ὁ σωτὴρ ἡμῶν," 412.

45. Sawyerr, *Creative Evangelism*, 86ff., 121ff. Compare also Mulago's *Le pacte de sang et la communion alimentaire*, 171-87.

46. Dickson, *Theology in Africa*, 185ff.

Christian hope." Dickson thus sees the key to an understanding of the cross for Africa as an event that heals and confirms relationships within society (cf. 1 Cor. 10:16-18). He points out also that African religion understands sacrifice to be, as in the Bible, a means of cementing the relationship between the worshiper and his kinsmen to God. Jesus' death, as the perfect sacrifice of one who lived an exemplary life, fits him to be regarded as the perfect Ancestor, who has died yet lives to have communion with his people. The concept of Jesus as ancestor is one to which we shall return again below. These explorations suggest that there are aspects of christology and soteriology that are not totally alien to African thought.

African women theologians are also beginning to take a fresh look at christology from a feminist perspective. Feminist theology in Africa, as we have suggested above, tends less to polarize the feminist-masculine divide than to see them as complementary.[47] From this perspective Jesus is seen as a symbol for all humanity, female as well as male. A common theme, however, is that of relating the passion of Christ directly to the suffering of women.[48] Part of this sense of suffering has been caused by the domination of the church in Africa by male structures,[49] and a preliminary task of African feminist theology is to uncover such oppressive structures.[50] The theme of the African woman's suffering has been approached from different perspectives.

Therese Souga[51] takes her point of departure from the Gospel narratives to demonstrate Jesus' concern for and empathy with women, and to argue that African women share with many of the women who appear in the Gospels a common lot of exclusion, weakness, silence, and

47. Anne Nasimuyu-Wasike, "Christology and an African Woman's Experience," in *Faces of Jesus in Africa*, 70.

48. Rosemary Edet and Bette Ekeya, "The Church of Women in Africa, a Theological Community," in *With Passion and Compassion*, ed. V. Fabella and M. Oduyoye (Maryknoll, 1988), 4.

49. A common theme in Third World feminist theologies; compare also women's writing on Dalit and Minjung theologies.

50. Edet and Ekeya, referring to Rosemary Nthumburi's paper "On the Possibility of a New Image for an African Woman" (presented to the EATWOT Women's Commission in Port Harcourt, Nigeria, in 1986).

51. Therese Souga, "The Christ Event from the Viewpoint of African Women: A Catholic Perspective," in *With Passion and Compassion*, 22-29.

the bearing of burdens. For her, Christ is in solidarity with women, because it is they who "incarnate the suffering of the African people" and it is from this suffering that the message of Christ liberates. Louise Tappa[52] shares this desire to interpret Scripture and the history of the early church from the perspective of women. For her, the two stories intertwined in Mark 5:21-34 provide a paradigm that demonstrates the way in which Jesus overcomes the taboos and exclusion that characterize women's place in African society.

Anne Nasimuyu-Wasike[53] has adopted a more pragmatic approach to christology. Her field survey of African women of different social and educational statuses is a salutary exercise in African oral theology that reveals the actual role of Jesus in their lives today. Again the predominant attitude towards Jesus on the part of her informants was to focus on his role as hope, refuge, strength, and comforter in their position of marginalization and exclusion, hardship and burden bearing, in home, society, and the church. For Nasimuyu-Wasike, Jesus' attitude to women was revolutionary and "counter-cultural,"[54] and she points out that Jesus not only freely associated with women on the margins of society but also frequently speaks of women in his parables. Her model for a christology in the African context would also include the symbol of "Jesus as Mother," the nourisher of the weak, while her interpretation of the more common models — liberator, healer, eschatological redeemer — takes on a new light as they are viewed from a woman's perspective. A basic problem that is common to all christologies in Africa, however, is the apparent lack of any real parallel in African religions to one who combines what Tillich has termed "transcendent roots with historical functions."[55]

52. Louise Tappa, "The Christ Event from the Viewpoint of African Women: a Protestant Perspective," in *With Passion and Compassion*, 30-34.

53. Nasimuyu-Wasike, 70-81. For approaches making use of oral materials see also the articles of Elizabeth Amoah and Mercy Oduyoye in *With Passion and Compassion* and Teresia Hinga's examination of an independent church in "An African Confession of Christ: The Christology of the Legio Maria Church in Kenya," in *Exploring Afro-Christology*, ed. J. Pobee (Frankfurt am Main, 1992), 137-44.

54. Nasimuyu-Wasike, 73, 77.

55. Tillich, vol. 2, 89.

2. Community and Participation

In African religions the place of the community is of central importance, and the religious community is identified with the civil community.[56] As we noted above, Mulago drew attention to this aspect of African culture, when he discovered the focal point of the religious thinking of the Bantu of Rwanda Burundi to be vital union, a union that extended in ever widening circles from the individual to the family, tribe, and nation, and that survives death itself in the union of the living with the ancestors.[57] Mulago's views were reiterated in his contribution to *Biblical Revelation and African Beliefs*,[58] in which he extended his findings to other Bantu groups. Life, according to Mulago, is essentially "existence in community," for "the life of the individual is grasped as it is shared." It is both empirical and superempirical, that is, it is life here and now and life beyond the grave.

These two aspects of life are inseparable and interdependent. There is a real continuity between the living and the dead, for life in community is participation in the sacred life of the ancestors: "[I]t is the extension of the life of one's forefathers and a preparation for one's own life to be carried on in one's descendants."[59] This represents a "community of blood." God himself is the ultimate source of life, and he is its fullness. The degree to which a person participates in the life of the community is determined by social rank, beginning from the invisible order — the founders of clans, culture heroes, the ancestors — down to the visible order of the king and queen mother, the heads of clans and families, and, finally, the individual. The key to Bantu customs, according to Mulago, lies in the fact of the community, in the "single principle of participation."[60]

Mulago's emphasis upon the importance of the community has been shared by several other African theologians. Some have pointed out the similarity between the African idea of participation and the

56. See E. Dammann, *Die Religionen Afrikas* (Stuttgart, 1963), 222.
57. See Mulago's *Une Visage africaine de Christianisme: l'unité vitale bantu face a l'unité vitale écclesiale* (Paris, 1965).
58. Mulago, "Vital Participation," *BRAB*, 137-58.
59. Mulago, "Vital Participation," 139-40.
60. Mulago, "Vital Participation," 145.

biblical concept of "corporate personality." Bonganjalo Goba, a South African, has given this theme extended treatment.[61] He reminds us that in ancient Israel the individual represented the community, his actions affected its welfare, and the basic unit was the household to which the individual belonged.[62] Goba finds the situation very similar in traditional Africa.

> As in Israel the concept of corporate personality manifests itself in everyday relationships, so also in Africa most communities are held together by a web of kinship relations, and within these relationships every form of evil that a person suffers, whether it be moral or natural evil, is believed to be caused by a member of the community.[63]

John Pobee has discovered a similar base in the Akan worldview: for him Akan ontology is at root *"cognatus ergo sum"* — I am related by blood, therefore I exist. This, Pobee believes, is an element that Africa shares with the biblical faith, and is therefore a basis upon which a dialogue may be begun.[64]

The application of the African concept of the community to Christian theology has proceeded so far broadly along three avenues: its relevance for our understanding of the Godhead, for our understanding of the church, and for our understanding of the communion of saints.

In its application to the doctrine of the Trinity, it bears some similarity to Augustine's analogy of shared love,[65] centering on relationships within the Godhead, an approach that may well be more meaningful than the traditional credal concept of "persons." Foremost in this approach have been the Catholic theologians Nyamiti and Mwoleka.[66]

---

61. Bonganjalo Goba, "Corporate Personality: Ancient Israel and Africa," *BTSAV,* 65-77.

62. For a discussion of solidarity in ancient Israel see G. von Rad, *The Theology of the Old Testament,* vol. 2 (London, 1967), 231ff.

63. Goba, "Corporate Personality," 68.

64. Pobee, *Towards an African Theology,* 44ff. To similar effect is the proverb, common in many Bantu languages, that "man is only really human in the company of others."

65. Augustine, *De Trinitate,* iv.4, viii.12, ix.2, also *Confessions,* xiii; for a discussion of Augustine's doctrine see J. N. D. Kelly, *Early Christian Doctrines* (London, 1958), 271-79.

66. So also Mercy Amba Oduyoye, *Hearing and Knowing; Theological Reflections*

Nyamiti takes his point of departure from the role of the ancestors and their place in the community, which unites the living and the dead.[67] The mystical relationship between the living and the dead, which is characteristic of African religions, he sees as corresponding to the relationship that through Christ links the Christian community to God. This God-human relationship is achieved by death (of Jesus) and continues after death, in that "through Christ's death and resurrection a mystical relationship has been established between him and the rest of humanity." The idea here is that in traditional thought a person's relationship to the family is continued, though in an enhanced form, after death: similarly the relationship of the Christian to God is transformed by the death and resurrection of Christ.[68] For Nyamiti Jesus is the perfect ancestor, more specifically the brother-ancestor of African tradition. He elaborates a detailed parallel between the role of the brother-ancestor and that of Christ. Like the African ancestor, Jesus shares in the human nature of his descendants, and like them he attains this ancestorship by undergoing death. He is also, as they are, mediator between the living and God, and by virtue of his human and divine life the model of conduct for his descendants.[69] Consequently Nyamiti emphasizes the solidarity of Christ with this church — "his descendants" — "Christ is not Head alone; he is Head and members together."[70]

Nyamiti uses the ancestor-descendant analogy also to elucidate the

---

on *Christianity in Africa* (Maryknoll, 1986), 144-45, where the Trinity is understood as the pattern for human society. Mwoleka's views will be discussed in chapter 6.

67. Charles Nyamiti, *African Tradition and the Christian God* (Eldoret, n.d.), 45ff., and subsequently in *Christ as Our Ancestor* (Gweru and Harare, 1984), part 2.

68. Sawyerr would disagree; for him Jesus differs from the ancestors precisely because "unlike the ancestral dead of the Africans, Jesus Christ, once dead, now lives." Sawyerr, *Creative Evangelism*, 93.

69. Nyamiti, *Christ as Our Ancestor*, 15ff. Nyamiti's other parallels between the role of Christ and that of the African ancestors seem to me less convincing. He sees it also as part of Christ's ancestral role that he may send calamity upon his people for their neglect of communion with God, and that he reveals himself through earthly means (such as priest and sacrament) just as the ancestors were believed to reveal themselves in animal forms. He recognizes that the ancestor analogy has differences as well as parallels; the most important is that Christ's nature, being rooted in his divinity, is essentially different from ours, and his mediatorial role is based on his redemptive work accomplished in his death and resurrection.

70. Nyamiti, *Christ as Our Ancestor*, 49.

relationship between God and Jesus, and indeed he sees it as more helpful within the African context than the biblical father-son analogy. The ideal ancestor is

> a personal parent of another person, of whom he is the archtype (*sic* — archetype) of both nature and behaviour, and with whom he is entitled to have a regular sacred relationship through communication of some sort.[71]

On this view the life of the Godhead within the Trinity becomes the exemplar of all human ancestorship; God is ancestor, not only because he generates the Son and is the "Prototype" of the Son but "because there exists between him and the Son an intimate relationship of sacred communication of nature and love through the Holy Spirit."[72] The Spirit, then, is the expression of mutual love and self-giving between God and Christ, which corresponds to the traditional notion of sacred communication between ancestor and descendant. The Spirit, therefore, becomes an essential element in the ancestor-descendant analogy as applied to the Godhead. Nyamiti's exploration into the meaning of the Trinity is an interesting attempt to approach this aspect of Christian dogma from within African categories, and from an ethical rather than a metaphysical point of view.[73]

The relationship between the community in African thought and the Christian church seems more obvious and straightforward, but is not, surprisingly, one that has been very extensively explored,[74]

---

71. Nyamiti, *African Tradition*, 48; in *Christ as our Ancestor*, 23, Nyamiti distinguishes between God, who is the "parent-ancestor," and Jesus, the "brother-ancestor."

72. Nyamiti, *African Tradition*, 48; *Christ as our Ancestor*, 64-65.

73. Compare R. L. Ottley's comment that "the Christian doctrine of God has been more intelligently grasped and stated in proportion as the metaphysical conceptions have been replaced by ethical ideas" (*The Doctrine of the Incarnation* [London, 1946], 569). For other discussions of Jesus as ancestor see especially Bediako, *Jesus in African Culture*; Francois Kabasele, "Christ as Ancestor and Elder Brother," in *Faces of Jesus in Africa*, 116-27; and Bujo, *African Theology in Its Social Context* (Maryknoll, 1992), to be discussed in the following chapter.

74. Mbiti's remark is apposite: "African traditional life is largely built on the community. Since the church is also a community of those who have faith in Jesus Christ, this overlapping concept should be exploited much more on the African scene particularly in terms of the family, the neighbours and the departed" ("Christianity and African Culture," *JTSA* [1977]: 26).

though Mulago, as we have seen, did draw out in some detail the parallel between the traditional society and the church as the community of God sharing in the divine life. Harry Sawyerr, from an Anglican point of view, has also, like Mulago, explored this theme within the general context of the place of the sacraments.[75] Sawyerr believes that "kinship in Africa provides us with a very significant concept on which African Christians could build the concept of the church as the Great Family."[76]

His main interest, however, is not in the visible church but rather in the place of the departed. He stresses that in Africa the departed ancestors are very important indeed.[77] Just as the African community embraces the living, the unborn, and the dead, so the church is militant on earth and triumphant in heaven. Christian doctrine, he believes, should address itself towards presenting the church as a body that not only transcends the earthly community ties of family and tribe, but also preserves the solidarity of the living with the dead. Sawyerr believes that in this way the ancestors could then "be readily embraced within the framework of the universal Church and be included within the communion of saints."[78] He goes on to discuss the fate of the non-Christian ancestors, and believes that there is biblical and theological warrant for prayers for the unconverted dead, and that this would fulfill a deeply felt need of African Christians.[79]

The fullest treatment of the place of the ancestors within the context of Christian theology came from Fasholé-Luke, in his contribu-

75. Sawyerr, *Creative Evangelism*, 105ff.

76. Sawyerr, *Creative Evangelism*, 91.

77. Quoting Baeta's dictum that "whatever others may do in their countries, our people live with their dead." C. G. Baeta, ed., *Christianity and African Culture* (Accra, 1955), 60.

78. Sawyerr, *Creative Evangelism*, 94.

79. Compare Mbiti's discussion of the departed in his *New Testament Eschatology*, 154-55. He tentatively suggests that certain features of the Akamba concept of the afterlife could be introduced into Christian practice, including prayers for the dead and the idea that the departed may intercede on behalf of the living. He believes Christianity should take very seriously the place of the departed and that "the act of embracing the Christian faith need not mean a complete severing of mutual interest between the departed and the survivors." Nyamiti's *Christ as our Ancestor*, despite its exhaustive discussion of ancestorship, effectively skirts around the theological problem of the non-Christian dead.

tion to the Sawyerr *Festschrift*, "Ancestor Veneration and the Community of Saints."[80] Fasholé-Luke urges the Christian church to take seriously the deeply felt concern of Africans for their ancestors. The way to do this, he believes, is by developing the neglected doctrine of the communion of saints in such a way that it avoids the dangers both of syncretism and of spiritual schizophrenia — intellectually rejecting the ancestral cults while engaging in them to satisfy emotional longings. Fasholé-Luke sees a distinction between worship offered to the supreme being in traditional Africa and the veneration offered to the ancestors. It is this distinction that "provides a genuine basis for the development of a doctrine of the communion of saints which will be acceptable to the universal church and satisfying to African Christians."[81]

Like Sawyerr, Fasholé-Luke is hopeful about the fate of non-Christian ancestors, and sees the sacraments of baptism and the eucharist as one way of incorporating the ancestors into the Christian community. The *sanctorum communio* implies "fellowship with holy people of all ages and the whole company of heaven," and participation in the sacraments "gives us a signpost to the road along which our theologising should travel."[82] This theologizing takes its point of departure from the death of Jesus, which is for the whole world and the merits of which reach to all: "Thus both Christians and non-Christians, receive salvation through Christ's death and are linked with him through the sacrament which he himself instituted." The ancestors may be included, in Fasholé-Luke's view, in the communion of saints, and the eucharist may be the occasion for prayer on their behalf that the all-sufficient sacrifice of Christ may be effective for the non-Christian departed. Conversely, it may also be anticipated that the Christian dead will intercede on behalf of the living.

What Sawyerr and Fasholé-Luke are pleading for here is that the real concern of Africans for their dead not only should be acknowledged but also should be linked in a meaningful way to the traditional Christian doctrine of the communion of saints.[83] Sawyerr advances biblical

---

80. E. Fasholé-Luke, "Ancestor Veneration and the Community of Saints," in *New Testament Essays for Africa and the World*, ed. M. Glasswell and E. Fasholé-Luke (London, 1974), 209-21.

81. Fasholé-Luke, "Ancestor Veneration," 212.

82. Fasholé-Luke, "Ancestor Veneration," 216.

83. "We would suggest," writes Fasholé-Luke, "that veneration of our ancestors

support for his suggestion that the non-Christian dead may be included in our prayers (Mt. 27:52ff.; 1 Cor. 15:29; 1 Pet. 3:18), while Fasholé-Luke proceeds on the more philosophical ground of the infinite worth of the sacrifice of Christ and its mediation through the sacraments of the church. What the *sanctorum communio* article of the creed originally meant is probably, as Kelly has said, an insoluble problem,[84] but it does not seem on any understanding to have included the non-Christian dead, which is the issue raised here. This is one of those gray areas of theology on which there is little biblical evidence.

3. Eschatology and Sacrament

The place of the dead leads us naturally into the question of eschatology, and how Christian eschatology may be dealt with within the context of African ideas. Perhaps no one has returned to this question as often as John Mbiti.[85] His approach to eschatology in African religions takes its starting point from his view of the concept of time in

---

in Africa and our passionate desire to be linked with our dead in a real and genuine way can be satisfied by the development of a sound doctrine of the communion of saints" (Fasholé-Luke, "Ancestor Veneration," 220). An interesting Asian contribution to this discussion has come from C. S. Song. Commenting on the way in which missionaries to China failed to discern this deeply felt aspect of Chinese religion by forbidding ancestor veneration, Song stresses that ancestor worship was understood not so much as communion with the *dead* as with the *living* (so also Mbiti's preference for the term "living dead" to denote the ancestors: *African Religions and Philosophy,* 25ff.) For Song, too, the celebration of the eucharist, as a remembrance of Christ, is also to experience Christ as "the centre of the family to which we belong," which includes also those who have passed beyond this life. The eucharist thus "gives us assurance that the loved ones who have gone before us are also present with us through Jesus Christ" (C. S. Song, *Third Eye Theology* [London, 1980], 153ff.).

84. In the Eastern church it seems to have meant originally "the participation in holy things," i.e. the eucharist, but the more usual understanding of "communion with the departed saints" is also attested quite early: see Kelly's discussion (J. N. D. Kelly, *Early Christian Creeds* [London, 1972], 388ff.).

85. Mbiti's numerous writings on this theme indicate how central it is to his interests: see particularly his contribution "Eschatology" to *BRAB,* 159-84, and *New Testament Eschatology.* For an excellent general survey of Mbiti's theology, see Kwame Bediako, *Theology and Identity,* 303-46.

Africa, a view that has been much debated.[86] According to Mbiti the main feature of the idea of time in Africa is the virtual absence of the future: time is therefore two-dimensional, having a present and a long-past, and moves backward rather than forward, as does the linear view of time.[87] The golden age consequently lies in the past, and African mythology is more concerned with the *Urzeit* than with the *Endzeit*.[88] African thought therefore has no futuristic eschatology and no hope of a future resurrection.[89] Clearly such a view of time has important implications for the relationship of biblical eschatology to African thought. This problem Mbiti attempted to tackle in his doctoral thesis of 1963, which probably still remains his most significant contribution to African theology.

New Testament Eschatology in an African Background is a study of the "encounter between New Testament theology and African traditional concepts" as found among Mbiti's own people, the Akamba of Kenya. Mbiti shows that Christianity was introduced by Western missionaries with a fundamentalist outlook on the Bible, and consequently the Akamba converts were presented with a futurist eschatology that depended on a literal understanding of biblical symbolism. Such a view of a new world in the heavens represented a radical discontinuity with the traditional worldview, but seems to have been willingly accepted at a popular level by Akamba Christians.

> This whole conceptual area is new to the Akamba and other African peoples, in that traditionally they never thought of or expected, a future world situated somewhere in the heavens. Both in terms of time and geography, African peoples are undergoing a radical change in their conception as far as their understanding of the hereafter is concerned.[90]

---

86. For a critique of Mbiti's understanding of time in Africa, see my "Time in Traditional African Thought," *Religion* 7 (1977): 117-26, and F. Gillies, "The Bantu Concept of Time," *Religion* 10 (1980): 16-29.

87. See especially *African Religions and Philosophy*, 16ff., and "Eschatology," 159-84.

88. "Eschatology," 163.

89. Compare Mbiti, "Some African Concepts," 55.

90. Mbiti, *New Testament Eschatology*, 90.

In Mbiti's view, this development has had deleterious results for two reasons. First, it has encouraged a pietistic approach, which directs attention to the other world to the detriment of active Christian involvement in the present. Second, it has resulted in the separation of eschatology from christology. According to Mbiti, this dilemma stems from a fundamental misunderstanding of New Testament eschatology. From his comprehensive survey of the biblical evidence Mbiti concludes that, although there is a linear understanding of time in parts of the New Testament, this is not its only, nor even its main, emphasis. Rather, this is one of "fulfillment" or "consummation" in Christ, in which time is subject to eschatology rather than eschatology being dominated by a linear view of time.[91] Thus while time illuminates the "horizontal" dimension of eschatology, Christian eschatology also has a "vertical" dimension, which is basically nontemporal.[92] The vertical dimension confronts us with the reality of what Mbiti calls "the nearness of the spirit world," and finds its outward expression in the liturgical life of the church. This aspect of eschatology does not depend upon the linear concept of time, and is not, therefore, embarrassed by such problems as the time of the parousia, which plague the futurist approach. It also has points of contact with other, including African, cultural systems and can, in Mbiti's view, be convincingly conveyed through them. Accordingly, the Christian doctrine of the Spirit and of the sacraments can provide a "way in" to a relevant eschatology for Christians in Africa, for in the events of baptism and the eucharist the "physical and spiritual worlds converge, as do also the dimensions of Time."[93] In the sacraments eschatology and christology are brought together; they are eschatological events that have Christ as their focus.

In the strict sense, Mbiti admits, worship of this type is alien to Akamba traditions, as also to those of other African peoples. There is, however, in Africa a widespread practice of offerings, prayer, and sacrifice,[94] which bears some relation to eucharistic worship. Mbiti sees other

---

91. Mbiti, *New Testament Eschatology*, 49-50.

92. Mbiti, *New Testament Eschatology*, 61.

93. Mbiti, *New Testament Eschatology*, 91.

94. See especially Harry Sawyerr, "Sacrifice," *BRAB*, 57-82, whose paper ends by calling on African theologians to work out a response to the persistence of traditional sacrifice in Africa.

possible points of contact in the various Akamba rituals, and he discusses the most important of these. The naming ceremony *(kuimithya)*, which takes place soon after a child's birth, signifies the acceptance of it as fully human and as a member of society. Circumcision of both sexes represents a rite of maturity in which the initiate is "born anew" into adult society. Akamba religion also knows of a sacrificial communal meal, at which offerings are made to the departed and which signifies not only remembrance of the dead but also their fellowship with the living. There are also cleansing ceremonies that aim at removing disharmony from society. While the broad similarities between these ceremonies and aspects of the Christian sacraments are clear enough, they cannot, according to Mbiti, be regarded as sacramental in meaning or intention. He sees the essential difference as the fact that Akamba rites rarely invoke God directly; even when a direct prayer to God does occur, it is rather of a petitionary nature than of true worship or fellowship.[95] In contrast to these Akamba rites the Christian sacraments present worship at its "most intense and real,"[96] in which eschatological and christological realities are conveyed. These realities are mediated through the Holy Spirit, the eschatological gift and guarantee of the Christian eschatological community. According to Mbiti, the theological problem for the Church in Kenya (and by implication elsewhere in Africa) is how the real significance of baptism and the eucharist can be "presented intelligently to a people which lacks sacramental concepts."[97] In other words, how can the sacraments be related to the traditional African worldview in a way that avoids the misleading emphasis on the future that characterized the more fundamentalist missions?

Mbiti's approach is less one of adapting traditional ceremonies to fit Christian sacramental ritual than of seeking to incorporate specific traditional elements into sacramental worship. The Akamba rite of the naming of children could find a place in baptism since both share the underlying ideas of a new birth. Further, the concept of incorporation into the community that naming involves fits in well with baptism as incorporation into Christ. Prebaptismal instruction would provide an ideal vehicle for expounding Christian doctrine, taking the sacraments

95. Mbiti, *New Testament Eschatology*, 95-96.
96. Mbiti, *New Testament Eschatology*, 90.
97. Mbiti, *New Testament Eschatology*, 116.

as its central feature. The circumcision ritual, especially in view of the Pauline teaching (Rom. 2:25-29; Col. 4:11), also lends itself to being reinterpreted in baptismal terms. The traditional implications of circumcision, such as the attainment of adulthood and completeness of personality, may have their counterparts in such baptismal concepts as the new birth and new covenant. However, one aspect of the Christian sacrament has no counterpart in Akamba ritual, namely the idea that the baptism joins the believer in fellowship with God.[98] For the Akamba the living are linked to others in the world of the living and in the world of the dead, but there is no conception of unity with the Creator. Christian baptism therefore introduces a quite new dimension, in that it "opens the door into the world of the I-Thou relationship between God and man."[99] This "dialogue of communion" finds its fulfillment in the eucharist, which unites the eschatological emphasis on the new community with a christological one, the centrality of Jesus as the focus of this community. For Mbiti, the eucharist is also of vital importance because it embraces time in all its aspects: the past is seen in the remembrance of the Last Supper, the present in the celebration of a common meal, and the future in the promise of the return of Jesus at the end of the age.[100] In sum, therefore, what Mbiti is trying to do is to find elements in Akamba traditions that "readily lend themselves to points of contact with Christian ideas and ceremonies." These will become "starting points from which the theology of the sacraments could be built," which may be "baptized" to convey Christian meaning.[101] The sacraments, as both Christ-centered and eschatological, are for him focal points in this process.

Mbiti's approach breaks new ground in its insistence that the true way into eschatology for Africa is not through futurism — which on his view of time violates the deeply rooted traditional worldview — but rather through an emphasis on a sort of realized eschatology that is mediated through the sacraments. The vertical God-ward aspect of Christian baptism and the eucharist provide the meeting point of past, present, and future, in real and immediate communion with God

---

98. Mbiti, *New Testament Eschatology*, 112.
99. Mbiti, *New Testament Eschatology*, 123.
100. Mbiti, *New Testament Eschatology*, 104.
101. Mbiti, *New Testament Eschatology*, 126.

through Jesus. Whether or not Mbiti's analysis of time in African thought is entirely satisfying, he has put African theologians in his debt by seeking to uncover the importance of the sacraments for Christian eschatology within the African context. In this he has introduced a new dimension into sacramental theology within the continent.

A good deal of discussion of the sacraments, by contrast, has centered around liturgical renewal. The aim of this is to attempt to formulate liturgies that will incorporate all that is good and lasting in African traditional rituals, and so infuse new meaning into the Christian sacraments. Such experiments properly belong to the field of liturgics and are not really our concern here. Among those contributions that show theological depth, however, we may mention Sawyerr's proposals for the transformation of the eucharist[102] and for adoption of features of traditional adolescent initiation into confirmation.[103] One possible means of injecting theological meaning in liturgical renewal may be through a rediscovery of the doctrine of Holy Spirit, perhaps along the lines of the traditional concept of vital force as set out by Tempels and developed by certain francophone African theologians. Such an emphasis on divine life force, which inheres in all things, would also provide a starting point for Christian theological reflection on the religious attitude to the natural world, which is a fundamental feature of African tradition. As Mbiti has remarked, this should be a point of contact between African religions and the Bible, for both have cosmic implications.[104] Modern environmental movements have encouraged an increasing volume of theological writing on ecology and the environment. Africa, which has suffered less from the depersonalization that is the inevitable result of Western-style development, is perhaps better able to point the way towards the development of a theology of nature and the rediscovery of the sacramental universe.

I have tried in this chapter to explore some of the main areas in which African theologians have seen an element of overlap between concepts in African religions and those in the Bible. In some of these

---

102. Sawyerr, *Creative Evangelism*, 140ff.

103. Harry Sawyerr, "Traditions in Transit," in *Religion in a Pluralistic Society*, ed. John Pobee (Leiden, 1976), 85-96. See also the works cited in note 30 above.

104. "In the African world-view the well being of man is intimately connected with the well being of total creation. Similarly the Gospel has both community and cosmic implications." Mbiti, "Christianity and African Culture," 31.

areas — for example, that of the community — the similarities offer great potential for the Christian theology. However, it is clear that in others — most notably christology and eschatology — there are considerable problems to be overcome before African traditional religion can be of material help in explicating Christian dogma. Furthermore, most of the writings we have considered in this chapter have focused on particular and limited aspects of Christian doctrine, and as yet there have been few attempts to take the traditional worldview as a groundwork or model for a developed and systematic reconstruction of an African Christian theology as a whole. In the following chapter I shall examine in some detail two recent attempts at a radical reworking of the Christian faith from the standpoint of Catholic francophone Africa.

V

Two Theological Reconstructions

1. F. Eboussi Boulaga: Christianity as Myth

F. Eboussi Boulaga was born in Cameroun. He was ordained as a Catholic priest and was at one time a professor of theology. Subsequently he began to question Christianity as he had received it in the Catholic Church, and after retiring from his teaching position returned to his home village to reconsider his faith. He then left the priesthood and the Jesuit order, and later took up the chair of philosophy at the National University of the Ivory Coast. Boulaga is not widely known outside francophone Africa, and little of his work has been translated. The most complete exposition of his thought is found in his *Christianisme sans fêtiche*,[1] and it is on this book that my exposition of his thought will concentrate.

Christianisme sans fêtiche is a radical protest against what Boulaga sees as the imposition of an alien form of religion upon Africa. It is also, more positively, an attempt to reconstruct what he calls a recapture of Christianity. It is not an easy book. Boulaga's argumentation is dense and concentrated, and his language in places obscure. He also lapses from time to time into philosophical poetics, which do not always make

---

1. F. Eboussi Boulaga, *Christianisme sans fêtiche* (Paris, 1981); English ed. *Christianity without Fetishes* (Maryknoll, 1984). Page references are to the English edition. See also his article "The African Search for Identity," in *The Churches of Africa, Future Prospects*, ed. C. Geffre and B. Luneau (New York, 1977), 26-34.

his thinking as precise as the reader would wish. Nevertheless Boulaga has something very important to say, and his thought deserves a wider audience than it has yet attained. His radical critique of the Christian faith may well be compared to those of Bultmann and Bonhoeffer in the West, with whom, strange to say, Boulaga seems to me to have a good deal in common.

Boulaga's book revolves around four questions that reflect the ambiguity of being both Christian and African. He asks:

1. Can the status and functions of the doctrines of the Christian faith be the same for the African as they are in the world that gave rise to them?
2. Must the essence of Christianity always be based in creeds, rites, scripture, and one Lord?
3. Can Africans, who have seen their tribal world and the myths that enshrine it destroyed, accept the Christian faith's claim to be the only and absolute truth for all people? Moreover, can they accept this when Christianity has been imposed upon them by a dominant and alien culture?
4. Is not the God of Christianity an "other people's God," that is, the God of the dominant and privileged group?[2] As an important corollary, can one, against this background of the violent imposition of Christianity, take claims to "revelation" and "the Word of God" literally?

Western Christianity, argues Boulaga, has been destructive to Africa.[3] The traditional worldview was characterized by the missionaries as pagan, as unbelief, as an ignorance of true religion, and as idolatrous revolt against God. The whole of traditional society and culture was dismissed as an evil that needed to be extirpated before Christianity could come to fruition. Having thus uprooted Africans from their own culture, Christianity proceeded to impose upon them a form of "truth" quite alien from their own experience of the universe. This "borrowed space" was characterized by a quite different concept of what it means

---

2. A similar question was posed by the authors of *Black Theology, the South African Voice*, to be discussed in the following chapter.

3. Boulaga, 17ff.

to be a person. Acceptance of Christianity therefore resulted in an historical dislocation, a rupture with the Africans' sense of continuity with their past, and the shattering of their feeling of belonging to their ancestral culture.

In place of this, all missionary Christianity had to offer was an alien and transcendent dogma, which bore no relationship to reality as experienced by Africans or to their understanding of what it means to be human. Consequently any feeling for the ancient traditions that now remain are driven underground, and the result is a kind of guilt-ridden schizophrenia.[4] The ideological universe of Christian dogma then, as it were, floats free from real experience, and itself stands in danger of being rejected when the convert recovers the capacity for self-reconstruction and the basis of deeply felt tradition.

In Boulaga's view the foundations of this type of Western Christianity are to be found in the Greek emphasis on reason and the Judaic stress on history. Both contributed to Christianity's assumption of arrogant superiority vis-à-vis other religions. From this base Christianity was able to launch a frontal attack on "paganism" as grossly materialistic, in that it located the deity in physical objects (the fetish), and pictured God in crudely anthropomorphic terms. By contrast, Christianity saw itself as a coherent, logical system of superior knowledge, based on truths divinely revealed. Its dogmas were therefore to be accepted without question, and the validity of these dogmas was guaranteed by the powerful institution of the church. Opposition was beaten down by the violence of incontrovertible argument, and the pagan was coerced into accepting a faith that found its support in a technologically more advanced imperial culture.

This pretense to domination, argues Boulaga, is hollow. It is fundamentally a Christianity of violence, a "supernatural terrorism," which declines as the colonial power that upholds it declines. Like imperialism, its secular arm, it is too sure of its own claims and cannot let go of its assumption of monopoly of the truth. But these truth claims are themselves ambivalent. Not only do they represent a closed system of circular argument, which excludes the possibility of dialogue, but they also are open to the same kind of rationalism that Christianity itself used to destroy paganism. Take for example, argues Boulaga, the Christian view

4. See p. 14 above.

of history. Christian theology claims that God has broken into the human world in concrete historical events, and that these events constitute divine revelation. The events, it is claimed, have a demonstrable historical basis; however they may have been "written up" by the biblical writers, there is nevertheless a secure kernel of historical fact, demonstrable by the findings of historical criticism. In Boulaga's view the whole idea of historical revelation is false. Such a historical kernel, if it ever existed, he argues, can never be proved to be the irruption of God into history, that is, the event cannot be demonstrated to be God's act. Both the fact and the interpretation on which the concept of sacred history are based are illusory.[5] The worse result of this historical positivism has been to denigrate the value of myth, which for Boulaga (as we shall see) is a basic mode of representing the divine and has an essential function to play in religion.

In addition to the problems for the African of the rationalism and the historicism of Christianity, there is also its irrelevancy. It has failed, he believes, to reach the real issues facing African societies today. Christianity has its formulae and ideals, but these are not brought down from heaven to earth in any practical way. Ideals of equality, unity, and so on, remain as ideals only, appropriate only to what Boulaga ironically calls "the invisible no-place where souls gather," and are not translated into real terms. For the African the real world is one of the continuity of existence as exemplified in his or her relationship to ancestors. Christianity has demanded the renunciation of this relationship, but it has failed to replace it with anything equally real. The convert has thus been extracted from all that makes him or her a true person, and fed only on dogmas that do not relate to experience. One significant response to the estrangement brought about by the advent of this alien form of religion embodied in Western Christianity has been the rise of the African independent churches.[6] The aim of these churches, as Boulaga sees it, is to preserve the tribal man and woman, both as individual persons and socially, as they are confronted with the bourgeois and scientific Western world. They are a demonstration that the African need not break with the ancestral past to become a Christian and that con-

5. "Christianity calls history," comments Boulaga, "what everyone else calls mythology." Boulaga, 51.
6. Boulaga, 63ff.

tinuity is possible. This is so because in the independent African churches Christ is re-presented, is reenacted in the founders, prophets, and charismatic leaders of these churches. The original deed of Christ is reeffectuated in a "creative interpretation, or better in a prophetic actualisation, a fulfilment." What Jesus did in the beginning is now recreated in different circumstances; there is re-presentation of the initial Christ-event, which is the coming of the kingdom of God, in a new context.

How is this brought about? For one thing, the African churches reenact the mystery of healing through their message of victory over death. The redemption they seek is a redemption that bestows "a fulness of reality in all the conditions of human life"; it is a healing, a deliverance, from all evil and oppressing forces rather than from personal guilt. These churches thus partake of the nature of mutual aid societies, whose energizing principle is love rather than dogma. They are a radical and spontaneous expression of Christianity in that the revelation they impart is not found in a deposit of doctrine mediated through Western cultural history, but rather in the activity of re-creation. The African churches have brought to light an important truth: Christianity is not a body of belief that can simply be reimposed at different times and places — the very distance that separates us now from its sources of tradition, such as the Bible, makes this impossible. Our conditions now — our "space and time" — are not the same as those of original Christianity, and therefore these sources cannot simply be taken over as they are. There can be no absolutes for all times, all cultures and circumstances. On the contrary, Christianity's existence is always relative to particular times and groups of the human race. Its basic principle is that it is linked to a past that can never be repeated,[7] and that the network of symbols that belong to that past Christian tradition cannot have relevance to reality here and now. The authentic faith of the African churches has seized upon the fundamental characteristic of original Christianity as a praxis, which deals with the situation of the particular needs of its recipients in all their experiences of anxiety and domination. This dynamic reenactment of what Christianity really means has led, in the independent churches, to the formation of new living communities that are conditioned by their own historical circumstances and that

7. Boulaga, 73ff.

function to transform and triumph over the sociopolitical conditions in which we live in Africa today. All this is far removed from the missionary church's demand for obedience to a dogmatic religious ideology that floats free from any base in real experience.

Herein lies a clue to how the African Christian may resist the imposition of a bourgeois Western Christianity and forge out a faith that will no longer be felt as alien to him or her. A start can be made by recognizing the value of African spirituality. This concept is indeed difficult to define, but may in essence be said to consist in a manner of self-understanding and of living out one's relationship with the earth, the living, and the dead in such a way as to resist the threat of estrangement. African religious traditions must thus be seen as a vital, reacting force, which "creates antibodies to resist aggression from without."[8] The point of departure here is that of the violent aggression of outside forces upon one's culture and society. African tradition should be seen as a self-consistent system that opposes the closed system of Western missionary Christianity. Not, indeed, that African tradition is a kind of *Summa* — all temptation to play the same kind of ideological game as Western dogmatics does must be rejected. African systems, properly understood, are vital and living, no tidy system but full of loose ends, and they evolve spontaneously in the cut and thrust of polemic against them. They are not so much formal structures of dogmatic theology as the "dialectic of the living spirit"; their coherence is one of inner experience that should govern our hermeneutic of the gospel, so as to evolve what Boulaga calls "forms of authentic Christian existence in the African condition." Basic to this approach is the conviction that "it is possible to have one's identity in something other than oneself."[9] This concept of the person in others, which is really another way of saying person in community, plays an important role in Boulaga's thought. It is on the one hand a reaction against what he sees as an excessive Western individualism, on the other an underlying factor of African experience. What does he mean by this?

For all people, in all cultures, argues Boulaga, the spiritual is a "given" over which we have no immediate control, for it is there in the realities of our existence. It is the "order into which humans insert and

8. Boulaga, 77.
9. Boulaga, 80.

110

lose themselves and against which they have to understand themselves as persons." For the African, the spiritual is found especially in the ancestors. To be a person is to take these givens and insert them into the framework of life. Boulaga seems to be arguing that our spiritual and cultural belonging, determined for us by the unalterable facts of our birth and the tradition of which we are part, is the only active basis of our existence in this world. Our life must therefore be lived out in this context. The aim of life should be correct "insertion" into the given order. This demands that we seek harmonious order within the community. It is the social aspect that is important, not the individual. Sin is not personal guilt because of an offense against God, but simply disorder in the community resulting from incorrect "insertion." Even death does not abstract the person from the community. The departed become spirits who are still dynamically involved with the living as their ancestral guardians and instructors. Even in death, therefore, the person is not an isolated individual, for personhood is found outside himself or herself within the community.

Boulaga can now move to his central thesis, which he terms the "Christic model." He seeks to express the meaning of Christ as he sees it before the processes of dogma got to work, Christ, as it were, "upstream from where dogma begins." Dogma is only credible, in Boulaga's view, when it expresses the experience of God that gave rise to it; abstracted from this experience it is meaningless and incredible. The only true starting point therefore must be the experience of the person. If the gospel story is to transcend its original purely local and historical context and become true in our experience today — that is, if it is to be experienced both individually and communally — two conditions need to be fulfilled. First, the questions and issues that characterized Jesus' time must still be relevant questions and issues for us today; if this is not so, then the life of Jesus will have no meaning for us. Second, the gospels must provide us not with a purely limited content, applicable only to their own time and context, but must provide us with a model that is applicable to all times and places — that is, it must be capable of "appropriate reinterpretation." This reinterpretation Boulaga calls the Christic model.[10]

How can the questions of Jesus' time be in any sense valid for us

10. Boulaga, 85.

today? It is true, says Boulaga, that Christianity arose out of a particular and peculiar set of circumstances. However, the problems of this bygone age may still be ours today insofar as what he calls "the problematic of the universal" — the problem of existence in this world — is still with us. Obviously the original circumstances surrounding the rise of Christianity, its original problematic, cannot simply be repeated per se; but they can be "reinvented," they can recur again and again in human experience. Such reinvention is possible in that Christianity, too, arose out of the spiritual "given" of its own traditions and history, that is, the Judaism of its age. And it came to be by evolving and judging itself from that starting point as "tradition rediscovered."[11] So too the African Christian, from the experience of alienation due to the imposition of Western missionary Christianity, must reinvent his or her Christian faith again from his or her own spiritual base, own set of "givens."

Jesus' ministry was determined by the given tradition of Jewish spirituality into which he came. This was not a simple one, but rather one of tensions, conflicts, even violence, which shaped and affected the Jewish people. Jesus himself came into conflict in one way or another with all the contemporary interpretations of Judaism of his time — with the Pharisees, Sadducees, Essenes, and so on. His ministry defined itself essentially in protests and controversies, and its real characteristics emerged through these conflicts. In so doing, Jesus made his protest against the illegitimacy of theocratic power (Sadduceeism), ritualism (Phariseeism), ethnicity (Essenism), and so on. Jesus' message was then not merely another doctrine, but rather creative action, born out of confrontation with the ferment around him. In him the religious world stands under judgment, because with Jesus the eschaton has come and exposes the simply finite nature of the religious movements of his age. In Boulaga's words, "It relativises such systems and demonstrates that they need to be transcended if one seeks salvation. The presence of God is immediate, rendering obsolete these systems which would set themselves up as mediators." God is therefore "right here, pointing men and women to the divine mystery by pointing them to their own proper reality. The presence of God makes reality the only possible media-

---

11. So also at 115: "The Good News is tradition understood and grasped. It is tradition's reconquest, its recovery from forgetfulness, routine, conformism and betrayal. It is tradition rediscovered as a constitutive spontaneity, as a gushing spring."

tion."[12] This eschatological principle, that is, God as concrete demand, is to be understood under the metaphor of God's parenthood. We cannot, Boulaga argues, know God as he really is; we can only respond to him in the "image" that he presents to us. This image is the human, the likeness and image of God. "The eschatological God therefore can be mediated only by the humanity of human beings in their concrete acts within the context of society." We thus "become" children of God in the creative acts of our humanity. This is the real meaning of faith. Faith is not belief; it is the creative freedom of the human person sharing with the creative spirit. God as father is a metaphor for this spirit creator, which calls us to a true humanity. "Humanity effectively realised," writes Boulaga, "is the true manifestation of this force, and entry into its dynamism, into its insertion into the world. This process of realisation, this actualisation, can be called 'conversion,' and its anticipated 'result,' 'faith.'"[13] In this sense to call God "Father" is a performative — the name involves performance. The focus of this performance, this action, is the creation of a community and of seeing our neighbor as the re-presentation of God. Such a community will be one of brothers and sisters, and will use power only as a means of service to others. The focus of value here is the value of the other person, not a focus on beliefs, rituals, or observances. As with the ministry of Jesus, it will seek to renew society from within by surmounting its evils and discriminations. The importance of Jesus' work therefore lies not in its content but in the model or paradigm it sets out. As paradigm it has three aspects: (1) openness to the eschatological God who confronts us; (2) the community that makes the demands of God a possibility; (3) the wider circle of a society that becomes reworked and transformed by the creative spirit of this community. Here we have an ever-widening circle that will reach out to all people. The Christic Model is the realization of person in community as the image of God, as his re-presentation. The person and life of Jesus thus

> furnishes the model of a life that achieves the fulness of itself, not only after having taken on its conditionings and determinisms and integrated them into a conscious and responsible activity and com-

12. Boulaga, 105-6.
13. Boulaga, 110.

mitment, but also after having undergone its destiny and receiving itself from the other.[14]

The significance of Jesus' life does not make it a hypothesis to be accepted and believed as dogma; rather, it is a living model to be re-presented.

Let us recapitulate this somewhat complex argument. The Christic Model derives from the life of Jesus. In his ministry the "given" conditions of his life (the Judaism of his time) undergo transformation, and the cultural religious forms of that Judaism are transcended through the advent of the direct reign of God. This model is not grounded in some unprovable kernel of historical fact, for its validity does not rest in anything one can lay hands upon. Rather, we are in the realm of "myth." Myth is neither fiction nor the product of bad faith. On the contrary, it is an integral part of the gospel, the hermeneutic by which we can recognize what the gospels really are, that is, "a process of general applicability."

Herein Jesus is presented to us as one who is a fulfilled being in accordance with his own tradition, and who yet transcends the limitations that are found in that tradition. He thereby creates the possibility for self-fulfillment in others. "The new definitive human beings," argues Boulaga, "are those who create self by choices, at the heart of the voluntary community with which they will be in reciprocity of being."[15] Such self-fulfillment goes beyond death, for to create new life one must (as did Jesus) die. It is this creative act of self-giving, not a doctrine, that we are called upon to accept in the Christic Model.

Myth is central, for it is the basic method of representing the divine. Denial of myth results in the desacralization of the universe and the loss of the sense of God's immanence. Paradoxically, Christianity itself, though it denigrates myth, is riddled with mythological language quite as much as paganism, and even rational theology cannot avoid such language. Demythologizing is not just a matter of jettisoning a few inessentials, like Adam and the demons! "The partial denial of myth does nothing for reason." What Boulaga wants to do, therefore, is not to demythologize, but remythologize, or rather accept the mythical

14. Boulaga, 127.
15. Boulaga, 113.

114

element as essential to the gospel. "Jesus Christ," he writes, "does not come to abolish myth, but to fulfil it." We cannot speak of God in any other way than through mythical language.

For Boulaga the most meaningful form of myth is that which tells of death and rebirth and which is common to all humankind. In the history of religions the most basic form of this mythology is found in the figure of the archetypal Mother. In mythology the mother figure may be pictured as the creatrix (the one who gives birth to all life), the earth mother (the source of agricultural production), and as the mother of the Mythical Hero. While all these aspects of the mother figure have relevance to the common religious experience of humankind, it is the last that is of most usefulness to Christian theology. The mythical hero is not an individual. He is rather a symbol or type of the fulfilled person, one who takes up within himself the authenticity of the human condition by his integration into the group-society and by his obedience to its laws. He takes upon himself, too, suffering and death, "the path which humanises and personalises through the active abandonment of self." The hero figure therefore — and here is Boulaga's point — is a *repeatable* model. The understanding of what life beyond death means is determined by the structures of each society. Where there is genuine integration of the individual into the group, immortality is understood in terms of the perpetuation of the group itself as an entity. When this "genealogical principle" breaks down (as in urban societies), this becomes inadequate, and the need for belief in individual immortality begins to take hold. In such circumstances the social or tribal community is replaced by spiritual communities, which make the mythical hero figure into a god who is worshiped and who assures the individual of personal salvation beyond death. In consequence a gnostic dichotomy between body and spirit, natural and spiritual worlds, begins to take hold. This kind of situation, as Boulaga interprets it, was the historical matrix in which Christianity was born.

What then is the function of this archetypal mother myth for the Christian faith? It can address what Boulaga sees as the only question that the Gospel message answers, namely, "are human beings the prisoners of the conditionings of their birth, and hence their bodies, their families and their tribes, or can they merely assume these, deliver themselves from them, and enjoy real survival?" That is, are we conditioned by and imprisoned within the genealogical principle, or can we have the liberty to become fulfilled human beings? The Virgin Mother of the myth symbolizes birth and life. In the case of Jesus this life is fulfilled in the new life of the resurrection and in the formation of the new community. Through this new community Jesus is now present in a mediated form — "Jesus has been reborn in the form of the community."[16] The mother figure, Mary, is now the Mother Church in which men and women are reborn to new life. Jesus is thus the figure, the symbol, of the fulfilled human being, who in his resurrection releases from within himself a new creative force of being for (and in) others. Jesus' life, death, and resurrection therefore are not "history," but find their real meaning as myth. They do not provide us with information about God, or doctrines to be accepted and believed. This cannot be, because God as he is, in his essence, cannot be known. Rather, the Christic Model is the new experience of the initiated "who experience in their existence the emergence of the Christic form." It is a way of existing, a manner of being, that opens us up to the infinite, but at the same time is being for others in community. In the incarnation of Jesus we do not *know* God as he is; rather, we *experience* a new mode of being.

The death and resurrection of Jesus can be understood within the context of the African ancestors.[17] Just as Jesus' life confronted and challenged the society of his time, so his death restored order to society, for because of it and its results he now acts within society through those who re-present his being in his spirit. And just as the ancestors, though now dead, influence and reorder the community of the living, so Jesus' post-resurrection life is a life beyond individuality, presented now in his followers and thus freed from the limitations of space and time. Jesus has fulfilled his genealogy, his tradition, but he has also transcended it in the church he has left. Through the church his presence and that of God himself may now be perceived, for "God comes in the representation and configuration of society and the world, but only in personal form."[18] This is not revelation, for God comes to us only "as if," only as metaphor. It is persons in community who are "his real and finite

---

16. Boulaga, 142.

17. Boulaga, 149; compare the interpretation of the death of Christ in the context of the ancestors by Bujo, discussed below; also Kwesi Dickson, *Theology in Africa* (London, 1984), 185ff.

18. Boulaga, 154.

representation." This re-presentation of God consists in the actions of living and working for the good and the true in a commitment of love. This does not reveal any new truths about God; rather, it shows God by action; it is an ethic rather than a revelation, the fulfillment of true humanity rather than the acceptance of a dogma. The Christic Model is Christ continued and expanded in the new community of those who have experienced Jesus.

The concluding part of Boulaga's book[19] is an exploratory search for an ethic and an authentic faith, which will be credible and vital to the African experience. Africans today, he argues, no longer live within their original genealogy; they are part of the complex pluralistic world, which demands that different cultures, civilizations, and religions coexist. The price of this coexistence is in what he terms "endless adjustments and reinterpretations" of belief and cultural values. Such a complex society in which different values interact he calls a "civil" society, the essence of which is to safeguard that society's welfare and survival in good order by refusing any pretensions to monopoly of truth to which ideologies and religions lay claim. In such a context Christianity, too, will need to put aside its claims to absolute truth in the interests of the common good. In common with other ideologies it will have to look for similarities and areas of agreement that make for human communication and transformation. In the context of civil society, the Christic Model takes up all that is good in the deposit of one's genealogy, one's cultural inheritance. In doing so, however, this genealogy is at the same time transcended. It bursts out of its original form as it is subjected to existential and communal reinterpretation, and there result new forms of creative activity. Such a reinterpretation of the sacred takes place through concrete human beings, through whom God mediates himself. This manifestation will differ in each successive generation; hence its content cannot be determined in advance. It is a kind of *force vitale*, which takes on a new manifestation in each new historical and social context. Essentially it is "myth" — it is not merely recounting but reenacting, an existential re-creating again and again on the part of the community. God thus becomes present in those who speak and act in his name.[20] This is not simply in *what* they say — the content — but rather in *how* they speak and act. What is at stake

19. Boulaga, 163ff.
20. Boulaga, 173ff.

here is not a particular belief, but a mode of existence, being in the image and likeness of God, and in freedom from alienation. Such re-presentation of God is the "task of expressing the inexpressible, manifesting the invisible by means of the visible, the non-mediate by means of the mediate."[21] Such re-presentation, whether within the cult or outside of it, is not absolute. It is a provisional representation of God through concrete humanity as working, sexual, and political beings. This is possible only in the community, for only here is the incompleteness of individual faith transcended.

How is this to be applied to the African situation? Boulaga advances proposals that will enable the African Christian to transform the alien Christianity that has been imposed upon him into something that is viable for modern civil society. This will not, he reminds us, tell us *what* God is, but it will speak of him only in the context of and relative to our social relationships and our finite nature.

First, he argues, truth must be personalized if it is to be credible. This does not simply mean seeking its relevance to the individual, but rather exploring how it may be integrated within our historical destiny. Essentially then, truth is relative. It has no meaning apart from our understanding and experiencing of it and the circumstances in which we affirm it. Truth is the advent of a new human liberty, "to be a person is truth shining forth." It is the emergence of the person as person within the determinants of this world. In a passage somewhat reminiscent of Bultmann, Boulaga writes:

> In this perspective Christian doctrine can and should be understood in its entirety as the description of the modalities of the human being's emergence as a person in the determinations of the action and the word within this world, in availability to the creative might which refers one only to oneself.[22]

Knowledge of God is thus to be found neither in deposit of dogma, nor yet in solitary meditation, but only in the real act of becoming of the person, of fulfilling one's humanity in society. The glory of God turns out to be humankind, alive and fulfilled in the company of others.

21. Boulaga, 176.
22. Boulaga, 192.

Furthermore, faith must be a process of historicization. The "historicity" of Christianity does not rest on the historical fact of Jesus, nor yet in the events of his life. It rests rather on the fact that it was born out of a given situation in history, a situation of the shock of cultures in conflict. The essence of Christianity therefore lies in its response to the challenges and questions thrown up in the context of human history. The "model" begins not with some ideal world, but from our own experience and existence. This distinction between the "ideal" and the real may be understood in terms of what Boulaga calls redemption and salvation. Redemption is what takes place in this world, and is present in the visible material process. This we can know in experience. Salvation on the other hand pertains to the spiritual invisible world, the beyond; that we cannot know. The common error of Christianity, as Boulaga sees it, has been a gnostic suppression of redemption in terms of salvation, that is, in the linking of the Christian life to the beyond, to an invisible kingdom of the heart. In consequence redemption is rejected as less important. For Christianity to be relevant, salvation "will have to be converted in a redemption of the terrestrial biological existence."[23] To do this we shall have to reassess the sources of Christian tradition. The Bible can no longer be regarded as an infallible guide, but its specific limitations as a book of its own time need to be acknowledged. It must therefore be interpreted not dogmatically but aesthetically; it offers not rules or doctrines, but figures, types, myths that have the power to inspire and to enchant, and that can only be played and danced out in today's existence. It is a treasury of metaphors, which re-create the presence of God by bringing home to us the original power of Christianity and by fusing that past in a dynamic way with our present experience. This is not, to be sure, the way of the learned theologian. It is essentially a nonelitist and popular Christianity. In such a manner does Jesus communicate with us, beyond the doctrines of Scripture, upstream from where dogma begins. Christianity is not universal in the sense that all are or ought to be Christian. Rather, it is but one historical example of something that *is* universal, namely "the eternal act of the redeeming love of God." Its monopolistic and intolerant claims to truth and its violent will to conquest therefore need to be renounced for an ethic of nonviolence, which will enable Christianity both to be inserted into and to transcend the genealogy of Africans.

23. Boulaga, 206.

Boulaga's book presents so many different issues, and there are so many currents and crosscurrents in his thought, that I shall conclude this section by pointing up only those of his most important contributions to African theology that seem to me to provide a basis for further dialogue. Boulaga's critique of received Christianity as a religion of aggression that has been victorious because of its violent imposition upon African culture is in keeping with emergent African theology in general,[24] and although perhaps overstated (at least in respect of some of the Protestant missions) is no doubt substantially historically correct. More important is his philosophical critique of such a Christianity of triumphalism. The Christian faith, Boulaga has argued, if it is to be acceptable to Africans, must be understood as essentially relative; it exists only in a local historical manifestation, not as an absolute. It can exist, therefore, only as the Christianity of a specific cultural milieu. Faith needs a concrete reality in which to exist, and it cannot rightly exist in disembodied abstract creeds and ideologies that are discontinuous with and disjunctive of the genealogy, the inherited culture, of a particular people. Furthermore, Christianity's truth-claims are in any case undemonstrable, for they move only within the argumentation of a closed circle of logic, and are provable only on the basis of their own premises. Fundamental to these truth-claims is the claim to revelation through history and Scripture. But for Boulaga revelation is an empty concept. God cannot be known as he really is, for he reserves his ipseity to himself alone. To claim to "know" him in salvation history will not help. To locate God in a historical event is just as idolatrous as to locate him in an idol or fetish, for neither can we know the event as it really is, nor can we ever interpret it infallibly as revelation. We can know God only in metaphorical form, as "myth." We see God's image only in people in community and as expressed in the reenactment of our genealogy in the concrete conflicts and trial of our time. Of this fulfillment of "person in community" the ministry of Jesus provides the great example, the Christic Model, which must then be re-presented, reenacted in the turmoil of our time.

One could wish that Boulaga would have entered into sustained dialogue with European theology, which he professes to stand over against so sharply, for it could be claimed several of his ideas were

24. See further chapter 6.

120

already subjects of debate on the nineteenth- and twentieth-century European scene. His almost Barthian emphasis on the ipseity of God is countered by a most un-Barthian rejection of the validity of the concept of revelation (even in Christ); his enthusiastic Bultmannian espousal of the significance of myth is combined with a most un-Bultmannian refusal to demythologize, for to him myth is the essence of religious language, which religion cannot do without. A radical rejection of history is also combined with an emphasis not only upon the existential but also upon the reality of genealogy, which is by implication to espouse the validity of history. Perhaps it is existentialism that provides us with a useful key to Boulaga's thought. Truth is relative, and what is important is not so much what you commit yourself to but rather *how* you do so; God is imaged in humans (especially humans in society), and the glory of God is represented in the fulfilled human — one seems here to hear the voice of a Kierkegaard or (in Boulaga's emphasis on fulfillment through death) of a Heidegger. These paradoxes in Boulaga's theology would, one would think, make a useful starting point for further dialogue. They raise indeed large issues. It will not be easy for Christian theologians to jettison the concept of sacred history, nor to dismiss the idea of a historical kernel behind the Christian faith (a faith, by the way, that emerged from a genealogy with very strong convictions about the acts of God in human history). The Kerygma and Myth exchanges and the seemingly endless quest for the historical Jesus make this all too plain. Nor will it be easy to abandon the idea of revelation, however understood. This is too firmly rooted in the Judeo-Christian tradition, with its conviction of a deposit of the acts of God contained in Scripture. But in another sense Boulaga is quite right to remind us that all our talking about God is ultimately metaphor (or, in his terminology, myth) and that, as Calvin once put it, God stammers out his word to us in human speech, full as it is of fallibility and contradiction. He is also surely right to remind us that the Christian faith is not, in the end, a matter of credence given to disembodied dogmas, but of life and of deed, and of human transformation. These are important lessons in any theological context.

2. Benézét Bujo: Christianity as Ancestral Theology

Bujo is also a Catholic theologian. He has studied in Europe and received his doctorate in moral theology from the University of Würzburg. For the past ten years he has been a professor in the faculty of Catholic theology at Kinshasa in his native Zaire. Bujo has published widely in French and German, and the most significant outworking of his thought was contained in the initial lectures of the annual series on Third World theology initiated by the Catholic faculty of the University of Frankfurt.[25] As in much recent African Catholic theology, Bujo takes his point of departure from Vatican II's openness to other religions and cultures, which he sees as having special relevance in the need of African theology to break away from its present eurocentrism.

Bujo's book falls into two parts. The first is a kind of prolegomenon, in which he examines the main features of African society, the colonial and mission impact upon it, and African writers' and theologians' reaction to this situation of conflict. In the second part he gives us his own attempt at a reconstruction of African theology, concentrating especially upon christology and ecclesiology. Bujo is particularly critical of a theology of inculturation that fails to address solid issues and seeks to appeal to an academic public outside the continent rather than to the African in his or her own need and context.[26] For him the liberative and cultural aspects of theology must be wedded. For this to happen, there is a pressing need for the African to rediscover roots, and it is to be hoped that this will enable him or her to relate ancestral religion to modern society. In doing so the African must not idealize the past as a lost paradise nor denigrate it as idolatry. African tradition, according to Bujo, saw life as a unity — religious, political, social — and was infused with the concept of the wholeness of life, which is "liberation" in the true sense. The idea of liberation therefore is inherent in

---

25. Benézét Bujo, *Afrikanische Theologie in ihrem gesellschaftlichen Kontext* (Dusseldorf, 1986); English ed. *African Theology in its Social Context* (Maryknoll, 1992). Page references are to the English edition, except where otherwise specified. Robert Schreiter, in his foreword to the English edition, regards Bujo's book as among the most original theological contributions to appear from Africa. Bujo also contributed "Auf der Suche nach einer afrikanischer Christologie" to *Der andere Christus: Christologie in Zeugnissen aus aller Welt*, ed. H. Dembowski and W. Greive (Erlangen, 1991).

26. Bujo, *African Theology*, 71.

the concept of life as understood in African tradition. African "cultural theology" is rightly understood as also "liberation theology."

In traditional society religion was a force that bound together the community as a balanced whole. This wholeness of society depends upon the concept of life, which pervades the whole community. Bujo here closely follows earlier writers like Tempels and Mulago,[27] who see society as cohering by means of a vital force that flows through that society as a kind of mystical bond. In the African hierarchy God (understood in a basically monotheistic sense) is seen as the source of all life. This divine life is conveyed to the living through the channel of the first ancestors of the family, clan, and tribe. While this is obviously true in the biological sense of physical generation, this is not the only, or even the most important, aspect of such ancestral life. Rather, it is a metaphysical or mystical concept, enshrined in all that makes life worthwhile. The ancestors have bequeathed to their descendants all their wisdom, including custom and law, which serves for the well-being of the society. In addition they (at least ideally) provide the living with a model of life in all its aspects. To ensure the continued well-being of the community, the living need to follow this ancestral model of the full and complete life, and to make the example and indeed the experiences of the ancestors their own. In the hierarchy of being, all members of a group, even the least, have the obligation to exploit and to strengthen the mystical life force of the community. Each good act, that is, each act in conformity with the model of the ancestors, adds to the life force of the community. The life of the community, therefore, is a mystical body that derives from the ancestors and that may be strengthened or weakened by the actions of its members. Sin is what detracts from the life of the mystical body. While all life comes ultimately from God, the ancestors play a special role as the medium through which divine life is conveyed to the living. Thus while the African worldview may be described as anthropocentric, it also puts God firmly as the source of all life. "When Africans honour the ancestors they are, at least, implicitly honouring God."[28]

In such a model the role of the ancestors is of primary importance, and the ancestral cult is the special (though not the only) place where

27. Bujo, *African Theology*, 17ff.
28. Bujo, *African Theology*, 23.

the increase of the mystical body is sought. In the funeral and ancestral rites, communication involves a mutual strengthening of both parties, and it therefore has both an eschatological and a salvific dimension.[29] The departed have, by their physical death, become spiritual beings, and by virtue of this are able to exercise a decisive influence upon the fortunes of the living. On the other hand, the living for their part ensure the happiness of their ancestors by keeping them in remembrance and by observing the ancestral cult.

The emphasis upon the fullness of life indicates that Africans have a concern for the future.[30] The African outlook is therefore eschatological in the sense that it looks beyond death, for the welfare of the living depends upon those who have passed beyond death. African death rites reflect this view in that they stress the role of the dead as guardian spirits of the living descendants. Despite their real physical separation they are still regarded as present, especially in the common meals, which are a kind of communion that cements the relationship between the ancestors and their progeny. In such death rituals the welfare of the community, in terms of numerous children, cattle, and so on, is assured. Thus the father, who by death becomes an ancestor, is the source of peace and prosperity, of life in all its fullness. At the same time the ancestors protect the life of their descendants from destructive influences, such as evil spirits, and from those who would seek to use life force for harm rather than good. It is not indeed that the ancestors are the ultimate source of life force: this belongs to God alone. Rather they are the indispensable channels through which this divine life force reaches the living.

It follows that no action is neutral; it always either increases the total life of the mystical body for its good or decreases it to the detriment of the community. This emphasis on well-being, on wholeness, indicates that "liberation," in the fullest sense of the word, is the most important aspect of African religion.

To recognize the fundamental role of the ancestors is to acknowledge that one's point of orientation lies in the past. It is the ancestors and elders who have taught us the art of living, and our own decisions for or against the fullness of life depend upon how far we embrace or neglect the ancestral heritage. Thus in African thought the heritage of

---

29. Bujo, *African Theology*, 24.
30. Bujo, *African Theology*, 29ff. — in contrast to Mbiti.

the ancestors is in a sense sacramental, it is a kind of sacred history that makes the present meaningful. Bujo compares this to the idea of narrative theology. By the reenactment and repetition of the deeds, laws, and so on bequeathed to us by the ancestors, a living memory is awakened so that these sacred deposits will bring their descendants out of misfortune and misery into liberation and victory. It is a kind of ancestral "exodus theology." Salvation, wholeness, and the meaning of life are inextricably bound up with the ancestors, who are the guardians of the present and the guarantors of the future. The future is existential possibility, the success or failure of which depends upon how far the heritage of the ancestors is actualized. So for Bujo the African does not, as Mbiti has argued, stand in a history that has no future and that moves only backwards to the golden age, but rather that very past points ever forward toward the realization of a salvation that is grounded in the ancestral tradition. It is therefore eschatological.

This possibility for the future depends upon humans themselves. Though God is present implicitly in every situation, the African outlook is essentially anthropocentric. The same applies to ethics. The African ethic is horizontal, between person and person.[31] This ethic, too, reflects the position of the ancestors. Respect for elders and parents is basically a reflection of the ancestral cult, and the good of the community depends on such respect given to elders. Ultimately it is the common good that determines ethics, for the community is, in essence, the extension of the ancestors into the realm of the living. So, for example, sexuality is for procreation of numerous progeny so that the ancestors can live on in their descendants. This is why childlessness is such disaster in Africa: it deprives the ancestors of a place in which their existence is continued and of a cult in which they are strengthened. Conversely, the taking of human life is permissible when, and only when, it is a means of removing a threat to the total life of the community. Possession of goods was also meant to contribute to the well-being of the group as a whole, and the acquisition of wealth, which is so characteristic of life in modern Africa, is in traditional life an offense against the solidarity of the clan.

In Bujo's view, therefore, when the colonizing powers and the Christian missions came to Africa they found a well-ordered and

31. Bujo, *African Theology,* 32ff.

functional society, which, while not perfect, did enable its members to enjoy the wholeness of life.[32] The missions, by and large, Bujo argues, worked hand in hand with the colonial powers, and with them took part in the radical disruption of traditional African societies. Among the factors contributing to this disruption were the conniving at the dehumanization of Africans as a source of cheap labor; the imposition of artificial borders that separated members of the same clan; the imposition of "Christian" names (ignoring the real and symbolic significance of names in African culture); the systematic rape of objets d'art (which Africans regarded as possessing a life-giving power); and, of course, as the basis of all this, a racism that regarded the Africans as inferior beings. In the religious sphere the missionaries especially undermined the ancestral cults that formed the backbone of the traditional structure. Polygamy, which was traditionally meant to ensure the continued existence of the ancestors, so-called magical practices, and the cult of the ancestors itself were all condemned. Early converts to Christianity learned too well from their European mentors and, in order to show they had become "civilized," showed an excessive zeal in condemning their "heathen" past, and adopted often quite inappropriate European practices. So, with very few exceptions, missionaries and early converts alike failed to analyze the structures of African society and religion and as a result missed the opportunity to create a truly incarnational Christianity. This sad state of affairs continued until the reaction of comparatively recent times, which was led by Africans who decided that it was high time blacks should be taken seriously by Europeans, both colonial and missionary.

In Bujo's view this reaction was twofold: literary and theological.[33] The literary reaction began with the négritude movement, whose leader, Léopold Senghor, argued that there could be no political liberation without cultural liberation, and that black culture needed to be set out in a positive way over against European culture.[34] Négritude indeed had its role to play, though probably it was more for the consumption of whites than blacks. Now it has its day, for it does not seem to have much

---

32. Bujo, *African Theology*, 37ff.

33. Bujo, *African Theology*, 49; Bujo does not discuss the contributions of political leaders in anglophone Africa like Nyerere and Kaunda.

34. Compare the approach of black consciousness discussed in chapter 6.

to say to the postcolonial situation. What is needed, thinks Bujo, is not a poetic attempt to recapture a lost paradise, but rather an attempt to reincarnate the ancestral world into the modern world. In this task, have African theologians gone any further than the advocates of négritude?[35]

Bujo identifies three main stages in African theology: the initial impetus through the work of Placide Tempels, a second stage of what he calls "self-awareness," and finally the critique of the younger generation.

Tempels's *Bantu Philosophy* (as we have already noted) advocated the then novel idea that Bantu thought comprises a logical and hierarchical system. Bujo lays a good deal of stress also on Tempels's later writings, which were more pastoral in intent, and on his subsequent involvement in the Jamaa movement. Tempels is for Bujo the father of African theology, whose exploratory ideas were taken up and developed by francophone theologians like Mulago, Kagame, and later Tshibangu. The problem with this school, as Bujo sees it, was that it did not really create a genuine theological synthesis, nor did it do much to address the new postcolonial period. He then turns to the practitioners of the "new quest" for an African theology, on whom he makes several perceptive comments. Mbiti, he feels, lapses into a kind of parallelism in his comparison of the biblical material with the African traditional religions; Nyamiti creates an African scholasticism. In any event, what Bujo thinks we need now is to discover again the genuine African tradition so that this cultural and religious heritage can be confronted with the biblical and patristic material. Neither should it be forgotten that many Africans today are unaware of their own traditions, and some customs have either fallen into disuse or else (like polygamy and hospitality) been perverted in modern society. Bujo would agree with Boulaga in seeing in the independent churches an attempt to retain valuable customs while at the same time integrating them into their Christianity. But the church as a whole, argues Bujo, has the responsibility of finding a balance between the traditional and the modern, and of distinguishing between those traditions that deserve to be retained and those that should not. Above all this should be a pastoral and not a purely academic task, and for it all the findings and methods of the social sciences should be brought in to aid theology. But cultural theology is not enough, and

35. Bujo, *African Theology*, 56.

indeed can degenerate into something sterile and academic, a theology that is for export only, or is more at home in the conference room, lecture room, and ecclesiastical hierarchy than it is in the African church. Theology needs to be a liberative theology if it is to address the post-colonial situation. As he quotes one seminarian as saying: "Father, if God speaks to us more in our customs and rites than through the drama of today's four million African refugees, then I am ready to hand back my baptismal certificate and have my name struck off the baptismal register. If that is the case then God doesn't interest me anymore."[36] Bujo feels there are some voices that plead for the oppressed and weak today, but on the whole the lifestyle of the priests and missionaries is starkly different from that of the people. If they are to be credible, ministers of the gospel will need to give up their privileged positions and stop behaving like politicians in power. African theologians also must not be satisfied with neat theories that they cannot put into practice, and still less with seeking international prestige either for themselves or for their theologies. Rather, African theology must address itself to the service of the poor and underprivileged. This will involve a complete restructuring of the whole concept of the church in Africa.

In the second half of the book[37] Bujo addresses himself to the question of what such a reconstruction of theology in Africa will look like. Christianity will only be congenial to the African, he believes, if it is a synthesis of the fundamentals of the Christian faith on the one hand and of the main pillars of African tradition on the other. The central concept of the latter is, as we have seen, the ancestors, including their role in "liberation" in the wider meaning he gives to the term. Ancestral concepts and practices should therefore inform the elaboration of the two most relevant areas of Christian dogma, christology and ecclesiology. In effect, as it turns out in Bujo's theological reconstruction, these two aspects are closely interrelated.

Bujo's christology is securely rooted in the traditional concept of the ancestors, and at the same time seeks to have consequences for the ethical life of the community. First, a rediscovery of the substance of the historical Jesus is necessary.[38] The New Testament writers express

---

36. Bujo, *African Theology*, 71 (my trans. of German edition, 75).
37. Bujo, *African Theology*, 74ff.
38. Bujo, *African Theology*, 76 — in contrast to Boulaga.

the significance of Jesus in titles that have a meaning within the culture of their time. Such titles now need to be reinterpreted in terms of the African context today, and this is even more necessary since Africans have received Christ in Western wrappings. Given the centrality of the ancestors to African thought and practice, Christ may best be expressed in terms of what Bujo calls the "Proto-Ancestor." As we have seen, in the African experience the peculiar words, rites, and acts of the ancestors have a special significance. They are an abiding rule of life, a rule that must be repossessed by the living, for upon them depend their welfare and wholeness *(Heil)*. Repossession and reenactment of this ancestral past is also (as we have noted above) to take a decisive step into the future, for it brings down the benevolence of the ancestors into the life of the community. In this context it is meaningful to speak of Jesus as the ancestor par excellence, for in him are fulfilled all the qualities and virtues that the African ascribes to his or her ancestors. In the African experience the last words of the father especially have decisive meaning, for they are regarded as exemplary and life giving, and they are in a sense normative for those left behind. Now the historical Jesus fulfills the highest ideals ascribed to the ancestors in African thought — he heals, he cures, he raises the dead, and so on: in short, he imparts life force in all its fullness. This love and power he bequeaths, after his death, to his disciples. This is a christology from below and provides a point of departure for a christology in the African context. However, Jesus is not just any ancestor, not even the original ancestor *(Urahn)*. Rather he is proto-ancestor, by which Bujo means that he fulfills within himself the authentic ideal of ancestor in a complete way, but he at the same time transcends this ideal and brings it to a new and full realization. In this he is unique.[39]

In the New Testament the person of Christ is inseparable from his proclamation of the kingdom; the kingdom is in fact ratified by his death and resurrection, and his raising from the dead initiates a new creation. It is precisely in his death and resurrection, with its soteriological meaning, that Jesus transcends the ancestors. The suggestion seems to be that the benefits accrued from the death and resurrection of Jesus have inaugurated a new creation, which far surpasses that of the living dead. Jesus is thus a kind of original form *(Urbild)* of all the

---

39. Bujo, *African Theology,* 80.

virtues and benefits that the ancestors longed for but could not attain to. He is proto-ancestor, the proto–life force that can never be superseded. The Jesus of history and the Christ of faith come together in the concept of the proto-ancestor, who by his proclamation, life, death, and resurrection has brought about a new relationship between God and humans, and thus between human and fellow human, and between humans and the world.

Our meeting place with God is in the incarnation of the Word, in which God becomes part of the world. Such an act of becoming flesh is, however, as much an act of revealing the nature of humankind as it is of revealing the nature of God.[40] In identifying himself with humankind as the incarnate proto-ancestor, Jesus takes upon himself all the strivings and longings of the ancestors and, as it were, makes their history his own. Not only is our place of meeting with the God of salvation therefore in him, but at the same time only in him can the ancestors be fully grasped. God has spoken to us in different ways and times (Heb. 1:1-2), and this includes speaking through our ancestors. Now he speaks to us in the Son, the ancestor from whom the whole community stems. The ancestors are thus types or paradigms, "forerunners or images" of Jesus, the proto-ancestor.[41] In other words, just as the experiences of the ancestors are normative for the African to attain wholeness, so these are realized in a unique and final way in the experiences of Jesus for our redemption, and especially in his death and resurrection. He as it were sums up in a kind of recapitulation (anakephalaiosis) the past and transcends it. This salvation in Christ is recounted, relived, and reexperienced in each generation. Another christological model that has been favored by recent African theologians, that of Christ as the master of initiation, also rests, in Bujo's view, ultimately on the ancestor concept, for the powers of initiation and the life force conveyed through this rite ultimately depend for their efficacy upon the ancestors.

For Bujo the concept of the proto-ancestor as a model for christology has several advantages. As a christology from below it accords well with the anthropocentricity of the African worldview. It is, further-

---

40. Bujo, African Theology, 82, referring to Rahner's comment that the incarnation is "the grammar of God's possible self-expression."

41. Bujo, African Theology, 83.

more, basically Trinitarian. The relationship between the Father and the Son may be seen as one of mutual interaction and sharing of life; in African terms it is a bond of vital union, life force, or divine power. Understood in terms of traditional theology, it is a bond of the Holy Spirit. This divine life of the Spirit is conveyed by the proto-ancestor to the community. In Bujo's view, the community also includes the ancestors themselves, for Jesus, in his work of bringing to completion and fullness the whole created universe also brings the ancestors into this fullness of life.

Christ the proto-ancestor has consequences for ethics and practical behavior. A keynote of Jesus' message and actions was the value of the human person. He advocated the rights of women, and he showed his solidarity with sinners and the outcasts of society. The salvation that he offered did not consist merely in divine revelation, but rather in the gift of the fullness of life at all levels. At the same time he called for a real change of heart, which would enable humans to break free from egoism and open themselves to the kingdom.[42] The radical teaching of the Sermon on the Mount underscores his emphasis upon interpersonal relationships and the humanization of all life. If one puts this in the African context, Jesus can be seen as the one who fulfills all the values of African anthropocentricity as exemplified in such characteristics as hospitality and concern for the family, for parents and orphans, and for the underprivileged. In other words, Jesus' ministry to the "poor" represents the fulfillment of all that is best in African culture. But at the same time his ministry transcends the limits of African anthropocentricity in that he extends these ethical values beyond the immediate kinship group to all humankind, regardless of race or ethnic belonging. This transcending of the traditional limits should characterize the Christian ethic. For the imitation of Christ, the proto-ancestor, is to assume personally Jesus' own deeds, passion, and resurrection, and all the possibilities which this brings. This will be to experience a kind of revolutionary dynamic that will enable us to break free from and transform a tradition that has become frozen and has lost its power of creativity. Sacred history is thus liberating power: it judges African tradition as well as exposing the postcolonial sins of corruption and abuse of power. The answer to these ethical dilemmas, which are the malaise of modern

42. Bujo, *African Theology*, 87-88.

Africa today, can only be found in the acceptance of Jesus as the proto-ancestor, the servant of God, who gives the value of the human person pride of place. "The modern African," comments Bujo, "can only tread in the footsteps of Jesus Christ when he sees him not as a tyrannical *kyrios*, but rather as proto-ancestor, whose legacy is an appeal to his posterity to toil unremittingly to overcome all inhumanity."[43] To accept Jesus as the proto-ancestor, then, means not just to stand by the cross and observe from afar, but to be on the cross and to suffer along with Jesus, for it is this crucified one with whom the believer can identify himself, the crucified as proto-ancestor. In him is the life-giving Spirit, and by the passion and resurrection he liberates, purifies, and humanizes African culture. This is the basis of an ethic for Africa today that will bring the ancestral ethos into dialogue with the Christian faith.

Christology, however, cannot be separated from ecclesiology, just as the ancestor or "clan founder" cannot be separated from his descendants. Bujo therefore proceeds to examine the significance of Jesus as proto-ancestor for the conception of the church. The exalted Jesus is the means through which God imparts his divine life to the world; he is, as it were, the proto–life source. We may compare this to models that Paul uses — Jesus as the last Adam (1 Cor 15:45ff.; Rom 5:12ff.), as head of the body (Col. 1:12), as head of all creation (Col. 1:15), and as firstborn from the dead (Col. 1:18; 1 Cor. 15:20) through whom God has reconciled all things to himself (Col. 1:19-20). The Johannine concept of "life" has similar implications (e.g. John 10:10-15; 11:25-26; 15:1-6; 6:32-58). This last reference is especially significant, since for Bujo the divine life in Christ is conveyed primarily through the eucharist. The eucharist is the means of nourishing and renewing the life of the community, life that is not merely biological generation, but rather mystical and spiritual. Jesus as proto-ancestor bestows life to all the community, and inasmuch as his followers share this divine life, they too become channels of the proto-ancestor to impart this same life not only within the church but further afield to the clan and nation. The church thus becomes the focal point from which the life of the proto-ancestor flows and spreads out to all humanity. Seen in this light, the eucharist, as the "ancestral meal" instituted by the proto-ancestor, stands at the heart of a genuine African ecclesiology. The purpose of

---

43. Bujo, *African Theology,* 91 (my trans. of German edition, 97).

the eucharist (as with some African death rituals) is to impart life in all its fullness for the welfare of the whole community. This life is the Spirit. The ancestral model is again seen to be Trinitarian, in which Father, Son, and Spirit are the source, imparter, and substance respectively of the divine life in the community.

An ecclesiology based on such an ancestral model presents a number of challenges to the life of the church. It was noted that in traditional society each individual member could, by virtue of his or her actions, either contribute to or detract from the vital force of the whole community. The life force that finds its source in God and in the ancestors is dependent for its efficacy in real life upon the actions of the members of the earthly "body." So within the church, each member has a role to play in transforming the conditions of postcolonial Africa by contributing to the divine life force of the whole. Religious leaders, bishops, and priests have the special task of service by which the life of Christ is spread and depends.[44] But the laity too have an essential part to play. "One cannot honestly speak," argues Bujo, "of a living Christian community when the laity are systematically excluded from any part in decision-making in their own church." For an undue sacerdotal authority that excludes dialogue will hinder the free flow of life force within the church. So indeed does a lifestyle on the part of the clergy that is alien to the gospel. In an impassioned plea to church leaders, Bujo urges them to renounce materialism and bourgeois values, and to live in a way that will demonstrate their solidarity with the poor and oppressed. They need, he argues, to address themselves more vigorously to socioethical issues such as the role of multinationals and capitalism, the contrast between the church's affluence and the context of deprivation in which it exists, and all kinds of dehumanization. To take the life of the eucharistic community seriously is not simply to speak and write about the oppressed, but to work with and for them. These values need to be fundamental for the training for the priesthood, so that theological theory will be conjoined with praxis and seminarians will have experience of sharing the real and basic needs of real people. In this sense, material projects like housing, water supplies, hygiene, unemployment,

---

44. Bujo also sees a role for the papacy in this model, as corresponding to the eldest son, who receives the father's inheritance and then imparts it to all the family in due measure so as to ensure meaningful life for all (Bujo, *African Theology*, 100ff.)

and so on will need to be addressed. This severely practical outworking of the fullness of life imparted by Jesus as proto-ancestor will enable us to overcome the abuses and dehumanization of postcolonial Africa. Thus, Bujo believes, an ecclesiology based on the model of Jesus as proto-ancestor will be able to relate in a meaningful way to Africans today. It is a model based on the religious experience of the significance of the ancestors, and at the same time founded on the biblical concept of the word of life, who brings life to his people and leads them through the Spirit into fellowship with the Father.

Bujo's reconstruction of Christian theology around the central African concept of the ancestors is a brave attempt to get beyond simple parallelism, and to try to create a synthesis in which both the traditional worldview and the basic doctrines of Christianity (in Bujo's case christology and ecclesiology) interact and complement each other. He is clearly correct in his contention that the christological titles of the New Testament are culturally determined and need to be modified to suit each different cultural milieu in which the gospel is incarnated. The choice of ancestral theology for this role is not, of course, new in Africa; it has been explored, in one way or another, by Sawyerr, Fasholé-Luke, Bediako, and others, and especially by Nyamiti. Bujo develops this concept with rather more attention to its significance in the totality of the traditional thought system, and he is doubtless correct that the role of the ancestors is in all African cultures the foundation of the religious life. Such a choice of ancestral theology is not, however, without its own problems. To begin with, the question may be asked whether the proto-ancestor model, though at certain points illuminating and effective, does not, when followed through with Bujo's thoroughness, run the risk of encasing christology in a straitjacket. Christ as ancestor — or proto-ancestor — as an illustration or paradigm is acceptable and useful. Worked through with the relentless logic that Bujo employs, however, it may seem to be too much of a good thing — after all, none of the biblical christological titles — Lord, Son, Christ, and so on — is subjected by the New Testament writers to such thoroughness. They are always part-truths, limited symbols that cast shafts of light on the mystery of the Godhead, but do not exhaust its many-faceted splendor. Bujo, of course, realizes this, and comments in passing that the proto-ancestor is not the only type of christology for Africa. One could have wished he would have expanded on this and indicated where other symbols and paradigms are needed to overcome these limitations. One such limitation, which Bujo mentions (again in passing!), is that the ancestors are not always all-good or all-perfect.[45] In most African thought-systems ancestors are sources of harm as well as of good, and indeed in some cultures become objects of concern only when they are neglected and when they make their displeasure felt by calamities or spirit possession. One gets the impression that for Bujo the darker side of the ancestors is unimportant, and that he has presented us with a somewhat idealized picture. But if Christ is to be seen as proto-ancestor, do we not need to tackle honestly the negative side of the ancestral cult and ask how Christ is *not* like the ancestors? This issue surfaces in the somewhat tangled attempt to incorporate the past (presumably pre-Christian) ancestors into the life of the proto-ancestor. It is not at all clear how the life force of Jesus is imparted to these biological ancestors, whether it is on the basis of a common grace (as the appeal to Heb. 1:1-2 would seem),[46] or by a kind of universalism derived from the efficacy of the resurrection. If Jesus is the mystical and spiritual proto-ancestor, how can he be related to biological ancestors who are not strictly within the community bound together by faith? Other theologians have tried to deal with the problem with rather more convincing results.[47] Indeed, is not the whole concept of ancestorship very difficult to accept unless it includes in some way the biological relationship that is ipso facto excluded in the case of Jesus as ancestor?

Despite Bujo's own warnings against romanticizing tradition, one is left with the suspicion that with Bujo the African past has been idealized in polarization with the evils of the colonial and mission heritage. While there were — and still are, no doubt — many good and wholesome things about the cult of the ancestors, one cannot assume that everything about it is capable of being utilized for an elaboration of Christian theology.[48] This is perhaps to raise the much wider issue for African theology today of the need to assess elements of discontinuity and of alienation in African socioreligious systems.

---

45. Bujo, *African Theology,* 79.
46. Though of course Heb. 1:1-2 must refer to the Jewish fathers as the forerunners of Christianity.
47. For example, Pobee and Bediako.
48. As is implied when Bujo deals with the issues of marriage.

VI

Political Theologies

1. Theology, Protest, and Socialism

Outside of the Republic of South Africa, African theologians have, until comparatively recently, seemed surprisingly little concerned to relate their Christian faith to political systems. Within the last decade or so, however, it has become evident — possibly because of the influence of South African black theology, possibly due to the wider emergence of liberation theology on the ecumenical scene — that we are beginning to witness a new interest in political issues. What Mbiti back in 1972 complained was a "neglected element" in African theology[1] is now coming more and more to the forefront.

The factors contributing to this former neglect of political theology have been analyzed from a theological standpoint by K. Ankrah.[2] Ankrah points out that the kind of Christianity that was implanted into Africa — especially by the Protestant missionaries — tended to be of the pietistic variety, with a dominant emphasis on the salvation of the individual; sociopolitical questions, if considered at all, were viewed as quite subservient to the individual attainment of eternal life. Alongside this was the stress on the doctrines of original sin and divine providence:

---

1. John Mbiti, "Church and State: A Neglected Element in Christianity in Comtemporary Africa," *ATJ* 1 (1972): 31-45. Useful background material to this chapter may be found in A. Hastings, *A History of African Christianity 1950-1975* (Cambridge, 1979).

2. K. Ankrah, "Church and Politics in Africa," *ATER*, 155-61.

humankind — especially "pagan" humankind — was regarded as corrupt, and society could therefore not be renewed by social action but only by divine intervention. According to Ankrah, evangelical missionary pietism tended to project the righting of earthly wrongs into the distant future and encouraged the passive acceptance of the injustices and inequalities of life here and now. In addition there was the alliance between missions and governments during the colonial period, involving, as it usually did, a doctrine of mutual coexistence, the missionaries' non-rocking of the ship of state in exchange for the benefits of the Pax Britannica or whatever other colonial power was involved. Thus, as Africans interpret it, the churches were all too often subservient to the ruling colonial powers and consequently relatively uninvolved in the struggle for political and social justice.

The problem with this view is not that it is necessarily incorrect — indeed, in general terms it can claim a good degree of historical justification; it is rather that it has tended to stunt the growth of genuine political theology in independent Africa. It has become all too easy, all too common, to bewail the ecclesiastical and theological shortcomings of the colonial period rather than addressing the problems of the post-colonial present.

There are encouraging signs that these backward-looking attitudes are changing and that African theologians outside the Republic of South Africa are also now taking seriously the task of making theological and ethical judgments on the problems of their own states in the light of their Christian convictions. This trend may be clearly seen in some of the papers from the Jos conference of 1975. Edward Fasholé-Luke, for example, in his introduction to some of the contributions dealing with these issues, agreed that the European missionaries were often characterized by conservative and colonial attitudes; he then went on to note, however, that it is far easier to fulminate against the past colonial era and against apartheid South Africa than to protest about the exploitation of black Africans by fellow black Africans. He concluded that independent Africa also needed a theology of liberation.[3] In the same vein, Desmond Tutu, himself a frequent victim of South African government policies, complained that African theologians have had remarkably little to say about important issues like military coups, oppression, exploitation, poverty, and disease

---

3. E. Fasholé-Luke, *CIA*, 358-59.

in their own independent countries.[4] His call for the church in Africa to exercise its prophetic role was reiterated in his speech after the murder of Archbishop Luwum in Uganda under Amin:

> Political leaders have often been let down by a sycophantic Church leadership, who should provide moral and ethical guidance, but who are content to be time servers. The Church in Africa is faced with this challenge of injustice, corruption, oppression and exploitation at home, and it has no option but to fulfil its prophetic vocation or seriously call in question its claim to be the Church of Jesus Christ.[5]

The postcolonial environment in Africa is, of course, by no means always friendly to Christianity. The case of Zaire is a significant one in this respect. Here the Mobutuan philosophy of *authenticité* led to the proclaiming of a secular state, the disenfranchisement of the Catholic Church, curtailment of freedom of worship, and the compulsory use of traditional (non-Christian) names. It also led to the temporary exile of Cardinal Archbishop Malula, the setting up of youth section committees of Mouvement Populaire de la Révolution (JMPR) within the major seminaries (both in 1972), and the temporary banning in the following year of the Episcopal Assembly as a subversive organization. Given the previous role of the Catholic Church during the colonial period, it was perhaps hardly surprising that Mobutu should have adopted such an avowedly anti-Christian stance. Significantly, these political moves did not stimulate any considerable theological response from a church that contained several outstanding theologians, although, as we shall see, there was strong ecclesiastical resistance to some of Mobutu's more blatant anti-Catholic policies. In one sense, the Zairean theologians had already been through their own period of theological *authenticité* long before, for the preindependence writings of men such as Mulago and Tshibangu were just such an attempt to deal with the real value of tradition. Perhaps this is why they felt no real need to engage in any radical new theologizing after Mobutu's political ideology was promulgated.[6] The course of the conflict between

---

4. Desmond Tutu, "Whither African Theology?" *CIA*, 368-69.

5. Desmond Tutu, *The Voice of One Crying in the Wilderness* (London, 1982), 114.

6. Kwame Bediako, in a personal communication, suggested this interpretation of the Zairean theologians' lack of response to *authenticité*.

the state and the Catholic Church in Zaire has been well charted in Professor Ngindu Mushete's address at the Jos conference.[7] According to Mushete, *authenticité* poses serious problems for the Catholic Church, partly perhaps because the "secular" state in Zaire has turned out, in practice, too often to appear anti-Catholic.[8] As an ideology, however, *authenticité* aims to get rid of the deleterious consequences of the past colonial heritage and to rediscover its African soul. It seeks to correct the idea that Christian Western civilization is the only possible one and is of universal validity. In its attempt to rediscover real African personality and integrity it also protests against Western individualism, which it sees as diametrically opposed to the all-embracing emphasis on the welfare of the whole social group in traditional Africa. *Authenticité* therefore seeks to overcome "mental alienation" and in Mobutu's ideology is "another name for radical decolonisation, total political, economic and cultural freedom." Thus "to be converted to authenticity is in practice to renew contact with those free men, our ancestors, who were creators of culture and civilization."[9] The challenge of this political doctrine to the church is for it to discern the specifically theological significance of such a recourse to *authenticité*.

The Catholic Church in Zaire from the early seventies found itself in conflict with Mobutu's Mouvement Populaire de la Révolution (MPR) on a number of issues, before it arrived at some kind of modus vivendi. From the beginning, however, it made no claims within the political sphere of the state. The church, rather, in its task to encourage people to live according to the gospel, was to serve the world in its particular Zairean situation.[10] At the end of 1973, after the conflicts referred to above, the bishops met to make clear their considered position on church-state relationships. They affirmed their belief that the "strength of common Bantu wisdom" on both sides could effect a

---

7. Ngindu Mushete, "Authenticity and Christianity in Zaire," *CIA*, 228-41, expanded from an earlier article published in *Cahiers des Religion Africaine* 8, no. 16 (1974): 209-390.

8. Mushete, "Authenticity and Christianity," 239 n. 33, quoting the XXIInd Plenary Assembly of Bishops.

9. Mushete, "Authenticity and Christianity," 231.

10. Mushete, "Authenticity and Christianity," 232, referring to the Acts of the XIth Plenary Assembly of the Episcopate in Zaire, March 5, 1972, *l'Église et l'État, l'Église au service de la Nation Zaïroise* (Brussels, 1972).

reconciliation. The Catholic Church, on its part, was a servant of the world in Zaire. It confessed it had been bound too closely to the colonial regime and henceforth determined not to be a "stranger" within the independent Zairean nation. It was

> anxious for the same collaboration, in the fullest confidence and with the most total sense of participation in the life of the nation, without however reaching a situation that implied direct intervention in the political domain.[11]

Mushete sees *authenticité* as resulting from the West's former cultural domination and from the consequences of this for the people, the culture, and the relationship between the people and religion. The Catholic Church was particularly vulnerable in this respect in independent Zaire (in a way the Kimbanguists were not) because of both its historical association with Rome and its own highly developed, almost monopolistic, system of organization, which might appear to pose a threat to the political system. As Mushete sees it, these factors especially bring into focus its theological task, which is one of the authenticity of the church's message.

> If it is not to perish the church of Zaire is called upon to Africanise itself as regards the personnel of the hierarchy and the laity, its mode of expression, its liturgy, and more profoundly, its theology.[12]

Its practical task in Zaire he sees as collaborating actively in development by bringing about a change in mentality, based on a sense of justice and fraternity. Of especial importance is that it should not appear as a foreign body in the nation; thus the Africanization of Christianity within Zaire is its most important task.[13]

By no means have all francophone Catholic theologians been so accommodating in the face of brutal political systems, and some have

---

11. Quoted in Mushete, "Authenticity and Christianity," 236.

12. Mushete, "Authenticity and Christianity," 239.

13. Mushete, "Authenticity and Christianity," 241. For an examination of the reasons for the decline in the influence of the Catholic Church in rural areas of Zaire and a plea to reconcile the preaching of the gospel to the new political identity, see Musempele, "The Church and Rural Development in Zaire," *ATJ* 6, no. 2 (1977): 38-42.

attempted to come to grips with sociopolitical issues in a much sharper and more critical way. Outstanding in this respect has been the writing of the Camerounian priest Jean-Marc Éla. His collections of essays[14] combine the insights of acute social analysis with those of critical theology. Éla's interests are wide-ranging. While standing firmly within the Catholic tradition, he is nevertheless ready to criticize his church for its Western dominance and orientation and to argue for a truly African Catholicism. He rejects what he sees as artificial attempts to resurrect or romanticize a past African tradition (he has some especially caustic comments on négritude and similar movements),[15] but is at the same time convinced that there are genuine values in "Africanness," such as the concept of the wholeness of life, the role of the ancestors, and aspects of cultural symbolism, that need to be integrated into Christian theology.[16] Éla's main emphasis, however, is on human liberation. The factors that threaten authentic human existence in Africa today are, he believes, part of the continuing legacy of colonialism; but the strength of Éla's analysis is that he also grapples with wider and more contemporary problems, such as the nature of the current world order and the misgovernment, corruption, and misuse of power that characterize independent African nations.[17] For him the heart of the gospel consists in addressing the great gulf between rich and poor, the strong and the powerless, and in the vitality of Christianity in taking sides in the struggle for justice.[18] In this he sees the Bible as the ground and rationale for liberating action. The task of theology is in praxis rather than in word; it is to "renounce *in absoluto* discourse on God and take sides with the groups caught in the struggle for a more just and humane society."[19]

The church-state dialogue that has taken place elsewhere in Africa (outside Amin's Uganda) has been of a more gentle kind, and has shown the tendency to see the place of the church as the servant of the world within its particular national context. One main concern has been with

14. Jean-Marc Éla, *My Faith as an African* (Maryknoll, 1988; English translation of the French, 1985); *African Cry* (Maryknoll, 1986; English translation of the French, 1980).

15. Éla, *African Cry,* 123.

16. Éla, *My Faith,* 13ff.

17. Éla, *My Faith,* 67ff.

18. Éla, *My Faith,* 102ff, *African Cry,* 132.

19. Éla, *African Cry,* 132.

"African socialism." This term has indeed been used somewhat vaguely by theologians, some of whom have shown a remarkable lack of discrimination in lumping together such odd bedfellows as Nkrumah's conscientism,[20] Senghor's African socialism, Kaunda's humanism, Nyerere's Ujamaa, and Kenyan Harambee. What similarities there are originate perhaps in the influence of the first named on English-speaking Africa. It should be noted that none of these movements constituted the Marxist challenge to the gospel that Shepperson and Baeta thought would emerge.[21] It is only in Portuguese-speaking Africa that Marxism is becoming an issue for the church, and there has been too little theological reaction from these countries as yet to indicate whether theology there will move towards the more radical acceptance of Marxist social analysis that characterizes Latin American theology of liberation.[22]

Perhaps the most significant theological contributions have been those that have attempted to relate the Christian faith to the political ideologies of Kenneth Kaunda and Julius Nyerere. Both Kaunda, the son of a Presbyterian evangelist, and Nyerere, a former teacher in a Catholic college, share a Christian background that they have never rejected, and that has to some extent shaped their political views. For Nyerere belief in the existence of God is indeed almost a postulate of the socialist society.[23] Kaunda, for his part, has expressed the view that the increased

20. On Nkrumah's relations with the church see especially John Pobee, "Church and State in Ghana 1949-66," in *Religion in a Pluralistic Society*, ed. John Pobee (Leiden, 1976), 121-44.

21. Christian Baeta, *Christianity in Tropical Africa* (London, 1968), 144-45. Worseley pointed out that the classical Marxist categories are Western and inapplicable to most of Africa. He also noted that African tradition was concerned about the individual as a member of the social group, and that religion is too important a factor in African socities to be rejected (Worseley, *The Third World* [London, 1967], 122-23).

22. But see Filipo Couto, "Zur Diskussion um einer afrikanischen Theologie," in *Zwischen Kultur and Politik*, ed. T. Sundermeier (Hamburg, 1978), 110-41. Perhaps the most forceful early contribution from Portuguese-speaking Africa was José Chipenda's "Theological Options for Africa Today," *ATER*, 66-72. Chipenda argued that African communities are "free" but not "liberated" — that is, free from external rule but not liberated from disease, ignorance, and other evils. This he regards as in part due to economic, military, and political dependence on foreign powers. The church, in Chipenda's view, is similarly dependent.

23. Julius Nyerere, *Freedom and Socialism* (Dar-es-Salaam, 1968), 17. For a similar view from francophone Africa at the time see Léopold Senghor, *Liberté* (Paris, 1977), 30.

material benefits that accompany technological advances are not without certain dangers, one of which is the possibility of losing sight of the religious aspect of life.

> Is there any way that my people can have the blessings of technology without being eaten away by materialism and losing the spiritual dimension?[24]

In an appeal to Zambian theologians he writes:

> The more sensitive theologians are beginning to explore what it means to be a Christian in a genuinely African or Asian way. I wish some of our African clergy showed more interest in this complex problem and put a little less zeal into turning their congregations into black versions of seventeenth century English Puritans.[25]

African socialism, as expounded by Kaunda and Nyerere, is neither anti-religious nor anti-Christian, and there are no inherent contradictions to be overcome as is the case in relating the Christian faith to Marxist ideology. There is a sense, in fact, in which African socialism raises issues that are of fundamental theological importance: the meaning of human existence, poverty, disease, injustice, and so on.[26] These issues, as the theology of liberation has shown, are the kind of questions with which theology must grapple if it is to be relevant in the world today.

One approach to African socialism by Christian theologians has been to draw parallels between the primary concerns of the two systems. Similarities center around three main areas:

1. the estimate of the individual,
2. the role of the community, and
3. socioeconomic issues.

---

24. Kenneth Kaunda, *A Humanist in Africa* (London, 1966), 54.

25. Kenneth Kaunda, *Letter to My Children* (London, 1973), 17.

26. J. Mutiso-Mbinda believes these questions, which "go beyond the secular dimension," are also raised by Kenyan Harambee ("Towards a Theology of Harambee," *AFER* 20, no. 5 [1978]: 287-95). For a general overview see my "African Theology and African Socialism," *ATJ* 17, no. 3 (1988).

At the center of Zambian humanism, according to Mijere, is the importance of the individual.[27] Kaunda has himself sought to relate his political philosophy to precolonial African societies in which, he believes, the individual was of primary importance, regardless of age, role, and status. This anthropocentricism he seeks to incorporate into Zambian humanism. Nyerere's explication of socialism moves along similar lines. He emphasizes that its basic purpose is not ideological, but rather the practical well-being of the people, involving acceptance of human equality.

> Socialism is an attitude of mind. The basis of socialism is a belief in the oneness of man and the common historical destiny of mankind. Its basis, in other words, is human equality. Acceptance of this principle is absolutely fundamental to socialism.[28]

Thus Nyerere's policies were aimed at being non-elitist, and assume the inherent equality of all. As a Lutheran theologian has commented, men and women are not a means, but the focus of development.[29]

The emphasis on the community is also claimed to go back to traditional society. For Kaunda the precolonial community was a kind of mutual aid society that, because of kinship ties, was all-inclusive. Its economic system was geared towards the needs of the whole society: it was anticapitalist and not conducive to the exploitation of one's fellow humans. The needs of the elderly and otherwise nonproductive were attended to by the group as a whole. The Ujamaa ideal, as outlined in the Arusha declaration[30] and the writings of Nyerere, is also centered on the community, as the very term ("familyhood") implies. This is also claimed to be rooted in traditional values,[31] where villages were grouped

---

27. M. Mijere, "The Theology of Zambian Humanism and its Implications for the Local Church," *AFER* 20, no. 6 (1978): 349-57.

28. Julius Nyerere, *Freedom and Socialism,* 93, referring to the Arusha declaration.

29. S. K. Lutahoire, "The Place of the Church in Tanzania's Socialism," *ATJ* 6, no. 1 (1977): 25.

30. The ideals behind Ujamaa were not new when it became official party policy in 1976; Nyerere had spoken and written of it earlier than this.

31. So Lutahoire bluntly states that "African Socialism is derived from the extended family of Old Africa" (Lutahoire, 26). So also C. K. Omari, a Tanzanian sociol-

together for both religious and economic (such as grazing and harvesting) purposes. Such means of production were owned communally, both land and animals being controlled by the clan or lineage.

These traditional ideals are claimed to have been taken over in Zambian humanism and in Ujamaa. Evidence of this is seen in the communitarian ideal (in which aspects of socioeconomic life are placed in the hands of the people), the anticapitalist emphasis, the attack on exploitation, and the desire for an economy in which there is as far as possible an equal distribution of wealth.[32] In Tanzania, for example, there is in theory no foreign exploitation, for the economy is in the hands of the people themselves. This policy is seen as the first step towards eradicating bribery, corruption, and exploitation. For Lutahoire the cooperation of Ujamaa villages is a means of freeing people from the evils of disease, poverty, hunger, injustice, prejudice, fear, racialism, and tribalism.[33]

Mijere has sought to analyze the implications of Zambian humanism for the local church. He sees it as part of the search for a national identity, and sees Zambian humanism as reflecting not only the ideals of traditional societies but also many of those contained in the Christian gospel. He argues that Christianity in Zambia needs to be incarnated in forms that relate to Zambian symbols. One such symbol is the building up of the life of small communities. He believes "the communitarian aspect of the Zambian philosophy of Humanism is also at the core of the rightly understood church."[34]

The role of the church therefore is to formulate its faith in terms of Zambian humanism, and its priests are to act as "midwives in the process of giving birth to Zambian Humanism."[35] The focus for this will be the local church. Like Bishop Mwoleka, to whom we shall turn below, Mijere stresses the correspondence between the community ideal

---

ogist, who writes, "Africans lived together for the common good of all members of the social unit" ("Emerging Themes on Rural Development Policy in Nyerere's Thought," *ATJ* 6, no. 2 [1977]: 14).

32. Compare T. Mussa, "The Importance of the Opportunity Which Christianity has in Ujamaa," *ATJ* 6, no. 2 (1977), 25-31.

33. Lutahoire, 25.

34. Mijere, 352.

35. Mijere, 356.

and the body of Christ. The same comparison appears in the Tanzanian Lutherans Lutahoire and Mussa. For Lutahoire the function of politics is to direct people towards constructive nationalism, in which each individual is expected to participate in the group or community. Leaning heavily on Nyerere's writings (especially *Church and Society*) Lutahoire sees Africanization and modernization as the joint task of the church and state together.[36]

The enthusiastic support given by these writers to their respective political systems does not clearly spell out the theological basis for the involvement of Christians, beyond pointing to certain common central aims. A more theological approach has appeared in the addresses of Bishop Christopher Mwoleka,[37] one of Nyerere's most enthusiastic supporters, who has himself lived in Ujamaa villages for extended periods. Mwoleka takes his stand firmly on Vatican II in its emphasis on the place of the laity in the service of the community. In Mwoleka's view the Christian faith is still too much regarded as a private affair[38] rather than having the community as its main thrust, and this has consequences detrimental to the social aspects of the gospel. Herein lies the challenge of Ujamaa. The church has the obligation to involve itself wholeheartedly in the task of educating citizens to ensure the success of the Ujamaa villages, for Ujamaa calls on the church to "reset her institutions and revise her methods of presenting the gospel message, bringing them into line with the Ujamaa set-up." Mwoleka interprets the doctrine of the Trinity as corresponding in the theological realm to what Ujamaa signifies in the social realm. Just as the Trinity reveals that "life is not life at all unless it is shared, so does the ideal of Ujamaa represent the sharing of life in the practical realm." The Christian life

---

36. L. Magesa would go even further: he argued that liberation theology in its Tanzanian manifestation will not, as in Latin America, condemn government policies, but on the contrary "it will insist on alignment with government action aimed at human freedom and it will show the theological insight of the aspirations and aims of Ujamaa." L. Magesa, "Towards a Theology of Liberaton for Tanzania," *CIA*, 514.

37. Collected as *Ujamaa and Christian Communities* (Eldoret, 1976). His "Trinity and Community" was reprinted in *Mission Trends no. 3: Third World Theologies*, ed. G. H. Anderson and T. F. Stransky (Grand Rapids, 1976).

38. Mwoleka, *Ujamaa and Christian Communities*, 11; compare Mercy Amba Oduyoye, *Hearing and Knowing; Theological Reflections on Christianity in Africa* (Maryknoll, 1986), 138ff.

must therefore be seen as the imitation of the life of the Trinity, that is, "the central mystery of a life that is shared." Ujamaa thus unites all men, in a down-to-earth practical way, in imitation of the shared life of the Godhead. The doctrine of the Trinity in this way becomes not an abstract intellectual dogma but a practical experience of sharing — "life is not life unless it is shared."[39] The gospel should thus be presented as a life, to be lived in community, which becomes "a taste of God's own life, the salutary sharing with our brothers of the good things of the earth." Such a sharing is practical and comprehensive; the earthly and the heavenly realms are not opposed, rather the spiritual involves acquiring and making use of the material goods of the world.[40] Mwoleka is attempting here a genuine theological reflection on political issues.

The decline of African socialism in Tanzania and Zambia has meant that theological analyses of these political systems have lost something of their practical relevance. At its best, however, the theological approach to African socialism served to highlight issues of genuine Christian and human importance, such as the sharing of life and the value of the individual. Thus the writings of Mwoleka and others are of more than simply passing historical importance.

Further south, in Zimbabwe, Robert Mugabe's more radical form of socialism found an enthusiastic theological apologist in the Reverend Canaan Banana. Banana's importance for Christian theology in Africa seems to me to be slight, and his writings too subservient to his political ideology to have lasting value. However, since he had become something of a cult figure before his retirement from the presidency following the reorganization of the Zimbabwean government at the end of 1987, he calls for more than a passing mention.[41]

Banana is an Ndebele, and was born in 1936. His early years were spent mainly in educational work or in the Methodist church.[42] The increased tension in the 1960s following Ian Smith's unilateral Declaration of Independence saw a radicalization of his political views and

39. Mwoleka, *Ujamaa and Christian Communities,* 19.
40. Mwoleka, *Ujamaa and Christian Communities,* 16.
41. The Lancaster House agreement made no provision for a president; Banana's retirement in 1987 was a return to this constitution.
42. For an interesting self-portrait see Canaan Banana, "Taking People Seriously," in *A Community of Clowns,* ed. Hugh Lewin (WCC for Urban Rurul Mission, Geneva, 1987), 241-44.

at the same time a questioning of the church's role, as he saw it, in acquiescing to social and racial injustice. A period of involvement in the WCC's Urban Rural Mission, in both Rhodesia and Japan, was followed by several years of theological study in Washington. On his return to Rhodesia in 1975 Banana was jailed and subsequently had his movements restricted. Three years later, his involvement in the politics of independence having crystallized, he dramatically left Bishop Muzorewa's delegation at the Geneva conference and pledged support to Mugabe's largely Shona ZANU (PF) party.

Banana has written and lectured widely (he has also been an honorary professor in theology at the University of Zimbabwe) but has emerged more as an apologist for the Zimbabwean socialist revolution than as a theologian of stature. The recurring theme of his writings is the conviction that Christianity finds its true fulfillment only in a Marxist-socialist political system.

Banana's point of departure, in common with that of so many emergent African theologians, is the missionary churches' failure to attack the problems of racism, inequality, and socioeconomic realities. The colonial church, as he puts it, was too high in the skies to take notice of the lowly peasant and too full of abstract ideas to feed the hungry. It was, in short, "a faithful chip off the old colonial block."[43] As part and parcel of the racist colonial system, it neither engaged in, nor even saw the need of, radical social change.[44] The answer to the divisions within society is, he believes, to be found only in a socialism that will interact dynamically with the concrete situation in Zimbabwe today. The opposition of socialism to capitalism, then, is not simply a matter of different opinions, but (in Mugabe's words) an opposition, "of morality versus immorality, of equity versus inequity, of humanity versus inhumanity, and — of Christianity versus un-christianity."[45] Banana's

---

43. Canaan Banana, *Christianity and the Struggle for Socialism in Zimbabwe Today* (Harare, 1988), 3.

44. This is not entirely true, especially as regards the Catholic Church: see I. Linden, *The Catholic Church and the Struggle for Zimbabwe* (London, 1980).

45. Mugabe, in his foreword (pages unnumbered) to Banana's *The Theology of Promise, the Dynamics of Self-reliance* (Harare, 1982). Banana himself put the point equally succinctly on page 120: "[W]hoever abandons the false promise of capitalism and works to make possible the socialist promise . . . has eternal life." Banana's other substantial publication is his *The Gospel According to the Ghetto* (Harare, 1980). For a

most important book, *The Theology of Promise*, consequently, is not simply an attempt to point up the common ground between Christianity and socialism, but rather a drastic identification of Zimbabwean Marxist-socialist theory in its entirety with Christianity. In pursuance of this thesis it is clear that Banana is much more informed by dialectical materialism than he is by the Christian faith as traditionally understood.

Like many other Third World theologians, Banana regards the tools of Western Christianity not only as inadequate for the African situation but as positively misleading, for they are, he believes, the product of capitalist cultures. What we need now, therefore, is not a theology that has been neatly systematized by a capitalist élite, but rather one forged out by the people themselves, by the poor and oppressed peasant masses who "have elementary rights to think, to reflect on their own life and their own faith in God."[46] This kind of theology will have to be a socialist one, for "the kingdom of God is realised in socialism."[47] As Banana understands the history of his nation, Zimbabwe has been systematically exploited by a Western capitalism that created gross inequalities along racial lines, and that brought into being a people dispossessed and dehumanized in its own land. Thus the Zimbabwean revolution against the illegal settler government of Ian Smith was essential to bring about the socialist kingdom of God. The violence of this revolution was a necessary one — it was "the violence of God," for the freedom fighters were actually doing God's work. Reconciliation involves the removal of injustice. Consequently, "true love was only possible through revolutionary endeavours — in this case through the barrel of a gun."[48] Violence and nonviolence should not be regarded as opposites, but as gradations on the same continuum. Protest and liberation will involve action at some point on this continuum, and there are some circumstances that can be changed only by violence. Such circumstances call for aggression in order to destroy unjust systems and create now just ones. This should not surprise the Christian, for Christianity itself, in Banana's view, is a revolutionary religion. We should

response to Banana from the academic community in Zimbabwe see I. Mukonyoro, J. Cox, and F. Verstraelen, eds., *Rewriting the Bible, the Real Issues* (Gweru, 1993).

46. Banana, *Theology of Promise,* 114-15.
47. Banana, *Theology of Promise,* 116, 25.
48. Banana, *Theology of Promise,* 141.

not therefore ask whether it is possible to be both a revolutionary and a Christian at the same time; on the contrary "anti-revolutionary Christianity is not Christianity at all."[49] Religion and politics are not two different things, they are rather different sides of the same coin. Since Christianity and capitalism are quite incompatible, the only true form of Christianity is socialism (Jesus, Banana informs us, was a socialist). This Christianity will accept the eschatological perspective of Marxism, of the continual progress of the whole of humankind "moving towards the future, transforming itself into a new creation."[50] In such a dynamic march of progress humans themselves are the keys, so that Christianity turns out to be "the expectations of God waiting to see what man can do for him."[51] The socialist kingdom will need to be brought about by the activity of the whole human community, which is struggling for a better life, and the arrival of the kingdom will be seen in the material welfare of the people. In all this, God is to be discerned in the acts of humans in their human striving in history: "[I]t is from that total burning historical eruption that the voice of the poor is heard." The task of the theology of promise is to "describe how God's Kingdom takes shape on earth through the historical events in which God manifests himself."[52]

All this fairly bristles with problems. To some of these — for example, the problem of violence, and the concept of God's manifesting himself in human history — I shall return below.[53] Nor is it within my competence to try here to evaluate Banana's political ideas — though it may be remarked in passing that Marxist-socialist experiments elsewhere in Africa, or indeed the idealist-socialist systems of Kaunda and Nyerere, give little ground for optimism. This should caution us from the start that no political system is a panacea for all material ills, and none can naively be identified with the kingdom of God. It is Banana's acceptance of Marxism, however, as though it were the only option for Africa (or anywhere else) today that raises most questions for the theologian. At this point I shall mention only two: its claim to be "scientific"

---

49. Banana, *Theology of Promise*, 106-7.
50. Banana, *Theology of Promise*, 15.
51. Banana, *Theology of Promise*, 106.
52. Banana, *Theology of Promise*, 113, 116.
53. See further chapter 8.

and its simplistic conception of history as progress through conflict. These are fundamental assumptions in Banana's thought, and both are almost certainly spurious.[54] Banana has, in fact, accepted Marxism in a quite uncritical way. There is here no dialogue (such as we find in Latin America and some European theologians) between the principles of Marxist thought and the Christian faith, but rather a drastic rewriting of the gospel to suit a particular political ideology: Banana has fallen into the very trap he accuses missionary Christianity of, that of the wholesale and unquestioning acceptance of an alien Western-oriented system. It is not surprising, therefore, that Banana comes up with some curious pieces of exegesis. He states his hermeneutical approach as follows:

> The gospels enlighten us, but do not determine the future. This is the same as to say that the Gospels are not a set of moral principles to guide our behaviour but a collection of narratives to illuminate the life of man in accordance with the examples of privileged peoples who lived the unique human situation.[55]

There is certainly an element of truth in this: the gospels are limited (as is all the Bible) not only by their cultural background but also by their once-for-all unrepeatable nature. In this sense they are certainly unique. But this does not exhaust their significance, which lies not in the fact that they are mere illustrations but in that they must also in some way be normative for us today. If they do not contain principles that, however much they may need to be reinterpreted within other (equally unique) situations, remain valid, it is difficult to see what value the Scriptures can have for us. In fact, Banana himself tacitly assumes this when he uses the gospels to justify his own position, especially in relation to capitalism. The message of the prophets is thus reduced to a blanket condemnation of a particular class, and the message of Jesus (on the basis of Luke 16:10-13) to the identity of salvation with poverty and condemnation with wealth. In a similar vein, Acts 4:34-35 becomes a blueprint for economic socialism.[56] The problem with this kind of the

54. See further chapter 7.
55. Banana, *Theology of Promise,* 102.
56. Banana, *Theology of Promise,* 131, 21.

use of the Bible is obvious; it ignores critical-historical problems and fails to get anywhere near to the real intention of the text. In consequence, one is left with the impression that what we have in Banana's writings is not a theology to be seriously reckoned with, but an attempt to justify a particular political ideology.

Under normal circumstances Christian theology has a twofold role vis-à-vis political systems. The first is a positive and supportive attitude towards all that is good in them, all that helps towards a just, humane, and equitable society. At the same time the church has a prophetic obligation, in subjecting all political systems to the judgment of the word of God and in exposing in them all that she sees as incompatible with his will. Perhaps the biggest danger is that theology in some African states with governments whose policies approximate Christian principles may lose sight of this critical faculty and obligation, and fail to expose the elements in these political systems that militate against the good of the individual and the community. The danger of Erastian compliance is a real one.

We turn now to the one country in Africa where the prophetic voice of African theologians has sounded its clear call for liberation in the face of much persecution, to the voice of South African black theology.

2. Black Theology

The church in South Africa has been called upon to operate in a quite different set of circumstances from that elsewhere in Africa. It is not our purpose here to go into the philosophy and practice of apartheid,[57] but some brief allusion to those circumstances is necessary if the black theology movement is to make sense. While apartheid only became a formal doctrine in 1947, political life in South Africa had been moving in that direction for some long time before this date. Land acts of 1913 and 1936 confined blacks to some 13 percent of the land, and the gradual abolition of non-white franchise and parliamentary representation also

---

57. A useful list of the earlier source materials may be found in the United Nations Centre against Apartheid, special issue, *Publications List and Comprehensive Indexes 1967-1983* (October 1983).

began in the 1930s. Apartheid has been described by John Kane-Berman as a "comprehensive and technologically sophisticated system, seeking continuing political and economic mastery of one race or class by another." In South Africa this system was enforced by acts of a white Parliament[58] that legally permitted the government to detain suspects indefinitely without trial and without access to solicitors, courts, or even their families (Suppression of Terrorism Act, 1967); to forbid political meetings (Riotous Assemblies Acts, 1974 amendment); and to silence the media, organizations, and individuals (Internal Security Act, 1976). Pass laws were designed to restrict black Africans to the Homelands, or to townships in which they had the status of migrant laborers, and to compel them to carry passes, which allowed them into white areas for limited periods. Within those white areas — in which the economy was concentrated — blacks had no rights of residence or ownership; they were compelled — if they found work — to live in townships or in officially illegal shanty towns, which were (like Crossroads) subject to government clearance. Wives and children of workers had no legal rights to join the family wage earner, and had to live in the Homelands or risk the husband and father being charged with "illegally harboring" his family. The Homelands themselves, recognized by no country outside South Africa, were a means of banishing the Africans, who constitute 80 percent of the population, to 13 percent of the poorest land, under a veneer of political independence, which had little meaning as the Homelands were politically and economically unviable. The educational system still provided separate and grossly unequal facilities for blacks, and those who did gain qualifications could expect to earn significantly less than their white counterparts. Opponents of the system could have passports refused or confiscated, be imprisoned or "banned." A person so banned had his or her movements restricted or was subject to house arrest, the person was not permitted to associate with more than one at a time, and his or her writings or speeches could not be circulated. A frequent method of silencing or attempting to discredit opponents was to accuse them of association with the previously illegal Communist party, and accusations of this kind were made against the South African Council of Churches in 1979. Desmond Tutu's response to this allega-

58. The 1983 referendum gave some political rights to Indians and Coloureds, but not to Africans, who constituted 80% of the population.

tion, inter alia, provides a vivid picture of the situation of blacks in South Africa until recently, and bears extended quotation:

> I want to declare categorically that I believe apartheid to be evil and immoral, and therefore unchristian. No theologian I know would be prepared to say that the apartheid system is consistent with the gospel of Jesus Christ. If Mr le Grange thinks that blacks are not exploited, repressed and denied their human rights and dignity, then I invite him to be black for just one day. He would then hear Mr Arrie Paulus saying he is like a baboon, and a senior police officer saying he is violent by nature. He would be aware that in the land of their birth, black people, who form 80% of the population, have 13% of the land, and the white minority of about 20% has about 87% of the land. In this country a white child of 18 can vote, but a black person, be he a university professor or bishop or whatever, has no franchise. A black doctor with the same qualifications as his white counterpart is paid less for the same job. Have any whites had their homes demolished, and then been told to move to an inhospitable area, where they must live in tents until they have built themselves new houses? . . . I doubt very much that the Minister would still be able to say that apartheid was not an unchristian and unjust system, where human rights are denied.[59]

Such then was the situation in which black theology operated in South Africa, a situation made all the more poignant for black Christians in that this inhumanity to man was perpetrated by a ruling minority that professed to be Christian upon a subjugated majority that is also nominally Christian. To quote Tutu again:

> The perplexity we have to deal with is this: why does suffering single out black people so conspicuously, suffering not at the hands of pagans or other unbelievers, but at the hands of fellow Christians who claim allegiance to the same Lord and Master.[60]

59. Press statement of October 11, 1979, in reply to minister Le Grange's attack on the SACC; the statement is reproduced in Tutu, *Voice of One Crying.*
60. Tutu, *Voice of One Crying,* 35.

It is unhappily true that Christianity has seldom been free from the taint of racism, latent or overt, not least within the Reformed tradition;[61] it is also true that the missionary expansion into Africa was all too often characterized by a curious paradox in that, while preaching the equality of all before God, it nonetheless tended to elevate white Christians into superior beings. In South Africa, however, this hardened into a political dogma, which found its religious mythology in the conception of the Voortrekkers of themselves as the elect of God, set apart to possess the promised land by dispossessing the heathen African, and it had its ecclesiastical outworking in the separate racial units that constituted the Dutch Reformed Church.[62] Black theology, then, is essentially the theological response to the dehumanization of blacks that resulted from the ideology of apartheid.[63]

John de Gruchy, a white Congregationalist, has attempted to analyze the factors that led to the emergence of black theology in the late 1960s.[64] According to de Gruchy most of the leaders of the movement were themselves products of the policy of separate development in that they were graduates of the new black universities and colleges. They tended to be suspicious of whites — including "liberals" — and contended positively and in a dynamic way for the dignity of "blackness." They were also influenced by similar emphases elsewhere on the continent — Nkrumah's African Personality, for example, and Senghor's Négritude — as well as finding encouragement from the gains attained by blacks both in the civil rights movement in America and in the various liberation movements elsewhere in Africa. Perhaps the biggest single factor, however, was the emergence within South Africa itself of black consciousness. This was foreshadowed in the work of the Univer-

---

61. See, e.g., Klauspeter Blaser, *Wenn Gott schwarz wäre: das problem der Rassismus in Theologie und christlicher Praxis* (Zurich and Freiburg, 1972).

62. For a full discussion of the historical origins of the churches in South Africa and their official attitudes to apartheid, see especially John de Gruchy, *The Church Struggle in South Africa* (Grand Rapids, 1979), 1-148.

63. Compare Karl-Heinz Dejung, "Reaktionen auf Schwarze Theologie in Südafrika: Uberlegung zur ökumenischen Relevanz einer Bewegung," *Theologie in Konfliktfeld Südafrika: Dialog mit Manas Buthelezi*, ed. Ilse Tödt (Stuttgart and Munich, 1976), 13ff.

64. See de Gruchy, especially chapter 4 (149-94), "Black Renaissance, Protest and Challenge"; also Lucia Scherzberg, *Schwarze Theologie in Südafrika* (Frankfurt am Main, 1982).

sity Christian Movement in 1969, and found its most eloquent spokes-man in Steve Biko, who founded the South African Students' Organi-zation two years later.[65] Its political arm was the Black People's Con-vention.

Though it may have taken the name, consciously or unconsciously, from the black theology movement in America, South African black theology had little to do with figures like Cleage and Cone, and even less with black power as a political ideology.[66] It may be said to have emerged as a coherent theological force as a result of conferences held in 1971, the papers of which were published in book form by the UCM in the following year. The book was immediately banned; it was even-tually printed in London in 1973 under the editorship of Basil Moore, a white Methodist.[67] Other shorter contributions to black theology appeared in *Pro Veritate,* the journal of the Christian Institute, until it was banned in 1977 in the repressions following the demonstrations that took place on Biko's death.[68] While there remained other forums for theological views in South Africa,[69] it is ironic that much of the important material written by black South African theologians was not available in that country until the reforms of Botha and de Klerk.

It was immediately clear from the appearance of *Black Theology, the South African Voice* (although it evidently escaped the attention of the official censors) that black theology was not primarily a racial affair. It did not say (as Cone seems to come close to saying) that God is on the side of the black people simply because they are black. "Black" to

65. Biko's writings, together with a memoir by Aelred Stubbs, have been collected in *I Write What I Like* (London, 1978). Biko was detained by the security police in August 1977 and died a month later, after being kept in custody naked and manacled and subjected to repeated beatings. He was thirty-one. See also United Nations Centre against Apartheid, special issue, *Steve Biko* (October 1977).

66. On the relationship between South African and American black theology see further chapter 7 below.

67. *Black Theology, the South African Voice,* ed. Basil Moore (London, 1973), reprinted in 1974 as *The Challenge of Black Theology.* Its original title was *Essays in Black Theology,* ed. Sabelo Ntawasa. Both Ntawasa and Moore were subsequently banned.

68. The Christian Institute was declared illegal at the same time; many of its staff were detained, and its white leaders, including Dr. Beyers Naudé, were banned.

69. Especially the *Journal of Theology for Southern Africa,* which at this time began to carry more articles by black theologians. This role has more recently been taken over by the *Journal of Black Theology in South Africa.*

these South African writers was less a racial designation than a sociopolitical symbol: it was primarily a synonym for oppression and exploitation. As Barney Pityana, a leading proponent of black consciousness, affirmed in an essay published in the same year as *Black Theology* appeared, blackness was a synonym for subjection and a symbol of those who are deprived of their rights, of the wretched of the earth.[70] Moore, too, could claim that to describe Christ as black was not to make a racial statement but to say that he comes to the poor and oppressed as one of them.[71] This view was reaffirmed at the Lutheran Consultation at Hamannskraal in 1974: "It does not aim at black exclusivism. It is simply a cry for help in the rediscovery of human dignity and it aims at liberation."[72] In Motlhabi's words, black "only secondarily connotes colour. . . . It denotes all the oppressed people in our country irrespective of colour."[73]

In order to appreciate this application of the term "black," it is perhaps necessary to look a little more closely at black theology's secular forerunner, black consciousness. In one sense, of course, it is not strictly accurate to describe black consciousness as "secular," for some of its leading proponents were deeply committed Christians, even though (like Biko himself) they may have had reservations about some aspects of Christian dogma and been highly critical of the churches in South Africa.[74] What was of vital importance in the development of black theology was black consciousness's dynamic philosophy of the dignity of blackness. This has nowhere better been set out than in Biko's address to the SASO in 1971 entitled "The Definition of Black Consciousness" and

---

70. Barney Pityana, "Macht und sozialer Wandel in Südafrika," in *Christus der Schwarzer Befreier,* ed. Theo Sundermeier (Erlangen, 1973), 62.

71. Basil Moore, "What is Black Theology?" *BTSAV,* 16.

72. Document of the Pastoral Institute of the Federal Lutheran Church in South Africa, Consutation at Hermanskraal, quoted in Sundermeier, ed., *Zwischen Kultur und Politik,* 143 n.5.

73. Mokgethi Motlhabi, "Black Theology: A Personal View," *BTSAV,* 77.

74. Biko saw the Christian missions as one powerful historical factor in the denigration of black personality and the destruction of African customs and culture, in that they led converts to "ridicule and despise those who defended the truth of their indigenous religion." Biko is not questioning, as he put it, "the basic truth at the heart of the Christian message," but rather attacking the attitude of those white missionaries who assumed that Christianity had a monopoly on truth and despised native customs and traditions. Biko, *I Write What I Like,* 93-94.

in his contribution to *Black Theology, the South African Voice,* "Black Consciousness and the Quest for True Humanity."[75] Black consciousness, according to Biko, is a necessary corrective to the exploitative dominance of whites in South African society, who seek to justify their position of wealth and privilege by the dogma of the inherent inferiority of black people. Black consciousness combats this situation by opposing white racism with an equally strong positive affirmation of the dignity and value of blackness, "the determination of the black man to rise and attain the envisaged self."[76] In contrast to the white tendency "to depict blacks [as] of inferior status," black consciousness aims to set black people free to see themselves as beings complete in themselves. Blackness is not primarily therefore a matter of skin pigmentation but of mental attitude,[77] in freeing oneself from the connotation that blackness means inferiority and in gladly acknowledging in blackness a positive dignity and the power of true humanity. For Biko the case for black theology rests on its ability to wrestle with the problems of the black man in daily life and to describe Christ as a God who fights against the lie of white domination.

The influence of black consciousness on black theology has been great. While Nyameko Pityana may have overstated the case when he called black theology an extension of black consciousness,[78] it seems clear that it was the latter movement that provided the mainspring for the "South African Voice." As Motlhabi put it, black theology was the religious arm of black consciousness and tried to "relate God and the gamut of religious values to the black man in his situation in South Africa."[79]

75. Both reprinted in *I Write What I Like,* from which page references are taken. It is interesting that Buthelezi also used the concept of "true humanity" for one of his papers in BTSAV.

76. Biko, *I Write What I Like,* 92. Biko describes this opposition in dialectical terms: "The thesis is . . . a strong white racism, and therefore the antithesis to this must be, ipso facto, a strong solidarity among blacks on whom the white racism seeks to prey. Out of these two situations we can therefore hope to reach some kind of balance" (at 90). Hence Biko regarded liberal anti-apartheid "non-racialism" as too weak to deal adequately with the situation in South Africa, and saw "integration" so defined as in fact a tacit unquestioned acceptance of white exploitative values.

77. Biko, *I Write What I Like,* 48; hence those blacks who supported the system, e.g. by joining the security forces of the oppressive regime, were not true blacks.

78. Nyameko Pityana, "What Is Black Consciousness?" *BTSAV,* 62.

79. Motlhabi, 77; compare Scherzberg, 40-44, who also sees black theology as a part of black consciousness.

Motlhabi's statement underlines what is perhaps the major concern of black theology, namely its attempt to deal with the existential situation in which black people find themselves in South Africa. Its concern is with blacks in the totality of the dilemma of oppression. It makes no claim to be absolute but addresses itself to a specific situation in time.[80] It is therefore an unashamedly situational approach to theology.[81] As such it is emphatically a theology of black liberation, but of the liberation of the whole experience — economic, social, political, as well as religious.

That black theology is a manifestation of liberation theology has been emphasized by Bonganjalo Goba.[82] In Goba's view the function of theology in the South African context is essentially to provide the guidelines for a Christian praxis by which the black Christian community can partake in the liberating activity of God in Christ.[83] This will involve analyzing the social and political situation in which blacks find themselves, in order to expose the contradictions within that society and deal with the racial conflicts inherent in it. The role of this "communal praxis" then becomes evident. It will have as its aim social change, and it is only insofar as the black church becomes involved in this process of change that its praxis is relevant. Such change, Goba believes, is intrinsic to the Christian gospel. Thus the basic question facing black theology is, "[H]ow can a black community begin to participate creatively and peacefully in the process of change?"[84] This kind of approach he regards as quite different from Western theology, because its central concern — that of the oppressed — is one with which Western theology does not deal. Western theologians have not been interested in the

80. So Ntawasa: "Black Theology grapples with existential problems and does not claim to be a theology of absolutes" ("The Concept of the Church in Black Theology," *BTSAV,* 111). Similarly Tutu's comment, made in the context of his discussion of black theology, that "all theology is provisional and cannot claim to a universal validity, for any relevant theology must accept the scandal of its particularity, which after all is the price of its relevance" (Desmond Tutu, "Church and Nation in the Perspective of Black Theology," *JTSA* 15 [1976]: 5).

81. So H. J. Becken, "Towards a Relevant Theology for Africa," *Relevant Theology for Africa,* 3; Motlhabi, 77; Theo Sundermeier, "Schwarzes Bewusstsein, schwarze Theologie," in *Christus der schwarzer Befreier,* 29.

82. Bonganjalo Goba, "Doing Theology in South Africa: A Black Christian Perspective," *JTSA* 31 (1980): 22-35.

83. Goba, "Doing Theology," 24.

84. Goba, "Doing Theology," 24.

problem of oppression, he believes, for they have operated within a quite different frame of reference.[85] Black theology therefore has a new theological methodology, which he describes as "theological reflection on hermeneutical praxis."[86] The basis of this praxis is to seek an understanding and analysis of existence in South Africa, which is first based on the black experience and then interpreted in the light of Scripture. The understanding derived from these two sources will in turn provide the stimulus for actual participation in the activity of liberation. Black theology, then, had as its primary goal confronting apartheid with the liberating gospel and thus contributing to the formation of a new and more just society. In that it seeks to change society, it is itself a communal thing — "religion is not a private matter," Goba believes, "but is a public praxis of the Christian faith, which seeks to transform the existing situation."[87] The church's obligation is thus to involve itself fully in transforming the political and social structures that oppress and dehumanize the black population of South Africa. Theology, on this view, becomes a "Christian communal praxis, a theology of the Christian community wrestling with concrete problems as well as providing alternatives in the process of liberation."[88] It is in this context that Christ may be described as black; Christ liberates because he shares our common humanity and shows that "God, in his forsakenness, suffers with us as the one who is crucified."[89]

Goba's article brings together a number of themes that are characteristic of black theology. Basically it was a new method in theology, which, like the theology of liberation in Latin America, finds its rationale in orthopraxis rather than orthodoxy.[90] Its central concern is humankind itself, suffering under an oppressive and dehumanizing system.[91] It therefore grapples with the problems of liberation and the use

85. Goba, "Doing Theology," 35.

86. Goba, "Doing Theology," 25.

87. Goba, "Doing Theology," 27; compare G. Gutiérrez, *A Theology of Liberation* (London, 1974), 10-11.

88. Goba, "Doing Theology," 35.

89. Goba, "Doing Theology," 27; so also A. Moyo, "Christus, Befreier oder Versohner," in *Christus der schwarzer Befreier*, 135-52.

90. E.g., Gutiérrez; R. Alves, *A Theology of Human Hope* (Washington, 1969); J. M. Bonino, *Revolutionary Theology Comes of Age* (London, 1975).

91. Compare Tutu, *Voice of One Crying*, 85-89.

and abuse of power. But unlike some American exponents of black theology, South African blacks see power as residing not with the powerful of this world, but with the oppressed themselves,[92] even as the supreme example of the almightiness of God is shown in his suffering in Christ for mankind. Black theology's base is also firmly in the Scriptures, interpreted through a hermeneutic that seeks to relate those scriptures to the black sociopolitical situation.[93] These themes have received their most extended treatment in the writings of the two leading black theologians in South Africa today, Manas Buthelezi and Allan Boesak, whom we now consider in more detail.

92. So also Tutu, *Voice of One Crying,* 46: "The Gospel of Jesus Christ teaches us that true power lies not with the powerful, but with the powerless for whom he specially cared."

93. Sundermeier can thus compare black theology's approach to the Bible with the "new hermeneutic" of writers like Fuchs and Ebeling ("Schwarzes Bewusstsein, schwarze Theologie," 19, 29).

VII

The South African Voice

1. Manas Buthelezi: Theology and True Humanity

Manas Buthelezi is bishop in the United Evangelical Lutheran Church, former president of the SACC, and cousin of the politician Gatsha Buthelezi. His writings are all too little known outside of his native South Africa, especially in the English-speaking world, perhaps because he has yet to commit his theology to a full-scale work. The most complete exposition of his views is still the seminar he delivered at the University of Heidelberg in 1972, shortly before his brief banning,[1] but he has also been a frequent contributor to theological colloquia in Africa[2] and to the *Journal of Theology for Southern Africa.* Like that of Boesak, Buthelezi's theology essentially addresses what he sees as the theological contradiction in the ideology and practice of apartheid, and it is only against this background that it can be fully appreciated.

Buthelezi acknowledges the seminal role played by writings of Senghor and Nkrumah, and also the importance of black conscious-

1. "Ansätze Afrikanischer Theologie in Kontext von Kirche in Sudafrika in Theologie," *Konfliktfeld Südafrika: Dialog mit Manas Buthelezi,* 33-132.
2. See, e.g., his three contributions to *BTSAV*: "An African or a Black Theology?" 29-35; "The Theological Meaning of True Humanity," 93-103; and *Theological Grounds for an Ethic of Hope,* 147-56. See also "Towards an Indigenous Theology in South Africa," *EG,* 56-75, and "Black Theology, a Quest for the Liberation of Christian Truth," *All African Lutheran Consultation on Christian Theology and Theological Education in the African Context* (Geneva, 1978), 52-59.

ness in pointing the way forward in South African blacks' search for identity. His own concern, however, is essentially theological and, despite the radical new situation in which it operates, stands firmly within the Lutheran and, further back, the biblical tradition. It is this, perhaps, that lends to his theology a pronounced ecumenical dimension. Even as he addresses himself to the peculiarly South African problem of racial conflict, he can still locate it within a much wider context; the localized problem of South Africa is to him part of the much larger problem of brotherhood of believers in Christ. South Africa's crisis is thus really the whole church's problem, that of the solidarity of humankind.

Christian theology, in Buthelezi's view, must be situational in order to be relevant. It must analyze the contemporary situation in which man finds himself with a view to exposing the central questions that confront him. It must then show how the Christian proclamation can address itself to these specific questions.[3] For black people in South Africa the primary problem is simply "Why did God create me black? What should the black person do in this world of white values?" This central question is one with which traditional Christian theology does not have the tools to deal. Western theology deals only with "white" questions; its whole scaffolding is derived from Greco-Roman thought, with appropriate modifications here and there to accommodate the accidents of European Christian history. To address the problem of the black person in South Africa, a whole new theological methodology is called for.[4]

This central problem — that of blackness within a world dominated by white values — is for Buthelezi fundamentally a theological one, and has two aspects.[5] First, there is the question of the meaning of life. Granted that all life derives from the creative act of God's will, can the dehumanization of the life of blacks in South Africa be part of God's plan? How may we answer the cry, "God, show me it is better to live

3. Buthelezi, "Ansätze Afrikanischer Theologie," 39.

4. Compare Bishop Zulu's comment that "the experience which has given birth to Black Theology is unknown to white theologians." "Whither Black Theology?" *Pro Veritate* 11 (1973): 11.

5. Buthelezi, "Ansätze Afrikanischer Theologie," 39; compare "African Theology and Black Theology," *Relevant Theology for Africa*, 18-24, and "Theological Meaning," 93ff.

than not to live"? The second question is that of the wholeness of life. In traditional Africa, religion and physical life belonged together — in contrast to later Western thought, which tended to separate the sacred from the secular. Life was a whole, both in that it was part of a continuity that extended from the dead to the living and in that life, in its true sense, was always believed to be lived under the presence of God himself. Life in its completeness *(impilo)* was both religious and physical, and these two aspects could not be dissociated. The kind of missionary pietism that separated the religious life from the flesh and blood life here and now — either by isolating converts from a lost society by bringing them into the safety of the mission compound, or by projecting blessedness into a hereafter to the neglect of present physical needs — this kind of piety, argues Buthelezi, drew a quite false dichotomy. It destroyed the sense of the wholeness of life that is as much part of biblical tradition as it is of African culture. These questions have a political dimension. Black people in South Africa experience life as one of powerlessness, in which they lack the means to fulfill themselves as they really should be in the sight of God. Their human personalities are dehumanized and systematically destroyed by those who have power over them because of the political, social, and economic machinery through which they operate. Their right to be themselves, to be really human, is rendered void by those who have placed them in subjection to the others' own way of life, and they suddenly come to the realization that they are but caricatures of what they are meant to be.

Clearly we may respond to the dilemma of Africans under apartheid in several different ways, most of them not specifically theological. Thus we may approach it from the ideological viewpoint, the economic, the ethical, and so on. For Buthelezi these are obviously valid grounds for the rejection of an oppressive and unequal system, for apartheid denies to humans what is a basic human right.[6] He is more concerned, however, with a specifically theological dimension. For him authentic humanity is far more than simply an ethical question; it is basically a

---

6. "Contemporary concerns for 'human rights' and 'human dignity' stem from man's quest for self-understanding and self-realisation in the face of dehumanising facets of modern life. Man's elementary possession in this world is *mutatis mutandis* his self . . . his right to selfhood is elementary to man's humanity." Buthelezi, "Theological Meaning," 93.

theological category.[7] Man is authentically human because both in his origins and in his redemption he is a creature of God. According to the biblical testimony man is created in God's image and likeness (Gen. 1:26). This is not an ontological statement but an existential one, for the "image" means the dynamic relationship that exists between God as creator and man as creature.[8] An essential aspect of this relatedness is that man is given "dominion" over the rest of the created universe (Gen. 2:7) as God's representative. To partake in true humanity then must also involve partaking in the dynamic of power — "to be human is to have power to be really human." It is precisely this power of dominion of which South African blacks are deprived, and such a denial of power reduces them to the level of "inhumanness." The real issue in South African society for Buthelezi, therefore, is that black people are denied the right to have dominion over even their own lives. They find instead that they are deprived of their God-given humanity by conditions that others have created through the exploitation of the others' own power of dominion. The argument has turned a full circle and returned to the original dilemma: "Is blackness an obstacle on the road to life we can do nothing about, or is it a context within which God has empowered the black to become truly human?"

Part of the reason for this situation is, according to Buthelezi, the result of the influence of Christian missions in South Africa. Operating hand in hand with the colonial regime, they saw it as part of their function to "civilize" the African, whom they regarded as lacking in culture. Real communication and love were neglected. The missions, on the contrary, described their task in terms of military campaign — "the conquest of the heathen," "the victory of the cross." In Buthelezi's view such an approach was actually a devaluation of the cross, which is not a symbol of might but of love,[9] and the true meaning of which is to point to the infinite worth of all people and the fundamental value of sacrificial service. Such sacrificial love, of which the cross of Christ

7. Buthelezi, "Ansätze Afrikanischer Theologie," 53ff.; "Theological Meaning," 94ff.

8. Compare Mpunzi's statement that creation is "the declaration of relationship. It declares the immediacy of God's relationship with me. It affirms that God loves me as a unique individual, as a father loves his children as unique individuals" ("Black Theology as Liberation Theology," *BTSAV,* 136).

9. Buthelezi, "Ansätze Afrikanischer Theologie," 63.

speaks, above all consists in personal sharing. Seen in this light, the essential principle of mission should not be one of "victory over the heathen" but one of mutual self-giving. Unhappily the history of the church in Africa did not develop in this way, and the dominance of the theology of might over the theology of service opened the door to the justification of the dominance of white over black and to the resulting exploitation of the native population. Worse, the Western world broke in upon blacks so violently that their faculty of choice was overridden. Traditional values became submerged, without providing a viable alternative to the Western way of life, nor did circumstances allow blacks to share fully in this new way of life. The traditional society, in which the concept of the sharing community had been of paramount importance, was destroyed by the rapid advance of a modern cash economy that exalted the role of the individual.[10]

The biblical witness in both Testaments, however, is that the right use of dominion is in service, not in domination. Creation should be rightly used so that its gifts may flow and circulate freely to all. The Christian concept of redemption also points to the divine intention that all may share in the wholeness of life. The Pauline "new creation" (1 Cor. 5:17), attained through the dying and resurrection of Christ and mediated through baptism, opens up for man the potentiality of fullness of life. This life does not operate in abstraction from mundane and created things of the world; rather, it is through them that God mediates his grace, just as the grace of baptism is mediated through the ordinary elements of water, human language, and the human minister. True humanity in Christ, then, does not consist in the bliss of the afterlife, but takes place here and now within the context of daily life on earth. Here again the same question is raised, but in a different form: Can the Christian reach full potential as a human if he (or she) lives under subhuman conditions such as poverty, slavery, and other humiliations? If not, does this mean that some people realize their authentic humanity as redeemed creatures of God only in heaven and not while they live as Christians in this world? Is this really God's plan of redemption?[11] Here then is the paradox with which Buthelezi's

10. Buthelezi, "Ansätze Afrikanischer Theologie," 82-86.
11. Buthelezi, "Ansätze Afrikanischer Theologie," 72ff.; "Theological Meaning," 97ff.

theology seeks to grapple: the Christian faith proclaims that man by his creation is given the power of dominion, and by his redemption has been restored to that dignity. The naked fact is, however, that black people live on the fringes of life and have not been permitted to realize the potential of their true humanity. They have thus become alienated from the wholeness of life — a condition that the non-black conscience has even found possible to rationalize and condone. Black people are thus caught up in a kind of economy of poverty in which they are alienated from the gifts of God. God does indeed offer his gifts to humankind, but black people are not in a position to receive them. It is true, argues Buthelezi, that man does not live by bread alone, but neither, in this world, can he live by the Word alone: both bread and the Word are needed to create the wholeness of life. Forgiveness in Christ does not remove humans from everyday existence; rather, the empirical life here and now in the social, economic, and political arena is our very point of contact with God. To live means to be in that arena in which one receives the life-sustaining gifts and shares these gifts with others. To be cut off from these gifts is to be alienated from the wholeness of life, and for Buthelezi this is poverty in its theological as well as its social sense. Such poverty has a deeper corollary: the Christian faith demands, as its basic ethic, love for one's neighbor. South African blacks, however, standing as they do on the periphery of life, are unable to fulfill this command. They may indeed be new people in Christ, but from the material point of view they are without the power and without the means to fulfill this Christian ideal — they are unable to love their neighbor in this practical Good Samaritan sense. Buthelezi notes that Christian (rather, we should say late Jewish) thinking has tended to identify poverty with blessedness, and thus to accept it as normal and necessary. But, he asks, should the poor continue to be poor so that the rich may have the opportunity to exercise the Christian virtue of charity on their poor (black) neighbors? Should not Christian love demand the eradication of poverty rather than merely its alleviation?[12] What Buthelezi seems to be affirming here is a standpoint that is both typically African and deeply Christian: life is one; the material and the spiritual cannot be divorced, for both come from God and both belong to life in its fullness.

12. Buthelezi, "Ansätze Afrikanischer Theologie," 97.

These main concerns of Buthelezi's theology — the emphasis on the wholeness of life, the problems of powerlessness and poverty, of racism and brotherhood — are not normally the concerns of Western theology. The latter, he believes, has too long dominated Christian Africa, and has been too much concerned with the intellectual approach to the Christian faith and an excessive desire to defend credal and ecclesiastical statements. In the South African context at least, orthodoxy of this kind has been totally inadequate to stimulate Christian praxis — "the ecclesiastical umbrella of confessions and of teaching has been lamentably ineffective against the storms of racism."[13] Christian theology in Africa, therefore, should break away from this European straitjacket.[14]

A further problem with Western theology (at least in its missionary form) Buthelezi believes to be its neglect of the existential dimension, and its consequent tendency towards what he calls "objectification." This is most clearly seen in the "ethnographic" approach to theology,[15] an approach that has something in common with that of some proponents of "African theology," but that Buthelezi regards as the special failing of European Africanists like Tempels, Sundkler, and Taylor. This approach seeks to analyze the traditional worldview and to "baptize" those elements that are in agreement with the gospel. It aims thus to "translate the Christian Gospel into a form congenial to the African mind." Fundamentally, in Buthelezi's view, such a method involves a paradox: it tends to romanticize the past and thus to isolate it from the harsh realities of the present time. "Who can blame the man," he asks, "who can see no sense in writing theological poetics about the golden age of the past, while at the very same time his present human dignity is daily being systematically destroyed?" For Africa is not static, and a Christianity that hankers after a "once upon a time" is in grave danger of appearing irrelevant in the Africa of today with all its problems and

13. Buthelezi, "Ansätze Afrikanischer Theologie," 8.

14. Thus Buthelezi writes that "without freedom to produce heresy theology is not possible" — taking "heresy" in its original sense of "choice" (Manas Buthelezi, "Mutual Acceptance from a Black Perspective," *JTSA* 23 [1978]: 74; also "Black Theology, a Quest," 52-59).

15. See also Buthelezi, "African Theology and Black Theology," 18-24, and "Towards an Indigenous Theology," 56ff. For a further discussion of Buthelezi's approach see my "Theological Methodologies in Africa," *Verbum SVD*, fasc. 1 (1983): 58-61.

pressures. Buthelezi therefore advocates an alternative theological method that he calls "anthropological." The point of departure here is not the past, but rather the Africans themselves as they exist here and now. Man is viewed not as "data" — an object of investigation — but as God's creature, the image of God to whom is entrusted the rest of creation; as "postcolonial" man, who is liberated by Christ from all that dehumanizes him. Thus it is the rediscovery of what it means to be human (as opposed to the ideological and confessional concerns that have marked the Western church) that is the task of theology in Africa. He writes:

> Put in a nutshell, the basic problem of an indigenous theology in Africa is properly not what kind of content such a theology should have (the ethnographic approach), but who should create it: the problem of its *causa efficiens*, the African man himself (the anthropological approach).[16]

Thus

> theology in Africa must reflect the throbbings of the life situation in which people find themselves. . . . A theology of tranquility and dogmatic polish in times of restlessness due to people's alienation from the wholeness of contemporary life can only be the product of dishonesty.[17]

Buthelezi's theological approach is both biblical and situational. While it takes its point of departure from the situation in which black people find themselves in South Africa today, it is equally rooted in the biblical faith, in which the twin poles of creation and redemption are fundamental. His stress on these aspects of Christian doctrine derives from his essential emphasis on true humanity as the focus of Christian theology, for, to him, the integrity of the human identity is what salvation is all about in South Africa today. "How can I be liberated to be my authentic self?" is for Buthelezi a variant of the ancient question, "What must I do to be saved?" This problem of human identity occupies

16. Buthelezi, "Ansätze Afrikanischer Theologie," 111.
17. Buthelezi, "Towards an Indigenous Theology," 70.

the central role because in the South African situation black Christians are being exploited in such a way that their very existence becomes dehumanized and because the exploiters themselves also claim to be Christian. The task of Christian theology, as Buthelezi sees it, is to relate the Christian proclamation to existence in just these conditions. As such it is less reflection than event. It thus has a dynamic liberating quality, and the content of theology becomes one of "doing the truth," of ortho-praxis, rather than of correctness of doctrine. It may indeed, in his view, not always be possible to establish a theoretical basis for action before one acts as a Christian — the theological reflection may be an after-thought to action. The struggle of the gospel therefore is "to further whatever promotes the well-being of man and to destroy whatever oppresses and keeps him in bondage."[18] This struggle may involve suffering, for "to be truly human means to dare to live for Christ, even to the point of suffering for others as Christ did." Such suffering is itself a cause of hope for a new humanity since "on the cross God transformed the experience of suffering at the instance of unprovoked violence into a medium of redemption."[19]

Manas Buthelezi's writings raise a number of important issues, not only for theology in South Africa, but also on the wider ecumenical scene. Few, I imagine, would quarrel with his emphasis on the situational nature of theology, or with his — basically Tillichian — concern that the gospel should address itself to the problem of the culture and society in which it finds itself. Nor again can we seriously doubt that much Western theology appears to have little to say in answer to the kind of questions that still confront black Christians in South Africa today. Granted these assumptions on which black theology proceeds, the two main issues I wish to look at a little more closely at this point are, first, Buthelezi's theological methodology and, second, his biblical hermeneu-tics.

Theo Sundermeier has pertinently questioned Buthelezi's sharp dis-tinction between the "ethnological" and "anthropological" approaches.[20]

18. Buthelezi, "In Christ, One Community in the Spirit," *ATJ* 7, no. 1 (1978): 33-42.
19. Buthelezi, "Violence and the Cross in South Africa Today," *JTSA* 16 (1976): 51-55.
20. Theo Sundermeier, "Theologie zwischen Kultur und Politik," *Zwischen Kultur und Politik,* 22ff.

In Sundermeier's view both are in fact "anthropological," although they operate in different dimensions. Both, he feels, deal with the question of identity, the one in the sphere of cultural alienation, the other within that of social and political oppression. But both have as their aim African selfhood in its wholeness. They may better be regarded, therefore, as overlapping and interrelated. Further, there are, as we noted earlier, leading "African" theologians who have themselves realized that a one-sided emphasis upon the past is sterile unless it also takes account of contemporary sociopolitical issues[21] — an excessive preoccupation with the past is now no longer an issue for most African theologians. One may also perhaps question whether theology can be so radically dehistoricized as Buthelezi appears to do. Buthelezi's interest in the past seems to be dominated largely by the deleterious results of colonialization and of the Christian missions in dehumanizing black South Africans. But it may be asked whether there may not also be a "black past" beyond this that may have some role to play in black theology. And indeed, not only have black theologians themselves sought in some degree to uncover this, but it is also what Buthelezi himself does by his adoption of the very traditional concept of "wholeness" of human life as the centerpiece of his theological reconstruction.[22] In so doing he has admirably demonstrated the immediate relevance of the "traditional" to the contemporary predicament of his people. Buthelezi's aversion to anything that approaches a "Homelands theology" is understandable, and his corrective necessary; but it may be that the lines between his two approaches are too sharply drawn, and that they are closer than he suggests. This does not, of course, at all invalidate his own approach; it merely draws him closer to his fellow African theologians outside of South Africa.

Our second question concerns his use of the Bible. Here Sundermeier has suggested that the hermeneutic of black theology veers towards that of the "new hermeneutic" of writers such as Fuchs and

---

21. See above chapter 2.

22. Buthelezi himself acknowledged that "African Theology" had the "merit" of drawing attention to "positive elements in what is traditionally African" ("African Theology and Black Theology," 20). See also Boesak's comments in Allan Boesak, *Black Theology, Black Power* (London, 1978), 151-52. Biko stressed the positive aspects of black traditional culture in his address to black church leaders in 1971 (Steve Biko, "Some African Cultural Concepts," *I Write What I Like* [London, 1978], 40-42).

Ebeling. There may, it is true, be passages in Buthelezi's writings that could be taken to support such an interpretation. Buthelezi recognizes that the word of God in the Bible is already in what he calls an "indigenous" form, in that it addresses specific people in a specific situation. The task of preaching, in his view, is to "unfold the message of the Bible to the situation of the hearer rather than to unfold and transpose the hearer to the message of the Bible."[23] The African therefore is entitled to interpret the Bible in the light of experience as a black person in the South African context, and Buthelezi believes that it is this approach by black theology that has made the Bible "an open book, in the sense of being a liberating actor, by enabling the black man to think creatively about his spiritual existence."[24] At the same time this does not mean that the primary task of exegesis is bypassed, as Buthelezi's careful exposition of Biblical texts makes clear. What Buthelezi seems above all concerned to do is to avoid a sterile approach to hermeneutics that has no relevance to the existential situation in which present-day humans finds themselves. For him there is no substantial definition of the gospel outside the context of the human situation in which that gospel, the "good news," generates hope. And there is, indeed, a close relationship between certain central categories used by Buthelezi and those found in the Bible. Foremost among these are the categories of wholeness and of poverty. Buthelezi's "human wholeness" is, as we have noted above, a traditional category, but it is also a biblical one, which has an important place in both Testaments.[25] The concept of poverty is more problematic, but it may be reasonably argued that Buthelezi's stress on poverty as alienation is not very far from that of the eighth-century prophets in Israel, although it does differ from the subsequent development of the term in late Judaism.[26] These are theological concepts to which we shall return in the final chapter.

23. Buthelezi, "Towards a Biblical Faith in South African Society," *JTSA* 19 (1977): 55-58.

24. Buthelezi, "The Christian Presence in South Aftica Today," *JTSA* 16 (1976): 8.

25. See further below, p. 202.

26. See below, p. 205.

2. Allan Boesak: A Black Theological Ethic

The most sustained exposition of black theology to come out of South Africa under apartheid was Allan Boesak's *Farewell to Innocence*.[27] Boesak, a "colored" Presbyterian minister, studied in America as well as in Europe and his native South Africa, and is therefore able to place his theology within a wide ecumenical context. He devotes considerable space in his book to a critique of the leading exponents of American black theology — Cone, Preston Williams, Deotis Roberts, and Wilmore, as well as Cleage — and to a discussion of its relevance to South Africa. Boesak describes his book as a "socio-ethical study on black theology and power," and it is his conviction that black theology "as reflection of the praxis of liberation within the black situation must have an ethic of liberation."[28] Here, then, the two recurring themes of his book are highlighted: the meaning of blackness and the ethics of liberation.

Black theology for Boesak is essentially a situational theology, determined by "the situation of blackness."[29] As such it grapples with such questions as "How can one be black *and* Christian? What has faith in Jesus Christ to do with the struggle for black liberation?"[30] Thus the black experience provides the "framework within which blacks understand the revelation of God in Christ." Blackness in this sense embraces the whole of black people's existence. It determines their way of life, which in South Africa excludes them from the privileges enjoyed by whites and from a truly "human" life. Blackness is therefore more than mere skin color; it is rather a "solidarity with suffering,"[31] for the black situation involves "slavery, domination and injustice; being forced to live a life of contradiction and estrangement in their own country."[32]

---

27. Allan Boesak, *Farewell to Innocence* (Maryknoll, 1977), reprinted as *Black Theology, Black Power* (London, 1978). Among Boesak's other important writings are his "Coming in Out of the Wilderness," *EG*, 76-95, and "Liberation Theology in Africa," *ATER*, 169-75. He has also published several collections of sermons and addresses: *The Finger of God* (Johannesburg, 1979), *Walking on Thorns* (Geneva, 1983), and *Black and Reformed* (Braamfontein, 1984).

28. Boesak, *Black Theology*, 142.

29. Boesak, *Black Theology*, 143; "Liberation Theology," 171.

30. Boesak, *Black Theology*, 10ff.

31. Boesak, *Black Theology*, 27.

32. Boesak, *Black Theology*, 29.

As we have seen, the black consciousness movement represented a powerful affirmation of the authentic humanity and dignity of black people, and Boesak sees its role in the development of black theology as indicating that "being black becomes a decisive factor in black people's expression of belief in Jesus Christ as Lord."[33] Black theology then seeks to come to terms with the black situation and to find an authentic Christian ethic for this situation. In Boesak's view this ethic needs to be one of total liberation. Though it is determined fundamentally by the situation in which blacks find themselves in South Africa, it does not have a narrowly racial base, for it seeks the liberation of all the oppressed, black and nonblack.[34] Hence black theology is to be regarded as one manifestation of a worldwide liberation theology, and it has its counterparts elsewhere in the Third World.[35] In common with these, black theology affirms that liberation is not simply one aspect of the gospel, but that it is "the content and framework of the Gospel of Jesus Christ," which "by making of theology a critical reflection on the praxis of liberation places the gospel in its authentic perspective, namely that of liberation."[36] Any theological attempt to justify the political system of apartheid therefore is pernicious because it tries to alienate the gospel from its true context of liberation. The Bible, on the contrary, from the exodus to the resurrection of Jesus, is a record of God's liberating activity.[37] The objects of this liberation in salvation history are the poor, as the first recorded sermon of Jesus makes clear (Lk. 4:18-19). Boesak writes:

> Liberation theology, by beginning with the Exodus, by making theology a critical reflection on the praxis of liberation, places the gospel

33. Boesak, *Black Theology,* 26-27. "Blackness does not in the first place designate colour of skin. It is a discovery, a state of mind, a conversion, an affirmation of being" (at 179).

34. Boesak, *Black Theology,* 144; compare "Coming in," 76ff.

35. Boesak, *Black Theology,* 7. While Boesak protests at those who would draw contrasts between black theology in America and in South Africa, he also clearly points out that, despite a common aim, they are by no means to be naively identified.

36. Boesak, *Black Theology,* 9. One of Boesak's criticisms of Cone is that he takes black theology out of the framework of liberation theology and makes his theme of liberation from white racism the ultimate criterion for all theology (at 143).

37. Boesak, *Black Theology,* 115ff.

in its authentic perspective, namely, that of liberation. It seeks to proclaim the gospel according to its original intention: as the gospel of the poor.[38]

The Christian West has obscured this central message of the Bible in two ways: historically and theologically. Historically Christian missions in Africa bear a heavy burden of responsibility for the present position of black people and especially for the denigration of the black heritage.[39] In addition, Western theology has steadfastly ignored the immediate central problems that are the concern of the non-Western world, problems of the dichotomy between rich and poor, oppressors and oppressed, white and black, and has hidden these problems behind a bland innocence (hence the original title of Boesak's book).[40] The theology of liberation, of which black theology in South Africa is a part, seeks to bring these kinds of polarities to light, and as such "denotes a fundamentally different approach to Christian theology, a new way of looking at the world."[41] In Boesak's view it was the primary contribution of American black theology to draw attention to the need to reorientate theology towards the theme of liberation and to draw out the relationship between theology and power. This new method in theology is not primarily rationalistic; it is in the first place one of a new ethic or praxis. The traditional ethic of white-dominated Christianity was, he believes, unable to take account of the black situation, for it failed to recognize God as God of the oppressed. A new theological form is demanded — a "new wineskin" — in which blacks can express the liberation they experience in Christ.[42] South African black theology is such a new method, one of "doing theology" or praxis. In this respect it is in agreement with Latin American theology of liberation, for which the activity of the church, in its effort to transform the world by service to others, is the starting point of theological reflection.[43] Thus black theology is essentially a theology of experience, a black experience that is shared by

---

38. Boesak, *Black Theology*, 10.
39. Boesak, *Black Theology*, 140; "Coming in," 82ff.
40. Boesak, *Black Theology*, 3.
41. Boesak, *Black Theology*, 2.
42. Boesak, *Black Theology*, 124.
43. Compare G. Gutiérrez, *A Theology of Liberation* (London, 1974), 7ff.

and articulated by the community; and theology itself becomes liberating activity rather than primarily rational reflection.[44] As activity black theology has to grapple with the problem of the ethics of power.

Power, in Boesak's view, is not in itself a negative thing. True, if it is understood in terms of power over others, it may be both evil and exploitative. Real power, however, is power shared with others, power "not as an alienated force, but service to others,"[45] that is, power for creative good. We saw above how Buthelezi emphasized the necessity of power as dominion over one's created self as essential to the Christian life. Boesak agrees that this is an essential first step. Using Tillich's concept of the "courage to be," Boesak sees the affirmation of one's own dignity as a prerequisite to the individual's challenge to illegitimate power. This is the "inner reality, the identification with one's self, self-affirmation." But this cannot survive without the other side of the coin, the "outward practical manifestation of this realisation." For "the power to be, the courage to affirm one's human dignity, must inevitably lead to the transformation of structures to fulfil its search for completion of wholeness."[46]

Power thus has a twofold aspect: the affirmation of one's own self-dignity as a human being and the consequent use of that affirmation in the service of others. The Bible (in the Genesis creation narrative and in Psalm 8) provides the theological grounds for humanity's special relationship with God but also shows that human power is grounded in the power of the Creator. True humanity therefore implies power shared in the service of others in this present, created world, rather than absolute power misused for selfish ends. The problem for black ethics is, then, not power as such, but the way in which power should be used to change oppressive socioeconomic structures. It is in this context that Boesak enters into dialogue with black American theologians insofar as their approaches touch on the situation in which South African blacks find themselves.

It is basic to Boesak's position that blacks in the Republic of South Africa do not simply wish to make their socioeconomic situation better — this would merely be to perpetuate the white values inherent in the

44. Boesak, *Black Theology,* 12-13.
45. Boesak, *Black Theology,* 47.
46. Boesak, *Black Theology,* 49-50.

apartheid structures. Rather they seek to change the system completely.[47] This, in Boesak's view, is precisely what American blacks like James Cone and J. Deotis Roberts do not do; and the latter in particular, Boesak feels, fails to present a sound critique of white society or to define exactly what he means by "equality."[48] For Boesak, transformation of society cannot come about by a superficial reconciliation; still less can it be effected by violence. Responding to Washington's[49] criticism of Martin Luther King, Boesak argues that King was right to reject violence, since "power which comes out of the barrel of a gun is . . . a falsification of authentic power." While retaliatory violence may be a final resort in response to oppression, he believes that this will bring about no real solution and that violence can never, ultimately, be justified.[50] To respond to violence by violence in the South African apartheid situation is to descend to the self-destructive power-ethic of white thinking, and blacks "seeing what violence has done to whites wish to have no part of that."[51] True power, on the contrary, is a gift of love, and power without love is at best inauthentic, at worst demonic. Love and power must be conjoined, and love must be the central element in the exercise of power.[52] This kind of power is supremely revealed in the loving and healing ministry of Jesus in service to men and women.

Boesak's attempt to delineate a theological social ethic for black South Africans, an ethic that seeks to transform the oppressive social structures under which they are forced to live, takes its point of departure from the existential situation of blacks in apartheid South Africa. There are, however, two other bases that intertwine with this situational foundation in Boesak's theology, and these are the biblical and the traditional. While one would anticipate that a Christian minister's (as Boesak then was) thought would be molded by the Bible, it might appear

47. Boesak, *Black Theology*, 133.

48. See J. Deotis Roberts, *Liberation and Reconciliation: A Black Theology* (Philadelphia, 1970).

49. Washington, *Black and White Power Subreption* (Boston, 1969).

50. Boesak, *Black Theology*, 70.

51. Boesak, *Black Theology*, 78. Buthelezi also condemns violence as inconsistent with the spirit of the gospel, although he realizes that many have so experienced white hatred that they have lost the sense of love and reconciliation (Buthelezi, "Violence and the Cross," 54). Boesak's later position on violence will be discussed below.

52. Boesak, *Black Theology*, 95.

at first sight surprising that a writer with such a penetrating concern for the dilemma of blacks in apartheid society should also have a place in his thinking for African traditions. Boesak's interest here is not of Buthelezi's "ethnographic" kind. Rather he is concerned to revive the real values of traditional Africa, which serve the interests of turning society away from the perversions of white domination and oppression to a more humane and just way of life. African tradition is therefore of value insofar as it contributes to the good of contemporary society:

> Black Theology must mean a search for a totally new social order, and in this search it will have to drink deep from the well of African tradition, to use what is good and wholesome for contemporary society.

Again, black theology

> sincerely believes that it is possible to recapture what was sacred in the African community long before white people came — solidarity, respect for life, humanity and community. It must be possible not only to recapture it, but to enhance it and bring it to full fruition in contemporary society.[53]

One aspect that is as important for Boesak as for Buthelezi is that of human wholeness. Wholeness is a unifying concept that seeks to integrate the complete life of men and women — the religious with all economic, psychological, and cultural values. But wholeness is also the ground of Boesak's theological hermeneutic, and as such, it provides a link between the Christian and the traditional. Wholeness in this sense is a concept that seeks to liberate blacks from a cultural dependence on the "departmentalised theology blacks have inherited from the western world" and to create instead a "biblical, holistic theology."[54] Black theology, in aiming at the totality of God's liberation, seeks to realize this wholeness and fullness of life.[55] It is in this sense that Christ may be described as black, for the black Christ may be received as a brother, whereas the Christ of the whites

53. Boesak, *Black Theology*, 151-52.
54. Boesak, *Black Theology*, 13.
55. Boesak, *Black Theology*, 141.

is foreign to black experience — he is, in Makhatini's words, "an *umlungu*, a white man [who] instead of becoming one of us, a brother, becomes our *nkosana,* the 'boss' himself."[56] This affirmation of the blackness of Jesus, the black Messiah, is a protest against the perversion of the name of Christ by whites who throughout (Christian) history have enslaved and oppressed blacks. To discover his significance for blacks today, it is necessary to stress the continuity between the "historical Jesus" and the "black Messiah," for this continuity has an especial relevance for those who are black. Consequently black theology is "not prepared to separate the reality of the historical Jesus from the reality of his presence in the world today."[57] Jesus indeed was truly the incarnation of God, but what brings him close to South African blacks is rather his identification with the poor and the suffering, among whom he was born and lived, and for whom he came. Boesak writes:

> He belonged to a poor, downtrodden people, oppressed and destitute of rights in their own country, and subjugated to countless daily humiliations under foreign rulers. He lived and worked among the poor, and from among these came his disciples.

Jesus, as Messiah, shared the same kind of deprivations that blacks in South Africa did:

> He knew what it was like to live without having a sense of belonging, to be ready to flee for his life at a moment's notice, to be on the alert constantly so as not to fall into traps of the informers. He lived on earth very much the same way as blacks are forced to live.[58]

Jesus is thus the one with whom blacks can identify, and is for them a black Messiah. However, he is also the one who overcame through his death and resurrection, by which he saves and liberates his people. Jesus' liberating activity affirms the infinite worth of the human personality and the love of God for the oppressed. He was, in this sense, a divine radical, a disturber of the established order, a revolutionary. As

56. Boesak, *Black Theology,* 56, quoting an unpublished paper by Makhatini.
57. Boesak, *Black Theology,* 41.
58. Boesak, *Black Theology,* 43-44.

black Messiah he takes the oppression of humanity upon himself and "restores wholeness to the broken and fragmented lives of those who trust him for their liberation."[59]

Boesak is deeply concerned to relate the black experience of liberation through Christ to the Scriptures, for to him the Bible is the ultimate criterion of theology. Thus while black theology is "critical reflection on historical praxis," it is at the same time "a critical reflection *in the light of the Word of God*" (Boesak's italics),[60] and all such reflection is to be judged by the gospel. The biblical *loci classici* here are the exodus narrative in the Old Testament and the synagogue sermon of Jesus (Lk. 4:18-21) in the New.[61] Boesak denies, however, that his use of scripture is selective, for he sees liberation as the central theme of the whole Bible. He believes that in the New Testament liberation has its base in the central events of the cross and resurrection: "Exodus and resurrection, cross and liberation, are not disparate entities, but are caught up in the same liberating movement, represent the same divine reality effected by the same liberating God."[62]

Although Boesak understands the exodus and Jesus' Nazareth sermon as real events, he uses them primarily as paradigms, by means of which the theological category of liberation may be applied to the contemporary situation.[63] Boesak's scriptural base agrees with the general approach of liberation theology, and his hermeneutical method has affinities with the "new hermeneutic." There are, I believe, problems involved in both these aspects, which are, of course, much wider than South African black theology. In Boesak's case the assumptions involved in such a methodological approach are susceptible to the kinds of ob-

---

59. Boesak, *Black Theology*, 43-44. For a sustained exposition of this type of christology see Takatso Mofokeng, *The Crucified among the Crossbearers* (Kampen, 1983).

60. Boesak, *Black Theology*, 12; so also at 121: "Black Theology should continue to cultivate self-critical reflection inder the Word of God within the situation of blackness." Compare Gutiérrez, 11: "[T]heological reflection would then be necessarily a criticism of society, and the Church, insofar as they are called and addressed by the Word of God."

61. Boesak's exegesis of Luke 4 stresses the literal meaning of "the poor," which is neglected by many commentators (Boesak, *Black Theology*, 20-26).

62. Boesak, *Black Theology*, 122.

63. Compare Moltmann's idea of the "exodus church" in *The Theology of Hope* (London, 1967), 30ff.

jections that have been raised against the use of Scripture in political theology generally. We shall come back to this problem, insofar as it affects Boesak's exegesis of the Bible, in the final chapter. However, Boesak's book remains a convincing attempt to grapple with the problem of a Christian ethic, based on the Bible, which will relate the gospel to the circumstances of oppression and exploitation.

3. The Second Stage in Black Theology

By the time Boesak's *Farewell to Innocence* appeared, in 1977, it seemed as though black theology was losing some of its initial momentum. This was partly no doubt due to the absence of an organizational base and thus lack of financial backing. The South African Students' Organization (SASO) and Black Peoples' Convention (BPC) had been banned by the South African government some years before. The Universities' Christian Movement, which had organized a black theology project, dissolved itself later when the Schlebusch Commission was appointed to investigate its activities along with those of the Christian Institute and the National Union of South African Students (NUSAS). After a lull of several years the prophetic mantle fell upon the Institute of Contextual Theology (ITC), a new organization with Frank Chikane as its secretary. Not long afterwards, of course, the political climate was also undergoing severe strains. On the one hand President Botha was attempting to relax some of the more blatant anomalies of apartheid; especially important in this respect was the scrapping of the pass laws, and the restrictions on the use of public facilities were also being eroded.[64] On the other hand, black (and some white) resistance to the whole structure of apartheid was becoming progressively more fierce and the government's response to it increasingly repressive. A state of emergency was declared in 1985, and thousands were arrested.[65]

Against this background a group of theologians and church leaders

---

64. Though of course these moves failed to tackle the central issue of the political representation of blacks. The tricameral parliament set up in 1984 gave representation to Indians and Coloured but excluded blacks.

65. It is estimated that during 1985 about 11,500 South Africans (including some 2000 children) were detained without trial, and a further 25,000 were charged with crimes of violence — though many of these were never brought to court.

of all races came together in Soweto to formulate their response to the political crisis in South Africa. The Kairos Document,[66] as it came to be known, was released in September 1985 and quickly ran through several reprintings, gathering ever more signatories. In the view of the writers, the critical dilemma facing the churches in South Africa was that in the apartheid conflict Christians were ranged against each other, and were to be found on both sides, for "both oppressor and oppressed claim loyalty to the same church."[67] Response to apartheid differed according to different theological presuppositions. The document identified three different theological responses. First there was what it called "State Theology." This had been the traditional response of the Afrikaner churches, and was simply an attempt to justify the status quo "by a misuse of theological concepts and biblical texts for political purposes."[68] The English-speaking churches, on the other hand, generally took a different option. Eschewing the blatant extremism of state theology, they made limited criticisms of apartheid, and pressed for reconciliation, nonviolence, and justice. This approach the Kairos Document terms "Church Theology." The fallacy it saw in this position was a futile attempt to reconcile irreconcilables — good with evil, God with Satan. There can be no true reconciliation, it argued, until injustice is removed, and there can be no true forgiveness without repentance. True justice in South Africa was therefore not a matter of reforms introduced by the white rulers, but rather of a complete change of the structures of whole apartheid systems. Nor is the question of violence a simple one. What was happening in South Africa, the Kairos theologians argued, was that violence was being employed by the state to suppress the legitimate aspirations of non-whites; it was an institutional, structural violence, perpetrated by the security forces and backed by the law. The document reminded its readers that there is a long Christian tradition that permits the use of physical force to defend oneself against oppression. Thus one cannot in the nature of the case simply rule out all violence as illegitimate for the Christian. The fundamental problem with church theology was, in the view of the Kairos Document, a failure to

---

66. *Challenge to the Church: A Theological Comment on the Political Crisis in South Africa* (Braamfontein, 1985).

67. *Challenge to the Church*, 2.

68. *Challenge to the Church*, 3.

recognize and to analyze aright the inherently violent structures of the apartheid system. Taking refuge in an other-worldly pietism, it failed to become involved in the active struggle to change the evils of the apartheid as an institution.

The only valid Christian response to apartheid was to be found in what the document calls "Prophetic Theology." The crisis of South Africa was not a simple racial conflict, but rather one between justice and injustice, the oppressed and the oppressor. The Scriptures witness to this sociopolitical conflict between good and evil by showing God as one who liberates the oppressed. Consequently, for the Christian "a tyrannical regime has no moral legitimacy." By subjecting the interests of the many to that of the few "it has made itself an enemy of the people and thus an enemy of God."[69] Love towards one's enemies, in these circumstances, may best be served by eliminating the oppression, removing the tyrants from power, and establishing a just government for the common good of all people.[70] To this end the Kairos theologians issued a challenge for action, including civil disobedience.

Less than a year after the appearance of the Kairos Document the South African government renewed its emergency legislation. Apart from draconian censorship laws, the Public Safety Act was amended to permit initial detentions for up to 180 days, in place of the original two weeks. Civil unrest and systematic repression continued unabated.[71]

It is not surprising, in the light of these traumatic events, that black theology took a new direction — or perhaps one should say, several new directions — and that, as Motlhabi has put it, a new stage in black theology appeared.[72] Some of the older voices were still to be heard —

---

69. *Challenge to the Church*, 19.

70. *Challenge to the Church*, 20.

71. Especially disturbing was the increasing involvement of children and their detention by the security forces. It has been estimated that between 30 and 40 percent of the 30,000 people detained in the ten months following the declaration of the state of emergency were under the age of 18. Equally tragic was the continued feuding between blacks themselves.

72. In the introduction to *The Unquestionable Right to Be Free*, ed. Itumeleng Mosala and Buti Thlagale (Johannesburg, 1986), xiii. This book is a collection of papers given at the Institute for Contextual Theology's conferences in 1983-84. For an overview of the "second stage," see my "Marxism, Black Theology, and the South African Dilemma," *Journal of Modern African Studies* 28, no. 3 (1990): 527-34.

Tutu and Boesak increasingly in their published addresses, Setiloane with his exploration of traditional theology, Goba and Maimela in books that addressed the sociopolitical issues[73] — but the urgent thrust of black theology increasingly passed to a younger generation of theologians: Itumeleng Mosala, Buti Tlhagale, Frank Chikane, Takatso Mofokeng, and others, both priests and academics. Their interests are in many ways more varied than those of their predecessors. The urgent issue of the legitimacy of violence has naturally provoked much debate,[74] but other and newer issues have also occupied these younger black theologians. There is, for example, a new interest in the origins of black theology in South Africa, an attempt to push its roots further back and to relate it especially to the African independent churches,[75] and there is also a greater openness to traditional religious values. An attempt is being made, too, towards a more coherent black christology, and a small but vocal feminist theology is also beginning to emerge.[76] Perhaps more significant is a sharpening of the concept of blackness, together with a much less critical approach to American black theology than was evident in earlier writers like Boesak. Above all, there has been a very apparent ideological shift on the part of several of the younger generation of black theologians, in that the underpinning of much of their theology is characterized by an explicit acceptance of Marxist presuppositions and analysis. Motlhabi indeed goes so far as to claim that "the historical-materialist sociological approach has become the

73. E.g., Desmond Tutu, *Hope and Suffering* (Braamfontein, 1983); Allan Boesak, *Walking on Thorns* (Geneva, 1983) and *Black and Reformed* (Johannesburg, 1985); Gabriel Setiloane, *African Theology* (Johannesburg, 1986); Bonganjalo Goba, *An Agenda for Black Theology, Hermeneutics for Social Change* (Johannesburg, 1988). Maimela's *Proclaim Freedom to My People* (Johannesburg, 1987) is largely a collection of earlier papers.

74. See especially *Theology and Violence: The South African Debate,* ed. C. Villa-Vicencio (Johannesburg, 1987).

75. See, e.g., the contributions of Mofokeng and J. Ngbane to *The Unquestionable Right to Be Free,* and Itumeleng Mosala, "African Independent Churches, a Study in Sociological Protest," in *Resistance and Hope: South African Essays in Honour of Beyers Naude,* ed. C. Villa-Vicencio and J. W. de Gruchy (Cape Town, 1985).

76. Itumeleng Mosala, "The Relevance of African Traditional Religions and Their Challenge to Black Theology," in *The Unquestionable Right to Be Free,* 91ff.; Mofokeng, *The Crucified among the Crossbearers.* For emerging feminist theology see the contributions by Bernadette Mosala and Bonita Bennett in *The Unquestionable Right to Be Free.*

basis for a black theology of liberation."[77] This African betrothal of the Christian faith with Marxist ideology remains significant, and, though some of the writers reflecting this approach have attracted more interest in the West than in their home country, it deserves more extended comment. In the remainder of this chapter I shall therefore attempt to review some of the younger black theologians' writings, examining particularly their use of Marxist thought to explicate their theology.

The second stage in black theology is, even more that the initial period, a vigorous reaction against the assumption that Christian theology can be uncommitted. While earlier writers, like Buthelezi and Tutu, had rejected the Western approach to Christian theology as inadequate for the needs of the black church, the younger generation has gone further, attacking also concepts such as "contextualization," which have found acceptance in the Third World. Itumeleng Mosala, for example, sharply protests against the idea of "theological harmlessness," that is, a theology that claims it has a neutral base. For him the Western theological tradition is "a most pernicious religious version of capitalist ruling class ideology,"[78] based upon Western idealism. Mere "contextual" theology is also inadequate, for in South Africa it is espoused by the white privileged classes and does not adequately reflect the needs of the oppressed. "Contextual" theology is only valid, in Mosala's view, if the context is that of the exploited and oppressed themselves, reflecting their own standpoint. These views are endorsed by Frank Chikane, for whom theological neutrality means in practice siding with oppressors and thus maintaining the status quo and the privilege of the ruling class.[79] Theology is thus, in Maimela's words, essentially a matter of "taking sides with the victims of society against the victimisers,"[80] which in South Africa today means solidarity with the black majority against their white exploiters.

The primary task of black theology is seen (as in Latin American

77. Motlhabi, *The Unquestionable Right to Be Free,* vii.

78. Mosala, "African Independent Churches," 103. A selection of Mosala's papers reflecting his materialist hermeneutic have appeared under the title of *Biblical Hermeneutics and Black Theology in South Africa* (Grand Rapids, 1989).

79. F. Chikane, "Doing Theology in a Situation of Conflict," in *Resistance and Hope,* 101-2.

80. S. Maimela, "Current Themes and Emphases in Black Theology," in *The Unquestionable Right to Be Free,* 105.

theology of liberation) as the analysis of the society in which blacks have to live. The tools for this task should no longer be those of idealist philosophy but "the use of social analytical tools such as those developed by Marx and other social scientists."[81] Buti Tlhagale, a Catholic priest who has worked extensively in Soweto, sees the South African church as faced with a crisis of faith, because institutional Christianity has, in the history of the nation, too uncritically and too easily accepted established political and economic structures, including the apartheid system. This has (as he puts it) "rendered the credibility of Christianity increasingly questionable."[82] In Tlhagale's view, if the Christian faith is to demonstrate that it is still valid in South Africa today, it will have to do so by using the approach of historical materialism, for only so can it show that it has something to say about the blatant inequalities in South African society. The starting point of this social analysis must be real people — black people — and the material conditions under which they live.[83] Thus he develops what he calls a "black theology of labour." Human labor in the Marxist understanding, according to Tlhagale, leads to collective growth, and thus to human beings becoming what they are meant to be. The biblical tradition is not incompatible with this, for in one biblical tradition at least, human action is part of a process of co-creation with God.[84] However, the situation in South Africa is a travesty of these ideals. In a white-dominated capitalist economy, black workers are merely objects in the production process; labor is not for self-realization but for the prosperity of the elite who control the means of production. For Tlhagale all "white" theology, despite its talk of the "option for the poor," fails to come to grips with this central issue. Black theology, on the other hand, seeks to be revolutionary. It is not concerned simply with the charitable alleviation of the lot of poor blacks; rather, it seeks to awaken an assertiveness in the workers themselves. "The more workers labour in accordance with their free will, in response to their material needs, the more the image of God becomes a reality."[85] Labor is for the benefit of the worker; capital is a communal, not a

---

81. Chikane, 102.
82. B. Tlhagale, "Towards a Black Theology of Labour," in *Resistance and Hope*, 126.
83. Tlhagale, 127.
84. A concept found in rabbinic Judaism and reflected in 2 Cor. 6:1.
85. Tlhagale, 130-31.

privileged, possession; and material goods are for all, not for the few elite. Herein lies the basis for a theology of labor.[86]

Tlhagale's concerns have been echoed in Mosala's concept of a "working class theology." He sees this as having its roots in the African past and as having been disrupted by the capitalist economy that accompanied the advent of Western Christianity into Africa. This traditional way of life he finds continued, despite mission Christianity, in the independent churches, especially the Zionists. Traditional religions, in Mosala's view, are the "product of two precapitalist African historical bases," namely primitive African communal societies and African feudalism. These were the social and economic contexts from which African traditional religions "took root and flourished."[87] Colonialism (and with it Christianity) introduced a new element, capitalism, which in the beginning coexisted with the old system but in time led to its decay and superseded it. African traditional religion therefore represents the "point at which the historical development of Africans was arrested and halted."[88] Consequently, he believes, it has an important role to play in the creation of a valid black theology, for a major task of such a theology is to oppose and contradict Western capitalism. The independent churches he sees as the logical successors, in economic terms, of traditional feudal African societies, and they are therefore to be regarded as examples of a working-class theology. They stand thus in sharp contrast to the capitalist mainstream churches; and, in Mosala's view, it is in them, with their working-class culture, that the real hope for theology lies. For him Marxist social analysis is a more fruitful model for the interpretation of the independent churches than any other model yet used by scholars.[89] Mosala's papers on this theme are characterized by a determinist view of the origins of development of religion and theology, derived in essence from his Marxist base. He thus quotes with

86. See also Mofokeng's emphasis on theology as the task of the community in Takatso Mofokeng, "The Evolution of the Black Struggle and the Role of Black Theology," in *The Unquestionable Right to Be Free*, 113-28.

87. Mosala, "Relevance of African Independent Churches," 97.

88. Mosala, "Relevance of African Independent Churches," 98.

89. Mosala, "Relevance of African Independent Churches," 110. Mosala goes so far as to claim that culture is not ethnic but based on class. If this is accepted, then presumably much "African theology" (i.e., cultural theology) would be rendered irrelevant.

approval the assertion that "it is a people's consciousness which deter-mines their being, but the social being that determines their conscious-ness."[90] Not surprisingly, any idea of religious charisma (in Weber's sense) is dismissed as part and parcel of an altogether pernicious West-ern idealism.

A somewhat similar point of view has been suggested by Takatso Mofokeng, with his emphasis on theology as a grassroots community praxis. Mofokeng sees the conscientization process of earlier black the-ologians as only an initial stage. In his view, it soon developed into what he calls "an instrument of theological reflection on the entire evolving liberation praxis," which was marked by, among other things, self-reli-ance projects.[91] In other words, black theology has become a mass participation movement, including black lay Christians as well as black theologians. Black theology therefore is now not simply (as originally) a theoretical reflection upon Christian action in the light of the Bible; in this second stage there is a reciprocal movement in which "the praxis of committed blacks falls upon the Bible itself, making it comprehen-sible." Scripture is interpreted in the light of black liberating praxis, rather than vice versa. We have arrived at this point at the problem of biblical hermeneutics, and the approach to hermeneutics plays a key role in the theology of the younger black theologians we have been discussing.[92] Many of the issues that they raise in this connection have indeed been raised before by the so-called new hermeneutic and by the more recent sociological approaches to the Bible, and I shall refer to some of these issues in the final chapter. In what remains of this section I will make only general comments on the Marxist stance of the second stage in black theology.

First, concerning their use of Marxist theory. There is a difference between adoption of the method of Marxist social analysis for an elucidation of the role of the Christian faith in our time on the one hand, and the much more complete adoption of Marxist materialism as a base for theology on the other. In the light of the powerful exposures

90. Mosala, "Relevance of African Independent Churches,"108.

91. Mofokeng, "Evolution of Black Struggle," 123.

92. For an analysis and critique of the biblical hermeneutics adopted by Mosala, see my "The Marxist Trend in Recent South African Black Theology: Is Dialogue Possible?" in *Mission Studies* 12, no. 6 (2) (1989): 77-86.

by Latin American theologians of the malaise of our times through the use of the first, few can seriously doubt its value. The adoption of Marxist ideology, however, is much more problematic for theology, for there are inherent contradictions between Christianity and Marxism that cannot so easily be reconciled. Some of these issues have been well discussed in the West, but black theologians do not seem yet to have come very clearly to grips with them.

Second, we may certainly agree that no theology is neutral, however much it may claim to be. All theologians have their presuppositions, and it is salutary to be reminded that too much Western theology has proceeded on the assumption that Western idealism has the monopoly on the truth. But this is an argument that cuts both ways. Theologians who work from a Marxist base have equally all too often proceeded on the assumption that dialectical materialism is likewise the only truth there is, and — perhaps more dangerously — that to question this assumption is to be an enemy of the poor and oppressed.[93] To quote, with apparent concurrence, that the premises on which Marx and Engels based their theories "can be verified in a purely empirical way,"[94] is not to prove a fact, but to take an option and express a preference for a particular explanation of the world. Marxism may indeed be a viable option for South Africa, but be that as it may, it remains one option among many possible ones, and one that is no more "scientific" than others.

Finally, there is the problem of language. Michael Polyani, in his great book *Personal Knowledge,* has well exposed the facade of much Marxist writing in its use of emotional rhetoric under the spurious guise of apparently scientific assertions.[95] Rhetoric is also a continual danger to any theology that expects to stir the heart as well as the head. When Marxist convictions are espoused to theological ones, the danger of overwhelming the reader by rhetorical bombastics is doubled. What is required is a calm and careful analysis of the meaning behind the emotive terminology — meaning that may well turn out to be loosely defined, inexact, and confused. Problems such as these seem to me as yet

93. A point well made by Lesslie Newbigin in *The Open Secret* (Grand Rapids, 1978), ch. 8.

94. So Mosala, "Relevance of African Independent Churches," 107.

95. Michael Polyani, *Personal Knowledge* (London, 1958).

to have been insufficiently considered by proponents of the second stage in South African black theology, and will need to be faced if it is to provide a genuine basis for a political theology that will be more than ephemeral.

The dramatic changes that resulted in the unbanning of the ANC, the release of Mandela, and the final dismantling of the apartheid state, and that culminated in free multiracial elections, have demanded that Christian theology in South Africa address itself to new issues. What Mosala has called "Black Theology after Mandela" has yet to take definite shape. White theologians like Villa-Vicencio and John de Gruchy are now turning their attention to issues of reconstruction,[96] and there is no doubt that the implications of this, too, will have to be a major part of the black agenda.

However that may be, what is so remarkable to those who stand outside of the dilemma of blacks in South Africa today is the extraordinary way, despite all to the contrary, in which black theologians have retained not only their Christian faith but also their conviction that reconciliation in that country is still possible. Their writings are a moving reminder of the power of the gospel of love in the face of almost impossible odds.

96. So C. Villa-Vicencio, *A Theology of Reconstruction* (Cambridge, 1994). The *International Review of Mission* 83 (1994) devotes the whole issue to the situation in South Africa and the way forward.

VIII

Enduring Problems

In the preceding chapters I have attempted to examine the writings of leading theologians in Africa, as far as possible allowing them to speak for themselves. From time to time I have offered specific criticisms of particular arguments raised by individual theologians. In this final chapter I shall attempt to isolate some of the most pressing problems that seem to me to emerge from African Christian theology today. Some of these problems have been made explicit by African writers themselves, but others have remained as underlying assumptions. Such issues need to be exposed, for they not only have an importance for the future of Christian theology in Africa but also have a much wider ecumenical significance.

These central issues are grouped around two main areas: first, the methodology or approach to dogma and to the Bible, and second, the place of the black experience in constructing theology. These two areas are equally the concern of both "African" and "black" theology (or "cultural" and "liberation" theologies). Indeed it should be evident now that a dichotomy between these two approaches cannot legitimately be sustained.[1] While they represent differing emphases, which result largely from historical factors, there is a unity in the theological task throughout Africa that derives from its common concern and its common sources.

---

1. See also above, chapter 2. It seems to me that Emmanuel Martey's otherwise informative book *African Theology* greatly overstates a supposed dichotomy between what he terms "inculturation" and "liberation" theologies in Africa.

Its concern is to relate the Christian faith to contemporary African life; its common sources lie in the Bible and Christian tradition on the one hand, and in the African heritage and present experience, in its widest sense, on the other. The use that theologians make of these sources, their assumptions as to their usefulness and authority, the relative weight they attribute to each — these factors will clearly affect both the method and the final result. In essence, however, there is no disagreement as to the fundamental sources that lie at the base of the task of theology in Africa.

1. The Theological and Biblical Method

African theologians are agreed that Christian theology in Africa stands in need of a new approach, a new method, that will not be determined by "white" or "European" presuppositions. The approaches inherited from the Western world are regarded as inadequate, both because they do not deal with the kind of questions that are relevant to the African context, and also because they lack even the means to enter into those problems.[2] Such problems may be ones of cultural or religious experience (such as the centrality of the ancestors) or sociopolitical concerns that have their roots in the legacy bequeathed by the colonial era. Either way, Western theology is seen as lacking the tools to take up these kinds of theological challenge.

It is clear enough that Western theology operates from Christian or increasingly post-Christian cultures, and not from cultures that, as in Africa, are to a large degree still dominated by a traditional non-Christian heritage. The closest parallels to the African situation in this respect lie not in modern Europe and America, but in the early centuries of Christian expansion in the ancient world and in the emergent Christianity of some Asian countries. In seeking answers to the relationship of the Christian faith to traditional African religion and culture, African theologians may find stimulation and guidance in these similar situa-

---

2. As Tutu remarked, "The white man's largely cerebral religion was hardly touching the depths of his African soul; he was being redeemed from sins he did not believe he had committed; he was being given answers, and often splendid answers, to questions he had not asked." Desmond Tutu, "Whither African Theology?" *CIA*, 366.

tions in the history of the church — the one in the distant past, the other very much still with us. Kwame Bediako has brilliantly demonstrated the relevance of the early church for the study of African theology, and the Ecumenical Association of Third World Theologians is doing good work in attempting to bring together Christians outside the Western world to discuss mutual problems.[3] At the same time, contemporary Western theology should not be too easily dismissed. Some African theologians have had a tendency to assume that to label something "Western" is to demonstrate its invalidity for Africa. African theologians who reject Western theology — or indeed any other theology — need to show that they have a clear grasp of what it is they are rejecting and that they have cogent arguments for doing so. It is also important that they ask whether what is called "Western" may not also have a solid base in the Scriptures and in Christian tradition. And after all, if Augustine — a North African — could so much influence a Luther, a Calvin, or a Barth, perhaps there is no great danger in the latter influencing contemporary African theologians. What is surely demanded is a critical discernment in adopting, with appropriate modifications, what is relevant and helpful in Western and European theology, while leaving aside what is not.[4]

A different side to this question has been commented upon with some sharpness by Benézét Bujo: the tendency of some African scholars to write and publish with a Western, rather than an African, audience in mind.[5] I have already noted the problem of the language in which theology in Africa is written, and it is significant that there have been exciting developments in vernacular languages. However, it is probably inevitable that any African theology intended for more general consumption will have to be available in English or French. What is less defensible is the tendency seen in some African writers to publish their work exclusively in the West (often at what are, by African standards, excessive prices) and with an eye to the plaudits of Western academics rather than to the usefulness of their work to the African church. Aspects of Third World theologies (not least those reflecting a degree of political radicalness) can

3. See especially the publication *Voices of the Third World*.

4. E. Fasholé-Luke, "The Quest for African Christian Theology," *JRT* 32, no. 2 (1975): 82.

5. Benézét Bujo, *African Theology in its Social Context* (Maryknoll, 1992), 72.

too easily become fascinating exotics for a Western élitist audience rather than a source of nourishment to Christian life in Africa. It is scarcely necessary to point out that the exodus of a number of gifted African theologians to positions in Europe and America (for whatever reasons) is also a trend that will need to be reversed if Christian thought in Africa is to reach its full potential. These questions of the language in which African theology should be done, the audience to which it is directed, its publication and distribution, and the return of the African theological diaspora to its own continent are all serious issues that need to be honestly addressed by the younger generation of African Christian leaders.

It is not surprising that because of the traumatic experiences of colonialism many African theologians have concluded that "white" theology was unable to deal from the inside with the problems of the oppressed and the poor. In this respect the voices of Latin American theology of liberation and of American black theology have struck a more sympathetic note. The danger here may be that the slogans of these movements may be accepted without a critical examination of either their inner coherence or the validity of their application to the African situation.[6] Writers like Jean-Marc Éla have amply demonstrated that the insights and methods of liberation theology can be applied to the African context to great effect, and, conversely, Allan Boesak made a thoroughgoing critique of American black theology.

The basic problem facing African theologians, as Kwesi Dickson has pointed out,[7] is really one of the theological categories in which

6. Ruvimbo Tekere's reaction to Latin American theologians in Brazil in 1980 was significant. While acknowledging their real contribution, he vigorously pointed out that they were themselves guilty of cultural oppression in that "the rich cultural attributes of the Indians and blacks have been ignored in conformity with the ruling dominant class." Such cultures were, he argued, also a gift from God, and a fusion of these cultural traditions with Christianity is critical for Latin American theology (*The Challenge of Basic Christian Communities*, ed. S. Torres and J. Eagleson [Maryknoll, 1981], 258). In essence Latin American theology of liberation was both Western and ideological and at that time in danger of becoming yet another theological imposition upon Africa and Asia. Fortunately discerning Latin Americans came to realize this and to acknowledge that they stood in need both of the typically African emphasis in theology of cultural liberation and of the Asian dimension of doing theology from the situation of religious plurality.

7. Kwesi Dickson, *Theology in Africa* (London, 1984), 119; also Tutu, "Whither African Theology?" 369.

they should work and of the need to forge out for themselves new and more relevant ones. What has not yet emerged with any clarity is precisely what these new categories are that will suit theology in Africa. Some of the leading concerns of African theologians, such as culture, humanity, poverty, and oppression, might well prove to be more viable as theological categories than the traditional divisions of systematic theology, and might help theologians to break out of the straitjacket of the Western dogmatic heritage. However, it could be argued that even the most innovative of African theologians have hesitated to jettison the parameters of Chalcedonian language. In Pobee's christology, for example, the definition of Christ as human and divine is accepted as a given. But the question of what exactly "humanity" and "divinity" mean in the African worldview (as compared with the Greek one), and whether this might lead to a deepened understanding of the person of Christ, is not really explored. In one way African theology has yet to move toward a more radical questioning of the received theological terminology. If it is accepted that all theological language is ultimately metaphorical, then the African theological task becomes one of seeking the appropriate African metaphors to replace those of the Western tradition.[8] This is most pressing in the area of christology, for if theology neglects this, whatever else it may be, it cannot legitimately claim to be Christian. This does not mean that African theology should concern itself with a restatement of the philosophical and abstract statements of the ecumenical creeds. But it must surely retain the centrality of Christ and seek to explicate his significance within the total being of the Godhead. As Maurice Wiles has remarked, Christian theology may begin with either the doctrine of God or the doctrine of Christ; but "the only rule that should have absolutely binding force is that these two areas of discussion must be allowed to interact upon one another all the time."[9]

8. In the earlier German edition of this book, I was inclined to agree with Wiles that "however innovative the theologian may, and must, be he cannot avoid the old imagery, even though his understanding of it may be radically different" (Maurice Wiles, *The Remaking of Christian Doctrine* [London, 1974], 121-22). Now I am not so sure that this is the way foward (at least for non-Western theology). It may well be that the old imagery does have to be abandoned if the Christian faith is to be relevant in Africa, and that African theologians have not yet gone far enough in reinventing new imagery.

9. Wiles, 41-42.

It seems to me it is precisely here where the most outspoken representatives of the view that there is a radical continuity between the idea of God in African religions and in Christianity appear to fail. What Idowu, Kibicho, Setiloane, and others seek to demonstrate really has little to do with the Christian doctrine of God, for they neglect the Christ-aspect, which is its most characteristic element. What these theologians are really doing is making a comparison between the concepts of God in Africa and in ancient Judaism; even if their case were demonstrated (and I personally do not think it is), it would scarcely be relevant. The specifically Christian aspect of the Godhead, the sharing of Christ in the being of God, will have been ignored.

Some of the attempts to delineate a christology in African terms were discussed above.[10] I suggested there that it was impossible to understand christology in abstraction from the whole area of the meaning of salvation. In South African theology the role of Jesus as the black Messiah who reconciles because he shares in both human tribulations and the life of God effectively unites what traditional dogma has understood by the humanity and deity of Christ. While such a politicizing of Christian belief may not find approval everywhere, it does have the advantage of acknowledging the centrality of the place of Jesus. Representatives of the adaptionist school have not infrequently failed to do this, largely because their main aim has been to seek a basis for Christian dogma in traditional culture. Because traditional African religions lack a clear sense of history and do not have historical founders, it is not easy to find such a contact point for christology,[11] and the christological models that have attracted most attention — ancestor, master of initiation, chief, and so on — all have a degree of timelessness about them. This problem perhaps indicates that a radical reorientation of the usual adaptionist approach is called for in the clear recognition that the central aspect of the Christian faith has no real parallels or points of contact in African traditions. Several leading theologians have stressed the fundamental importance of christology.[12] But we still await a

---

10. See chapter 4.

11. The "image of Jesus" for many independent churches is found in their founder-healers, which Boulaga sees as the way forward (see chapter 5 above).

12. Fasholé-Luke, *The Quest*, 84-89; Kwesi Dickson, "Towards a Theologia Africana," in *New Testament Christianity for Africa and the World*, ed. E. Fasholé-Luke and M. Glasswell (London, 1974), 204-5; John Pobee, *Towards an African Theology* (Nash-

full-scale attempt to delineate the significance of Christ from an African viewpoint. It is to be hoped that this will be seen as one of African theology's future primary tasks.

The problem of christology brings into sharp focus the difficulties facing the adaptionist approach. We saw earlier in this book how its earliest exponents, as exemplified, for example, by Mulago, attempted to draw out the essential foci of African religious systems and to relate these to corresponding aspects of the Gospel. Protestant scholars, by and large, approached the matter from the point of view of (in Idowu's words) seeking "to apprehend African spiritual values with the African mind."[13] It is probably true to say that some of the earlier attempts at adaptionism did content themselves with exhuming religious fossils, and against this Manas Buthelezi so rightly protested. African theologians soon saw, however, that such an approach was backward looking and largely irrelevant to contemporary Christian experience. African traditional religion consequently came to be regarded as useful only insofar as it contributed to the present needs of Christian living and understanding. Even when used with this careful eye for relevant features, adaptionism raises some pointed problems. A basic one has been the questioning of Christian scholars' whole interpretation of African religions. This issue was raised in a characteristically provocative way by Okot p'Bitek. His contention was that much of the systematic analysis of African religions has been done by Christian theologians, who have interpreted God in Africa in Christian terminology and categories. These scholars, he believes, are "intellectual smugglers," who have introduced Greek metaphysical conceptions into African thought. Consequently he feels that

[t]he African deities of the books, clothed with the attributes of the Christian God, are, in the main, creations of students of African religions. They are beyond all recognition to the ordinary African in the countryside.[14]

---

ville, 1979), 81-84; John Mbiti, "Some African Concepts of Christology," in *Christ and the Younger Churches,* ed. Vicedom (London, 1972); and even Bolaji Idowu, *BRAB,* 16, and Gabriel Setiloane, "Where Are We in African Theology?" *ATER,* 64.

13. Bolaji Idowu, *African Traditional Religions: A Definition* (London, 1973), xiii.

14. Okot p'Bitek, *African Religions and Western Scholarship* (Nairobi, 1971), 88.

A glance at some of the main writers whom Okot cites (Idowu, Mbiti, Danquah, Busia) reveals a good deal of justification for this contention. If African religion has been seen by Africans themselves through the prism of Christian theology, it need not be wondered at that these same theologians should find areas of agreement between the two traditions. What needs to be asked is whether these areas of agreement are inherent in the data or whether they are preconceptions in the mind of the (Christian) observer.[15] A basic challenge to exponents of adaptionism, then, is not only whether they have correctly interpreted the sources of Christian tradition, but equally whether they have correctly interpreted the African religious tradition, or conversely have allowed it to be molded to agree with their Christian presuppositions.

A second embarrassment to the adaptionist method has been the presence within African religions of "discontinuous" elements, those aspects of traditional religion that cannot by any leap of faith be reconciled to Christian teaching. It is to the credit of scholars like Nyamiti, Mbiti, Pobee, and others that they with integrity acknowledge that not everything in African tradition can or should be adopted and that those elements that are so absorbed may need some considerable modification before they can be of material usefulness.[16] The more significant opposite side to this is the ready adoption by African Christians of aspects of Christian doctrine that have apparently no relationship at all to traditional culture. Mbiti demonstrated fairly convincingly that in the realm of eschatology there is a radical break between Christian and

15. It could, of course, be argued that Christian theological categories are the best medium for describing African traditional religions, but as far as I am aware none of the scholars who take this approach has actually done this. The assumption here is that these categories are universal ones; clearly they are not, and such categories change even in the history of Christian theology itself.

16. Stanton has made the same point in the context of quite a different debate ("Incarnational Christology in the New Testament," *Incarnation and Myth, the Debate Continues* [London, 1979], 12-13). Stanton points out that though the earliest claims about the significance of Jesus were conditioned by the cultures in which they were formulated — for this was the only possible way the writers of the New Testament could express their convictions about him — yet each of these cultural categories was profoundly modified. "The earliest Christians," he writes, "stole the clothes of those to whom they were seeking to say something about Jesus, but those clothes had to be redeemed before they could be of use." Similar bespoke tailoring is called for from adaptionist theologians.

traditional ideas, and we noted earlier that christology provides another important example of discontinuity. Curiously, Christians in Africa do not seem to have too much difficulty (certainly no more than their European counterparts) in making the credal affirmations about the two natures in Christ, nor did Mbiti's Akamba Christians seem to have many problems in accepting a futurist eschatology that is (on Mbiti's view) so totally alien to their traditional thinking. If it is the case that African Christians can accept such radically new religious ideas without too much theological heart searching, does not this raise the question as to whether the adaptionist approach (and equally its supposed successor, incarnationism) may be quite misguided? Is the whole search for points of contact irrelevant?

Kwesi Dickson has raised a problem of a different kind in connection with the volume *Biblical Revelation and African Belief*.[17] This is the question of whether adaptionism does not begin at the wrong end. In its classic form it seeks first to discover the foci of African religions and then to relate them to Christian doctrine. Its point of departure is not the Bible or Christian tradition; it is rather African religious culture as a generic category. It is true that some aspects of this culture — the ancestors, the community, the world of spirits, and so on — may well be part of the present experience of the average African Christian, and to this extent they are valid points of departure. The hermeneutical problem here, however, is whether the African experience is interpreted in the light of the sources of Christian tradition or vice versa. There are occasions, even with the most sage of theologians, when the understanding of the biblical material seems to be molded by the African traditional worldview. The attempts of Sawyerr and Fasholé-Luke to accommodate the non-Christian ancestors seem to me examples of this. There is surely a need for care here, lest natural emotional attachment to African tradition shape, or perhaps misshape, the understanding of the sources of Christian tradition.

I do not believe that any of these objections is fatal to adaptionism as a method. Whatever its shortcomings, it seems to me to have considerably furthered our understanding of the African context, both cultural and religious, in which Christian theology has to operate, and to have led to thoughtful and even exciting explorations on how to give

17. Dickson, *Theology in Africa*, 204.

Christianity a more African face. Perhaps the most important question is what such adaption of aspects of African religion into Christian theology actually accomplishes at the level of Christian experience. Does it, on the ground, help towards the experiencing of the Christian faith in a more authentic way, or is it an academic exercise of little practical value? Advocates of the adaptionist method who are also entrusted with the care of souls should perhaps address themselves more fully to this question.

Black theology raises different hermeneutical problems. We referred earlier to Theo Sundermeier's remark that black theology approaches the Bible from the standpoint of the "new hermeneutic." According to this approach the function of *hermeneia* is not so much the canons of interpreting scripture as the way in which the scripture becomes clear to humans — a view close to Heidegger's understanding of *hermeneia* as a process of interpreting being or existence. This is not the place to examine this approach in detail, and at least in Buthelezi's case, as I suggested above, his approach to scripture is only partly comparable to the new hermeneutic. Boesak, however, does seem at times to use the Bible in this way, and his method merits closer examination. We saw earlier that Boesak tends to use biblical events, such as the exodus and Jesus' Nazareth sermon, as paradigms by means of which the category of liberation may be applied to the present situation. It seems to me there are exegetical problems inherent in this process, especially with regard to the exodus-event. While the Christian theologian may take the exodus as confirmation of his own social and political action, Biot rightly points out[18] this is not the interpretation that the biblical writers themselves give to the event. The exodus is, on the contrary, uniformly interpreted within the Old Testament as an example of God's act of deliverance (e.g., Deut. 5:15; 6:21-22; Amos 3:2; Mic. 6:4) in which the people were at best passive and at worst positively recalcitrant. Whatever else the exodus may have been, it was certainly never interpreted within the Jewish tradition as (as Gutiérrez has it)

---

18. F. Biot, *Théologie de la Politique* (Paris, 1972), 128. Fierro (*The Militant Gospel* [London, 1977], 147) finds Biot unconvincing here because he believes the important thing is not whether the political interpretation of the exodus has a basis in the Bible, but whether the event itself is biblical. This surely misses the point: given the fact that the Old Testament writers are less concerned with the historical "event" than with interpreting it in terms of God's activity, a biblical basis for a political interpretation is precisely what is important.

people's becoming aware that they are agents of history responsible for their own destiny.[19] The exodus in itself scarcely provides biblical and theological sanction for political action, although there may well be such sanction in principle elsewhere in the Old Testament. To use biblical passages in this way, it seems to me, results in a hermeneutical gap between the biblical happening (however one understands its historicity) and its application to circumstances in the present. Such contemporary applications are normally only convincing to those who are already convinced of the rightness of their action on quite other grounds — and after all, did not the Voortrekkers use the same exodus paradigm, with exactly the same strength of conviction but with such disastrous results? In his use of the New Testament Boesak casts his net wider, not only in the very full exegesis of Luke 4:18-19 but also in setting liberation within the wider context of the cross and resurrection of Jesus. However, his argument demands a much clearer spelling out of exactly how the cross and resurrection relate to liberation in a sociopolitical sense. How does one make the step from the New Testament interpretation of the cross and resurrection as a means of liberation from sin, guilt, and spiritual powers, to the cross as a means of liberation from racial, social, and political bondage? There is again a hermeneutical gap here, which Boesak (unlike, say, Gutiérrez) does not very clearly attempt to bridge. Despite his claim to have subjected his theology to the word of God, Boesak has not demonstrated from the evidence he uses that his understanding of liberation as a racial and sociopolitical entity has an incontrovertible basis in the Bible. If this biblical basis is not clearly spelled out, black theology in South Africa, like its counterpart in America, lays itself open to the charge that it is an ideology rather than a manifestation of Christian theology.

The difficulties raised here are part of a wider question of liberation theology's use of the Bible, and indeed of the much more fundamental problem of how exactly we understand the Bible. The basic task of hermeneutics has traditionally been understood to be to tackle the question of what the text meant to its original readers. Only when this question has been answered can the existential question of "what does it mean to me here and now?" be attempted. To bypass the stage of original meaning, insofar as it is recoverable, is to cut the biblical teaching loose from its roots, and may lead to some quaint and even perverse

19. Gutiérrez, *The Theology of Liberation* (London, 1974), 10-11.

interpretations, and such a method may be used to justify things that are fundamentally a-Christian. There is of course a strong trend within contemporary Third World theologies away from traditional approaches to biblical hermeneutics and towards interpretations of scripture more informed by non-Western cultural experience. While such approaches have produced some quite striking results, they do not seem to me to have invalidated the need to try (at least) to get at a meaning of the text informed by the original context — even granted the modern reader is alienated from that context by both time and culture.[20] The adoption of a Marxist hermeneutic by South Africans (notably Itumeleng Mosala) raises different problems, some of which I have discussed above.[21] Despite the insights that might result from a materialist reading of scripture, it does not appear to be a very fruitful way forward. The collapse of world communism (even though it should not perhaps be prematurely written off) seems to suggest that, for the time being at least, the Marxist approach to scripture is something of a blind alley.

Both Boesak and Buthelezi have approached black theology from another angle, from the standpoint of certain cardinal categories that are equally central to the Bible and to the experience of blacks in South Africa under apartheid. Do these provide a more stable link between the scriptures and the sociopolitical data? Two of the most potentially useful of these categories are those of true humanity, or human whole-ness, and of poverty. The former was indeed one of the basic ideals of black consciousness and has perhaps nowhere been more succinctly set out than in Biko's paper "Some African Cultural Concepts."[22] For Biko one of the most fundamental aspects of black culture is the importance it attaches to man, and one of the reasons for his rejection of Western values is that its individualism seeks to destroy "this most cherished of our beliefs, that man is the corner stone of society." This found theological expression, as we have seen, in Buthelezi's concept

20. But this is too large an issue for a fuller discussion here! For a good collection of papers that demonstrate varied approaches to biblical hermeneutics from the Third World (but that do not seem to me to justify the claims made in the editor's conclusion), see R. S. Sugirtharajah, *Voices from the Margin* (London, 1993).

21. See chapter 7, pp. 189-91.

22. In this paper, delivered in 1971 before a group of church leaders, Biko examined the role of African culture; the text is reprinted in Steve Biko, *I Write What I Like* (London, 1978), 40ff.

of the wholeness of life, which embraces the social, political, and economic dimensions as much as the religious. The basis for this human wholeness Buthelezi found in the biblical doctrines of creation and of redemption through Christ. Allan Boesak agrees that wholeness of life integrates all human values in one. While there is no one term in the Bible that provides an exact parallel to this concept of wholeness, the ideal itself is a very biblical one. Terms like *shālōm* in the Old Testament and *eirēnē* in the New convey very well the same basic idea. The former means at root "well-being," and not only covers physical health, but also can be used of political and social peace (especially in the later books of the Old Testament), as well as of salvation in a theological sense.[23] The New Testament usage of *eirēnē* shows similarly that there is, in biblical thinking, no sharp dichotomy between the natural and spiritual life, for life in all its aspects is a life lived before God.[24] The interpretations of black theologians at this point are substantially those of the scriptures.

Closely allied to the concept of wholeness is that of poverty. As used in liberation theology, with which Boesak is in agreement, "the poor" designates those oppressed by the unequal structures of this world. This is fundamentally the meaning of *'ani*, which, as Bammel defines it, implies not deserved poverty but rather those who are impoverished because they have been wrongfully oppressed.[25] From this it is a small step to the idea, found frequently in the Psalms and eighth-century prophets, of the poor as particular objects of God's mercy and care, not simply because they are poor, but because they are oppressed by the mighty. The heart of Jesus' message, that of the good news to the poor, derives from a similar base. The poor in Luke's Gospel are the outcasts and despised of society, especially the disciples themselves. In Jeremias's view, Jesus' use of "the poor" is similar to that of the prophets and denotes "the oppressed and the poor who are thrown completely

---

23. See, e.g., G. von Rad in *Theological Dictionary of the New Testament*, vol. 2, ed. Kittel and Friedrich (English translation, Grand Rapids, 1964), 403-5; also C. Westermann, "Shalom in alten Testament," in *Studien zur Friedensforschung*, ed. G. Picht and I. Tödt (Stuttgart, 1963), 144-77.

24. *Theological Dictionary of the New Testament*, vol. 8 (English translation, 1972), 310.

25. *Theological Dictionary of the New Testament*, vol. 6 (English translation, 1968), 888ff.: *dāl* and *'ebyōn* have a similar meaning.

on God's help."[26] The closeness of this to the concept of the poor in much liberation theology is evident enough, as equally is its remoteness from the kind of missionary pietism that exalted poverty (in others) as an indication of the expectation of blessedness in a future life. The biblical message is not one of the glorification of poverty for its own sake; rather it is one of the concern of God for those who are oppressed and of the demand to eradicate poverty at every level of life.

Categories such as these are theological in the truest sense, and provide a link point between the Bible and some central concerns of Christian theology in Africa. Exegesis along these lines does not merely isolate proof texts, nor does it proceed along debatable hermeneutical methods; it seeks, rather, an in-depth examination of biblical teaching within certain central areas of theological concern that are of immediate relevance to Christians in Africa. We are here moving into the area of "the black experience," a second large problem area for African theology.

2. Theology and the Black Experience

Both "African" and "black" theology stress, though in differing ways and to different degrees, the importance of African culture for Christian theology — culture, that is, in its widest sense, not merely of the African precolonial past, but as a present reality that responds to all the demands and challenges of the contemporary situation. The thrust of the call for an African theology, by both Catholic and Protestant scholars, has been the attempt to incarnate the Christian faith within African culture. On the religious side this was influenced by the rediscovery of the dignity of African traditional religions: from the ideological point of view secular movements such as négritude, black personality, black consciousness had considerable impact. These trends coalesced to open up theologians to the importance of African values, both past and present, which provided a springboard for the development of Christian explorations. These aspects were as important for political theologies as for the more explicitly cultural theologies of Africa.

---

26. *New Testament Theology*, vol. 1 (London, 1971), 113. Jeremias's discussion is illuminating, especially in his exegesis of Isa. 61:1ff. To similar effect, see Jürgen Moltmann, *The Church in the Power of the Spirit* (London, 1977), 78-80.

There are similarities here to what Tillich called the "theology of culture" (although Tillich probably would have found it as difficult to appreciate the theological values of African cultures as he did those of Japanese culture). Tillich's aim was to do theology from within culture and to integrate into theology all aspects of the culture in which it found itself.[27] John Heywood Thomas has a comment on Tillich that could with justice be applied to African theology. He writes:

> As itself a form of culture theology does indeed exemplify a very special form of the problem which a theology of culture recognises as central, viz. how the various kinds of meaning which make up our culture are related to the meaning which is revealed in religion as the meaning of life or the meaning of the world.[28]

This problem — the relating of meaning within culture to the meaning of religion (in this case Christianity) — is one that, although not enunciated in exactly these terms, has been an underlying concern of African theology. Two aspects of this concern are of especial importance: the meaning of traditional religions, and the meaning of the history of African peoples. Both raise issues that go far beyond the confines of the African theological scene.

We noted earlier in chapter 2 that African theologians have in general seen in traditional religion genuine religious values that are, in some sense, a revelation from God. In the mildest form of this approach, characterized in the works of writers such as Nyamiti and Mbiti, these values are regarded as a *praeparatio evangelica;* in the more drastic form, exemplified by Idowu, Kibicho, and others, African religion is seen as having a genuine salvific value. In either form they express the conviction that God is in one way or another at work in African traditional religions, and that he reveals his will through them to some degree. As the final statement of the Dar-es-Salaam conference of Third World theologians put it: "[W]e believe these religions and cultures have a place in God's universal plan, and the Holy Spirit is actually at work in

27. Especially in his *The Theology of Culture* (Oxford, 1959).
28. John Heywood Thomas, "The Problem of Defining a Theology of Culture with Reference to the Theology of Paul Tillich," *Creation, Christ and Culture,* ed. R. W. McKinney (Edinburgh, 1976), 280.

them."[29] This is an issue of much wider relevance than theology in Africa; it involves us in the question of the possibility of authentic divine revelation outside of the Judeo-Christian tradition.

We suggested above that Christian theology, taking its lead from the Bible, makes room for the self-revelation of God to all humankind in what has traditionally been called general or natural revelation. Karl Barth's contention that all religion is a form of unbelief, which is contradicted and displaced by the Christian revelation,[30] obviously has no relevance at all in this context. Hardly more acceptable to African Christians has been Rahner's picture of the sincere believer of pre-Christian religions as an "anonymous Christian," or a Christian in the making.[31] Such a view savors too much of religiocultural imperialism in claiming for Christianity all that is good in other religions. More relevant to our case perhaps is Jürgen Moltmann's "profile in the context of dialogue."[32] In Moltmann's view, fruitful interreligious dialogue demands not only a clear understanding of one's own faith, but also the sense of incompleteness that makes religious cross-fertilization possible.[33]

As yet few African scholars have attempted to tackle such problems in any depth.[34] They have in general been content to restate their conviction that, in some way, God is present in African religions, rather than argue a case or present a solution. That this conviction rests on a solid theological foundation few would deny. There is a pressing need, however, for a fuller argumentation both for the grounds on which it is believed that African traditional religion has a real revelatory value and for the extent to which it constitutes such a revelation. Two questions here demand an answer, one that addresses itself to this conviction in its extreme form, the other to it in any guise. The first we have alluded to already above: if there is a real salvific value in traditional religion, in what sense is the Christian faith necessary and unique, and on what grounds can it claim to be more meaningful? Why, indeed, should

---

29. *EG*, 270.

30. Karl Barth, *Church Dogmatics*, I/2 (Edinburgh, 1956), 299, 303.

31. Rahner, *Theological Investigations*, vol. 5 (London, 1966), 131ff., in his essay "Christianity and non-Christian religions."

32. Moltmann, 159ff.

33. Moltmann, 163.

34. But see Dickson's discussion in *Theology in Africa*, 37ff.

Africans follow the Christian way rather than the way of their fathers? I sense that in their enthusiasm to see African religions as the work of God, some of the more radical African theologians are somewhat embarrassed by this question.[35] It is certainly not at all clear from the writings of men like Idowu, Kibicho, and Setiloane how (or, indeed, whether) they as Christians (and Christian ministers) see Christianity as more ultimately salvific than African religions.

The other question is of more general application. If God reveals himself in traditions other than the Judeo-Christian one, how may the Christian discern what is truly of God in them? Obviously some elements — human sacrifice for example, or the slaughter of twins in some societies — are quite incompatible with Christianity (although perhaps no more so than certain passages in the Old Testament, so beloved of the Voortrekkers, like the extermination of the Canaanite peoples). Presumably one criterion of judgment is the New Testament and Christian tradition. But if this is the only criterion, are we not immediately limiting the possible contribution that traditional religions can make to our understanding of God? All the non-Christian religion can do in this case is to confirm what we already know from Christian revelation. If we grant that African religions contain within themselves in some way the possibility of the knowledge of God, how can we judge in what sense and to what extent they do so?

An allied aspect of this problem is the role of history in the construction of theology. Many African theologians seem to assume that God is at work in the history of all humankind, in "profane history" (to use Rahner's term)[36] as well as "sacred history." I suspect that it is the quite valid and understandable attempt to break free from the tyranny of colonial and mission history that has led to a renewed emphasis on the theological value of the past, on "African" history (as opposed to the history of Europeans in Africa). The assumption that the "Creator of heaven and earth, Lord of history, has been dealing with mankind at all times and in all parts of the world"[37] expresses the conviction that God has equally been at work in the history of African peoples, and that this

35. Gabriel Setiloane raises precisely this issue (with regard to himself!) in *ATER*, 64.

36. Rahner, 97ff., "The History of the World and Salvation History."

37. *BRAB*, 16.

history is one source of revelation of the nature and purposes of God. In one sense, of course, the very idea of the election of Israel implies, paradoxically, a universalist view of history.[38] Abraham Heschel regarded the Old Testament prophet as the "first universal man in history . . . who first conceived the unity of all men."[39] His point was that the prophets see God as the one whose universal purposes unite all human history in one. Should not all human history therefore be taken into account as a raw material of theology? This theological concern for history, especially the history of the people actually doing the theology, has attracted more attention from Asian theologians, and I may perhaps transgress geographical boundaries here to quote a succinct defense of this view from C. S. Song:

> God is already in Jesus Christ. That is why we must know how to begin with Jesus Christ. God is already in the history of Israel. For this reason we must study it. In the same way, God is already in human history on earth. Thus the data and events we encounter there constitute the subject matter of our theological inquiry. . . . To refrain from asking questions at this point is to flee back to the shelter of academic theology which is more interested in the metaphysics of God than the concrete acts of God in society and history.[40]

In principle one must agree with Song's statement: the evidence of Scripture and Christian tradition is too strong for the Christian to deny that "profane" history does represent the real acts of God, whether we call this "general revelation" or whatever. The problem I find here is not so much the fact that God acts in human history, it is not even that so many events in human history are fraught with dis-teleological questions; it is rather the difficulty of how we can interpret human history in such a way that we can correctly discern what God is about.

Within the biblical tradition we have interpretations of historical acts in terms of salvation history. The biblical writers expose what they

38. So G. von Rad, *Old Testament Theology,* vol. 1, 178.
39. Heschel, *The Prophets* (New York, 1962), vol. 1, 170.
40. C. S. Song, *Third Eye Theology* (London, 1980), 80: Song was disputing Torrance's view that theology should not take into account what it encounters in life and history.

see as the theological meaning of history, so that in effect these interpretations are really more important than the events themselves as the
materials of theology (although of course the different biblical writers,
especially in the Old Testament, are not always agreed on what to make
of the historical tradition). In our interpretation of history outside of
the Judeo-Christian tradition, we have no such interpretive guidelines,
so that the interpretation of profane history becomes a very subjective
thing, which depends upon very individual presuppositions. By all
means let us, as Song urges, "put our questions, despite the fact that
they are human questions"; but let us also remember that the answers
to those questions about the meaning of God's acts in history may not
always be self-evident, and that a humble caution is necessary lest we
be found to be merely giving divine sanction to our own ideologies.

Boesak's concern with history, in line with his emphasis on theology as liberation, is more attuned to the participation of the Christian
in God's saving acts in the present. Taking his cue from the Indian
theologian M. M. Thomas, Boesak argues for the reversal of the earlier
alliance of the church with the dominant powers and for the identification of its mission with those involved in a revolutionary struggle
against oppression. He believes that

> the work of Christ and his kingdom is discernible in the secular, social
> and political revolutions of our time, and that the Church's function
> is to discern it and to witness to it and to participate in God's work
> in a changing world.[41]

This approach is not so much one of reflecting on what God has been
doing in past profane history as of seeing in contemporary history a
theological imperative. Thus the task of the Christian faith is to "relate itself
dynamically to ideologies of the revolution to make them more human and
realistic, through bringing them under the criterion and power of the New
Humanity in Christ."[42] Boesak agrees that this is a risky business, for it
consists in an interpretative choice from inside a given situation, leading to

41. Allan Boesak, *Black Theology, Black Power* (London, 1978), 83.
42. Boesak, referring to M. M. Thomas's "Issues Concerning the Life and Work
of the Church in a Revolutionary World," in *Unity in Mankind,* ed. A. H. van der Heuvel
(Geneva, 1969), 89-98.

the commitment of the Christian to that situation. For Boesak this ethical imperative can be solved only within the context of liberation as symbolized by the exodus-event.[43] He believes that the failure of Christian missions to overcome what he calls ideologies of oppression and dependency has led Third World Christians to the conviction that the activity of God in human history is not confined to the church.

I am in agreement with much of what Boesak says, and his plea that the Christian should recognize the potential within the present situations, revolutionary or otherwise, and should commit himself or herself fully to them, insofar as they make for a truer humanity, is a necessary one. Black Christians in South Africa have shown the way to such commitment and have by their deeds often put the apartheid South African situation under the judgment of the Word of God. In this their fellow Christians elsewhere on the continent have much to learn, for oppressive and dehumanizing structures are still very much with us in Africa today. At the same time such commitment to social action must accept that it represents an interpretation of history — contemporary history — by the believer, subject as he or she is to human frailty and error. There will remain an inscrutability that does not in the same way inhere to the kind of revelation open to us in the scriptures. St. Paul's response to the mystery of God's acts in history (in his case the fate of his own Jewish people) was one of humble agnosticism: "For who has known the mind of the Lord, or who has been his counsellor?" (Rom. 11:34). At the same time this did not prevent him from involving himself with absolute self-commitment in the transformation of that human history.

African theology today, I believe, faces theological questions that are equally the concern of the whole church: the approach to the interpretation of scripture; the categories in which the theologian should work; the relationship of the Christian faith to non-Christian religions, to all human history, and to the dehumanization that is part of our world today. But above all, it faces the question that lies at the heart of all theology that calls itself Christian. This is the question that "incessantly bothered" Dietrich Bonhoeffer[44] and has been at the heart of all Christian thinking since the incarnation, namely who Christ really is for us today.

43. Boesak, 90.
44. Dietrich Bonhoeffer, *Letters and Papers from Prison* (London, 1967), 152.

Select Bibliography

Appiah-Kubi, K., and S. Torres, eds. *African Theology en Route.* Maryknoll, 1979.

Baeta, C. *Christianity and African Culture.* Accra, 1955.

Bediako, K. *Theology and Identity.* Oxford, 1992.

Boesak, A. A. *Black Theology, Black Power.* London, 1978.

Boulaga, F. Eboussi. *Christianity without Fetishes.* Maryknoll, 1984.

Bujo, B. *African Theology in Its Social Context.* Maryknoll, 1992.

Des Prêtres Noirs s'interrogent. Paris, 1956.

Dickson, K. *Theology in Africa.* London, 1983.

Dickson, K., and P. Ellingworth, eds. *Biblical Revelation and African Beliefs.* London, 1969.

Éla, J-M. *African Cry.* Maryknoll, 1986.

————. *My Faith as an African.* Maryknoll, 1988.

Fasholé-Luke, E. et al., eds. *Christianity in Independent Africa.* London, 1978.

Glasswell, M., and E. Fasholé-Luke, eds. *New Testament Christianity for Africa and the World.* London, 1974.

Martey, E. *African Theology, Inculturation or Liberation.* Maryknoll, 1993.

Mbiti, J. *New Testament Eschatology in an African Background.* London, 1971.

Mofokeng, T. *The Crucified among the Crossbearers.* Kampen, 1983.

Moore, B., ed. *Black Theology, the South African Voice.* London, 1973.

Mosala, I. *Biblical Hermeneutics and Black Theology in South Africa.* Grand Rapids, 1989.

Mosala, I., and B. Thlagale, eds. *The Unquestionable Right to Be Free.* Braamfontein, 1986.

Mwoleka, C. *Ujamaa and Christian Communities.* Nairobi, 1976.

Nyamiti, C. *The Scope of African Christian Theology.* Nairobi, 1973.

————. *Christ as our Ancestor.* Gweru, 1984.

Oduyoye, M. *Hearing and Knowing.* Maryknoll, 1993.

Parratt, J., ed. *A Reader in African Christian Theology.* London, 1987.

————, ed. *The Practice of Presence: Shorter Writings of Harry Sawyerr.* Edinburgh and Grand Rapids, 1995.

Pobee, J. *Toward an African Theology.* Nashville, 1979.

————, ed. *Religion in a Pluralistic Society.* Leiden, 1976.

Sawyerr, H. *Creative Evangelism, towards a New Christian Encounter with Africa.* London, 1968.

Schreiter. J., ed. *Faces of Jesus in Africa.* London, 1992.

Sundermeier, T., ed. *Christus, der schwarzer Befreier.* Erlangen, 1973.

————, ed. *Zwischen Kultur und Politik.* Hamburg, 1978.

Tödt, I., ed. *Theologie in Konfliktfeld Südafrika: Dialog mit Manas Buthelezi.* Stuttgart and Munich, 1976.

Torres, S., and K. Appiah-Kubi, eds. *The Emergent Gospel.* Maryknoll, 1978.

Tutu, D. *The Voice of One Crying in the Wilderness.* London, 1982.

Villa-Vicencio, C., and J. de Gruchy, eds. *Resistance and Hope.* Cape Town, 1985.

Index

215

Sacraments, 33-34, 43, 97, 100-103, 132-33
Sawyerr, Harry, 12, 14, 19, 41-44, 56, 63-64, 74, 82, 86, 96, 97-98, 103, 134
Senghor, Leopold, 13, 17, 36, 126, 143, 156, 163
Setiloane, Gabriel, 71-73, 84, 198, 209
Sin, 88-89, 111, 123
Socialism, African, 136, 143-53
Song, C. S., 210
Souga, Therese, 90-91
Spirit, 95, 100-101, 103
Sundermeier, Theo, 27
Sundkler, Bengt, 12, 19, 58, 63, 169

Tempels, Placide, 10, 19, 29, 32, 34, 36, 123, 127, 169
Temple, William, 65
Theology: feminist, 50-53, 90-91, 185; oral, 45, 56, 91; Western (African attitudes to), 13-14, 72, 107-8, 150, 160-61, 164, 169, 176, 186; Western (use of in African theology), 19-21, 45, 195-97
Thomas, M. M., 211
Tillich, Paul, 16, 81, 89, 91, 177, 186, 207
Tlhagale, Buti, 185, 187-88
Trinity, doctrine of, 33-34, 93-95, 131, 147-48
Tshibangu, T., 11, 35-36, 38, 127, 139
Tutu, Desmond, 14, 74, 138, 154-55, 185

Ujamaa, 143-48

Villa-Vicencio, Charles, 191
Violence, 150, 178, 183-84, 185
Vital union, 31-35, 92

Wiles, Maurice, 197